SALTED

Salted

A MANIFESTO ON THE WORLD'S MOST ESSENTIAL MINERAL, WITH RECIPES

Mark Bitterman

Photography by Mark Bitterman and Jennifer Martiné

TEN SPEED PRESS

Berkeley

The following material is reprinted with permission:

Pages 6 and 12, stone cutters in Pakistan, courtesy of Maqbool Bhatti

Page 12, Maras salt fields, courtesy of Leslie Trites

Page 18, Camargue salt works, courtesy of Mathieu Ginod

Page 20, *agehama-shiki* salt making, courtesy of Okunoto Endenmura

Page 52, drawing of Guérande solar salt ponds, courtesy of Jill Davies, adapted from oeilletdeguerande.com

Page 65, Maldon Salt Company, courtesy of Maldon Salt Company

Pages 118 and 150, salt pan floor, courtesy of Lennie DiCarlo

Published in the United States by Ten Speed Press, an imprint of the Crown Publishing Group, a division of Random House, Inc., New York.

www.crownpublishing.com

www.tenspeed.com

Ten Speed Press and the Ten Speed Press colophon are registered trademarks of Random House, Inc.

Cataloging-in-Publication data is on file with the publisher.

ISBN 978-1-58008-262-4

Printed in Singapore

Design by Betsy Stromberg

10 9 8 7 6 5 4 3 2 1

First Edition

Contents

TO MY MOTHER

Acknowledgments

My fantasy of sitting in a garret in Paris, smoking Gitane cigarettes and writing this book in monkish seclusion was not destined to be fulfilled. Instead of self-reliance and solitude, this book was born from the support of a huge network of amazing people. Above all, this book would not have been possible without Jennifer, whose eye for honesty has forced me to live and think more truly, and whose creative genius made a business out of our shared passions. Thanks to my boys Austin (ravenous appetite and gourmet tastes) and Hugo (enthusiastic cook and fiery collaborator) for being such good sports, and for insisting that even when I'm most distracted I can, indeed, wrestle.

Thanks to the rest of my family as well. To my mother, Jill, for not caging me as a child, and for backing me as a writer no matter how unruly that writing often was, and to my father, Howard, for his passion for eating—rivaled only by his passion for talking about it. Thanks to my brother, Aaron, for persisting in the idea that food is the most important thing in the universe; to my sister, Jennifer, for always laughing at my stories; and to my brother Shem for his encouragement and example as a writer.

A debt of gratitude to my dear friend Andy Schloss, who is as tough as he is brilliant, and whose generosity seems always to exceed my ability to abuse it. Loving thanks to my agent and friend Lisa Ekus for her high-octane inspiration and excellent whisky. Special thanks to my preposterously dedicated research assistant Evan Messinger. A very special thanks to the staff of The Meadow, who has tolerated my all-too-frequent absences from the business and my less-than-angelic temperament when I was not absent. Eternal gratitude to the crew at Ten Speed Press, and to my superb editor Melissa Moore and inspired designer Betsy Stromberg in particular.

Discovery: The Salt Road

There may be those who seek not gold, yet there never lived a man who desires not salt. —Secretary to the Ostrogothic King of Italy (528 CE)

At twenty years of age, I made the discovery that would change my life forever. I was somewhere in the middle of a very long, unstructured motorcycle trip across Europe, wandering from Wales to Slovenia, Vatican City to Denmark. My philosophy was that I should ride slowly, soaking up the scenery and stopping to look more closely at whatever caught my eye—a strange-looking tree, or a cow that approached the fence, or a toothless man. I'd maybe open a can of sardines and dump them on the crust of yesterday's bread, cut a tomato on top, and stare at whatever was there to be stared at. Some of the time I would camp alone, but often enough I would strike up a conversation and find myself at 3 A.M. drinking red wine from a barrel at the toothless man's cousin's ex-wife's vineyard, snacking on fried olives made by the ex-wife's attractive but mean-looking daughter.

When I made my discovery, I was motoring along on the picturesque D836 road from Paris to Le Havre. In the mood to splurge, I began looking for a *relais*—the French equivalent of an American truck stop, offering traditional food at affordable prices. Unlike the United States, where chain restaurants now dominate the roadside, France still has a good number of relais that exist as distinctive local enterprises. They buy local ingredients, cook specialty regional dishes, and serve them with locally made wines and spirits; thanks to them it is still possible to eat your way across the thousands of miles of French highways experiencing the country's dozens of traditional regional cuisines.

I rode for some time in search of a relais. Finally I asked a woman walking along the side of the road with a basket of beets under her arm. She pointed me in the right direction and minutes later I was seated at a nondescript relais drinking a glass of thin, crisp red wine and waiting for my steak.

The steak was superb. Firm in texture, like a fresh peach. With every bite the flavor evolved—from mild and sweet to something deeper and richer. The world floated away. I was one of Odysseus' oarsmen devouring the sacred cattle of Helios. Mythic.

Transported, I asked the waiter how they made the steak. This, evidently, was not a very intelligent question—his response was to return to the kitchen. I took a few more bites and tried again to engage the waiter, hoping to appeal to his pride.

Our conversation went something like this:

"Wow, this is the best steak I've ever eaten in my entire life, ever."
"I am glad."
"Um, how is this steak made?"
"It is a steak, Monsieur."
"Yes, but it is really good steak."
"Excellent."
"Um, so why is it so good?"
"Monsieur, it is a steak that has been grilled."
"Where did you get the steak?"
"It is from Michel-Paul's farm."
"Michel-Paul?"
"Yes, a man who raises cows."
"Um, okay. So what else?"
"It is steak, from a cow. It is cooked with the grill, and seasoned with the salt."

Aha! I looked at the steak more carefully. Hefty nuggets of opalescent salt were scattered across the surface, glistening in little wells of steak juice, each crystal a fractured composite of smaller crystals, within which were finer crystals yet.

"Where did you get that salt?" I demanded.

"That, Monsieur, is salt from Guérande. The owner's brother is a salt maker. This is the family's salt. They have made salt for hundreds of years in the traditional way."

And there it was. By dumb luck and a simple appreciation for a steak, I had discovered the heart of the restaurant, its connections to neighbors, family, and ancestral ways of life.

After lunch, I called my friends in Le Havre from the pay phone at the back of the restaurant and told them I would not be able to make it that day. Instead,

I rode off, fast now, gunning it toward the Brittany coast with the waiter's directions to find the salt maker.

This experience was one of several that shaped my love and respect for food. I was beginning to understand that all ingredients matter—a lot—and that, in virtually everything we eat, major revelations await the curious. Salt! Who would have thought?

Over the next decades, I discovered that there are multitudes of salts in the world, that their forms are legion, and that the ways to use them are infinite. A sense of never-ending possibility has fueled my interest and frustrated my comprehension. For years after my great roadside discovery, my outlook on salt could have been summed up as, "Wow." Yet over time my observations and thoughts—and my many conversations with salt makers and cooks—have coalesced into a greater understanding. From salt makers, I have learned how the most elusive and fleeting nuances of weather, ocean, land, and tradition are adamantine facts of the craft. Cooks have showed me how salting can become a portal into a more vital and personal connection to food. Both, in their own ways, are searching for truths as surely as any philosopher.

During that first long tour, and many subsequent ones, I picked up every imaginable type of food, from live eels to moldy cheese, but it was the salt that started to accumulate. Bags of salt would be tossed in cartons with journals, old pants, and spare motorcycle parts and secreted away. The collection was highly personal from the start. But over time it became more than that. Settling down with a family gave the salts space to breathe, and gave me even more time to research and cook with them. Old boxes were unpacked. Cupboards filled. Gradually the essence of my life took physical form: a lifelong pursuit of food and travel, curated in salt.

SETTING UP CAMP: THE MEADOW

I had always thought of my wife, Jennifer, as an art historian. She had worked at the Metropolitan Museum of Art, the Getty, and the Frick Collection and was now the director of a major art gallery in Portland. So I was surprised when she said one day that she wanted to quit her job and open a retail shop: "I want to surround myself with the things I love most."

What to make of that? My mind raced over the possibilities: Omelet pans? Lotion? Scratched LPs? Old Manolo Blahnik shoes? Paperbacks by Thomas

Mann? Cups? Half-filled photo albums? Burgundy? Antique mirrors? Books on Tai Chi? Mint? Jennifer is not an easy woman to categorize. All I could think of to say was, "Well, okay, I guess. Do you think we could find a spot for our salt in there somewhere?"

I drove out to inspect the spot she had selected. Located at the back of a courtyard on an obscure street in an even more obscure neighborhood in Portland, Oregon, was a small storefront painted in dark purples, blues, and greens. It had track lighting that hung down at the perfect height to shine directly into your eyes, creating the effect of staring into headlights as you enter a tunnel.

Perfect.

I spent the next five weeks painting, building shelves from old-growth Douglas fir reclaimed from demolished warehouses, designing and installing lighting, and buying jars for salt—meshing the realities of hidden nails and splintered wood with Jennifer's glowing mental image. We piled the newly built shelves and tables with buckets of fresh flowers, vintage vases, and jars of salt and hung the walls with a series of incredibly beautiful nudes drawn in Conté crayon, charcoal, and watercolor by a local artist. Then we invited all our friends over for a party, and opened our doors to the public.

Strangely, people were interested in our salt.

At the core of our business is an interest in sharing the excitement and pleasure of discovery. There are virtually no written signs in the store because we consider it our job to learn about our customers' needs, then educate them in person about what we have to offer based on what we've learned. Packaging, no matter how well intentioned or smartly conceived, does a very poor job of conversing with a customer. Plus, talking to people about food inspires a degree of candor that normally takes several martinis to produce. Within the space of an hour I may talk with a chef about problems he's having selling the owner on his passion for squid ceviche; with a tourist who is hungry for an intelligible and convenient way to make cottage cheese and peaches taste better; and with a neighbor who is surprising her husband with cassoulet for dinner.

This experience doesn't get old with repetition because it never really repeats. When a visitor enters the store and says, "Oh! Salt?" I hear surprise, curiosity, and a tinge of something else—a bond being formed. It feels like we're suddenly alone together, stranded in a strange space, trying to recapture something just beyond our reach, something like a déjà vu; and suddenly I have to try consciously to maintain an air of calm, cool collectedness. But—holding a pile of salt in my hands before a small crowd of people in The Meadow, surrounded by tables overflowing with seasonal flowers, opposite the chocolate shelves, flanked by a massive case bearing unusual wines, aperitifs, Champagnes, vermouths, bitters, and tonics, with a towering wall filled with more than a hundred artisan salts at my back—I sometimes begin literally to tremble.

SALT: THE FOOD THAT TIME FORGOT

For thousands of years we have been making salt from the sea or finding it in the land, and the world's thousands of regional cuisines have evolved in concert with the availability and character of regionally made salts. For most of human existence, salt has been scarce in the extreme, difficult to transport, and of dramatically varying quality. Salt was, literally, a treasure, and everyone everywhere who could make it would. Yet salt making was a challenging, physically demanding, risky job requiring the participation of an entire community. The salts that resulted were unique, each bearing a mineral and crystalline imprint of the elemental and human forces that wrought it. Salt was a natural, whole food, intimately tied to a place and a way of life.

When industrial methods of manufacturing and transporting salt emerged out of the technology and trade boom of the mid-nineteenth century, the uniqueness of salt began to be lost. Salt is now standardized, found mostly in three or four variously-colored, rather hefty cardboard boxes in the middle of supermarkets so vast that potato chips and cat food have whole aisles to themselves. Salt has a small slice of a shelf, and the salts on that shelf are all variations of the two basic refined salts produced by giant chemical companies: vacuum pan salt and industrial sea salt. Over the last century, salt has become commonplace. Most people have come to consume it routinely and indiscriminately, while paradoxically they have stopped thinking about it much at all.

That has begun to change. The organic food movement that has swept much of the Western world since the 1980s has caused us to think more about how our food is produced: What is the environmental cost of producing and transporting food? How are we treating food plants and animals? How are we treating farmers? What is the nutritional value of our food? All of these ideas and a host of others cannot be contained in the single concept, "health food." They have spilled over, and many people are now engaged in a far-reaching dialogue with their eating habits. All of this has helped shape and inspire a modern version of what might have been the first epicurean question mankind ever asked: What tastes best, and how can I make it taste better?

Thanks to an increasingly sophisticated understanding of how to use salt well in cooking, its use today is expanding into foods formerly off limits. For

example, *fleur de sel* caramels are sold in virtually every gourmet food store in the Western world. The combination has won over sweet-eaters and savory-eaters alike. Rare is the person who, after tasting salt in caramel, prefers it without. (The delicious—if less universally enjoyed—combination of salt and chocolate is also gaining popularity.) Salted caramel originated, or at least was perfected, in Brittany, where fleur de sel—one of the beautiful, artisan-made salts produced in the region—is sprinkled into the caramel in such a way as to keep the salt crystals from dissolving. If the salt were simply dissolved in cream before being combined with the burnt sugar, its deeper power would be lost. Instead of just salting to season, such salting is inspired by the salt itself—crystals, minerals, moisture, even the salt's own name—to result in a food that is greater than the sum of its parts. This subtle difference marks a shift toward thinking of salt as a strategic ingredient. Cooks are asking questions: What do you want salt to achieve for the dish? What salt will do this job best? How shall the salt be used?

In this environment, all-natural salts are staging an extraordinary comeback. While it might be an exaggeration to generalize that artisan salt makers are regaining ground lost to industrial salt manufacturers, there *are* actually scattered small communities or regions where artisan salt making is reviving. It's possible again to find a variety of hand-crafted salts.

MY METHODOLOGY: CHOOSING THE SALTS

I believe in miracles / Where're you from, / you sexy thing. —The Ramones

Virtually every region in the world makes salt, and most have been doing so since before recorded history. But the vast majority of saltworks that produced salt over the last hundreds and thousands of years are now gone, first falling victim to the industrialization of food production in general and salt production in particular, and then suffering a dramatic demotion in importance as the standardization of salt eliminated any regional character of the salt. Salt manufacturing was subsumed by the industrial-chemical machinery driving the modern global economy. It is a commonly held belief that the advent of refrigeration has replaced salting as a major way to preserve food, but we are in fact more dependent on salt now than ever.

The bounty of artisan salts available in North American, European, and Asian markets today is the result of a variety of forces, not least of which is an interest in reconnecting with our culinary and cultural heritage. Most of the artisan salts we find on the shelves of our favorite stores are themselves products of a desire among individuals, communities, and governments to find purpose in old ways. For example, the hugely popular salts produced in the Guérande region of France were on the brink of disappearing altogether before the region revived itself through a series of shrewd business and marketing initiatives (page 28). Guérande now serves as a model for salt makers everywhere hoping to save or revive their own salt-making traditions.

Tea, wine, and spices are traded through highly developed channels by sophisticated, well-financed merchants. Artisan salt, on the other hand, sits mostly in obscurity, with few telling its story. Salt makers are far-flung artisans and are not, as a group, equipped to communicate internationally. Thus many of the most ancient, authentic, fascinating, and delicious salts of the world are, at present, nearly impossible to find for all but the most experienced researchers and adventurous travelers.

The salts discussed in this book reflect this pull between popularity and obscurity, importance and intrigue. I've made every effort to insure that the commonly available salt brands, the major salt-making techniques, and the best-traveled and most interesting salt-making regions are covered. But because these salts only tell part of the story, I also spend considerable time with salts that are difficult or impossible to buy outside of their local markets. Each of these salts has its charm, its history, its secrets. Even if you never eat them, knowing about them can give you a richer appreciation of those artisan salts that do find their way to your table.

In some cases, I will withhold the name or exact location of a salt maker to preserve proprietary information granted to me in confidence by an importer or exporter. In other cases, I might not be able to disclose some information for my own professional reasons. More often than not, I have thrown caution to the wind and shared my secrets, putting the best interests of the salt maker and you, the reader, first.

THE SALT MANIFESTO: HONOR THY SALT

Everything should be made as simple as possible, but not simpler.
—Albert Einstein

Cuisine is characterized by a tension between two forces: technique and ingredient. Mastery of the culinary arts is a mastery of craft. On the other hand, all good cooks embrace the age-old concept of "honor the animal" and "honor the vegetable," meaning use your ingredients fully and respectfully. Culinary trends can lean more toward one side or the other, but technique and ingredient are inextricably linked. Technical skill works at the behest of making the most out of the ingredient, while great ingredients provide a lush palate with which to craft a meal.

We eat lots of things: animals, plants, fungi, bacteria. Salt is the only mineral we eat. Its international intrigue comes from the fact that it can be used to improve the flavor of all the others, and that it does more to enhance those flavors than any other ingredient. It is the only universal ingredient, and it is the most potent one. Yet salt in its own right can be as distinctive as any plant or animal. More so, in fact. There is no variety of plant or breed of animal that has been cultivated as food for as long, in as many places, and in as many ways as salt. It is not only the only universal food, it is the most varied. Honoring salt is not only important for understanding the bounty of nature, it is vital to the understanding of cooking and eating.

Using salts with character and integrity awakens us to the full potential of the ingredient. Salting mindfully, and with a basic understanding of a salt's properties and behavior, will lead inescapably to better nutrition and better tasting food. Master salt, and virtually every food will shine in a new light.

There are five good reasons to think independently and critically about salting:

1. Salting is one of the more ingrained habits in cooking, and all habits need to be questioned.

2. In understanding and mastering the principles behind salting, you become better equipped to get the best results for your individual cooking style, personal tastes, and unique nutritional needs.

3. At the least, appreciating the distinctive qualities of salt inspires clarity and distinction in our cooking. At best, appreciating them unleashes an elemental force in our diverse culinary traditions.

4. The risk is low and the payoff is high. No matter how pricy the salt you choose, it will likely be the least expensive ingredient in your dish—and if it comes off right, it will catapult the food's flavor into the stratosphere.

5. Using all-natural artisan salts is fun, easy, and satisfying on many levels. Once you start using artisan salts, you will never go back to refined salt.

The mission of this book is to make you think differently about salt and empower you to make food that is better in every way. My hope is to instill an appreciation for salt, to make salt more accessible, and to inspire cooking that benefits from taking advantage of the relationship of natural salts to all the other ingredients we eat. The book sets forth a categorization of salts that brings order to the multitude of salts out there and gives everyone from eaters to chefs—even salt makers—a framework for understanding and appreciating the salts of the world, and then using them to their greatest effect.

This book does not approach this challenge with a totally detached perspective. I believe salt awakens us to our senses and our instincts like no other edible substance. I believe it connects us to our environment and our traditions like no other substance of any kind. If we grant these suppositions—or maybe just allow them for the sake of argument—we open ourselves up to some ideas that may seem bold or extreme, but that are also fun and empowering. Here are the major assertions that inform this book:

1. Salt is the single most important ingredient in cooking and the single most powerful tool for improving the flavor of food.

2. No two salts are the same, any more than two varieties of mushroom are the same.

3. Some things do not belong in our food supply. Industrial salts like cheap sea salt, kosher salt, and table salt are products that few people want in their kitchens if they understand and face up to how they are made.

4. There is no equating industrial salt with artisan salt. Artisan salts are better than industrial salts. Think of industrial salt as you would think of open-heart surgery: use it only if your life depends on it.

5. Buying good salt can change the world by supporting traditional economies that preserve ecologically and culturally valuable resources. Buying standardized salt issuing from a handful of industrial suppliers supports one part of a globalized chemical industry.

6. Salt is not bad for you. On the contrary, it is very good for you. It is right and proper to use as much salt as you want so long as you are the one salting your food.

Honoring salt and using it well begins with a glimpse at the cultural and economic centrality of salt. It then explores salt's natural complexity and the artisanship behind it. With this in hand, we need a vocabulary and unifying framework for appreciating all kinds of salt from all parts of the world. Last, we can look at a variety of approaches, some traditional and some novel, to using salt in the ways that best suit you. An appreciation for salt—traditionally made in particular—changes our world for the better, leading to better tasting food, more empowered consumers, healthier populations, more sustainable food production, preserved natural environments, and a restored sense of belonging.

Salt is the prism through which the ingredients, dishes, and people of the world can be experienced in all their fullness and variety. Sprinkle the parchment-fine flakes of Maldon sea salt on homegrown butter leaf lettuce dressed in a shallot vinaigrette, and you will experience a chlorophyll dynamo that strums at the very heart of nature. Let fall dark crystals of Cyprus black flake salt on medallions of seared pork and plantains and you will feel the turgid rush of Incan discovery. Grind smoked salt on hand-churned ice cream and you will trade in your house for an igloo. Salt sates the alchemist's desire, transmuting food to fantasy.

THE LIFE OF SALT

HISTORY: FIRST BITE

With all thine offerings thou shalt offer salt. —Leviticus 2:13

Imagine that first person. Driven from the safety of her clan by the pangs of a sharp and terrible hunger, she takes the forbidden path. She pricks her ears for the sound of a panther stalking from behind, but hears only her own hushed breathing. Her bare feet slip occasionally on the moss that grows on the damp roots and fallen trees. But then she hears a soft roar ahead—not of an animal but of something else. . . . Suddenly she emerges from the jungle shadows into the fierce open light of the seashore. She shields her eyes for a moment with her hand, allowing the bright water to take shape before her, then quickly negotiates the jagged rocks to the water, mindful of the sharp pavement of barnacles under her bare feet. At the water's edge she glances over her shoulder once again to be sure she hasn't been pursued, then plunges, her golden form rippling through the cool, clear water, then vanishing. Clouds reflecting on the surface of the water scatter into a million points of light for a moment, then ripple back into focus. All is quiet beneath the surge of the tide. Then she surfaces, swims easily to the rocky shore, and climbs out. Salivating in anticipation, she cuts a piece of abalone from its pearly dome with a shard of broken shell and is about to eat when she spies a crust of white crystals sparkling at the bottom of an evaporated pool by her side.

Her mind races.

She has tasted this stuff before, licking at the silver lacework evaporated from her own perspiration after running through the tall savanna grasses. She knows its intimacy with her body, having tasted it in the blood licked from a scraped knee. She knows it from the waters through which she just swam. She reaches over and rubs the chunk of abalone in the salt, and bites.

We were innovative foragers, opportunistic in the extreme, relentlessly tasting everything in the environment to evaluate its nutritional potential; salting was something altogether new, perhaps the first seasoning ever applied, and by definition the most potent one. The food historian Felipe Fernández-Armesto said culture begins when the raw gets cooked because it is cooking that brings us together. But really, why would it not have started eons before the taming of fire, with that first primal cuisine, raw but wonderfully seasoned.

The first salt intentionally eaten with food would have startled the taste of even the most salt-jaded modern eater: raw seawater, rich in chlorine, sodium, magnesium, calcium, sulfur, carbon, potassium, bromine, and about seventy-five other minerals evaporated down to a dazzling white crust in the nook of a rocky tide pool. The crystals would have been flakey and brittle, dissolving instantly in an ionic explosion of bold, bitter pungency.

The first salted food may well have catalyzed the first great dietary revolution—the shift from eating whatever could be easily found to imagining ways to make food taste better. We started to mix flavors, sandwiching different ingredients together before biting. We boiled seeds, leaves, and nuts in salt water to leach out bitterness, soaked meats in brine or rubbed them with salt to tenderize, and stoked a fire to soften fibrous roots or sinewy meat.

THE NOMAD AND THE FIG

Heaven knows, a civilized life is impossible without salt. —Pliny

If we are correct in our assumption that salting came in the early days of our existence, when we were still foraging tirelessly for food, then it was not until a few hundred thousand years after our first salted food that hunting became a major source of food. Soon we developed weapons and hunting techniques sufficient to kill rhinoceroses. Having climbed this last rung of the food chain, we were now an elite hunting species: *Homo erectus*. We lived in a competitive landscape, and the quest for food and territory led us into Europe, Asia, and beyond. Lacking the shaggy pelts of the northern animals we encountered there, we killed them and wore their dried hides. We invented fire and thrived like this for hundreds of thousands of years, eating a variety of nutritious plants and animal meats, adapting our behavior and diet to our surroundings. There was no place we could not go.

Then one blue-white winter morning, Neanderthal man crested a frozen ridge and descended into the valley below. Neanderthals' (*Homo neanderthalensis*) increased intelligence gave them the ability to think more strategically about dietary needs. Rather than eating food as they gathered it, they hunted large game, then dried, smoked, or cooked it, and transported it to a safe place for storage during times of plenty. The Neanderthals who prepared and stored foods were often as not located near readily available salt, so while there is little archeological evidence of the fact, they likely collected salt and may well have learned to preserve food with it.

Historians disagree over when and where salt curing was discovered, but there is evidence that salt preservation has been practiced since before the last ice age some 12,000 years ago, and that salt-preservation techniques developed independently in geographically remote and culturally unrelated societies.

Neanderthals ranged broadly, and would have made use of various sources of salt. Salt deposits in the hills of Austria and Poland would have supplied them with a bold but blunt-tasting rock salt for feasts of woolly mammoth flesh, root vegetables, and berries. The shores of the Mediterranean and the Dead Sea, and salt springs and sea marshes across Europe and Asia would have provided seasonal access to crunchy crystals of solar evaporated sea salt to be sprinkled on deer, fish, and fruits.

After salting and cooking, the next great advance was the discovery of curing. Drying meat was likely the first method of preservation used, possibly practiced by Neanderthals as far back as 125,000 years ago, so it is conceivable that the tastier and more nutritious method of salt preserving was also not unknown to Neanderthal culture, which often subsisted on infrequent kills of large game that would have to sustain a community for several days or weeks.

Homo sapiens, our own species, appeared sometime between 150,000 and 300,000 years ago. Like our ancestors, we have very large brains, and our mouths reflect adaptations to a distinctly human diet: we have an overbite suited for cutting cooked meat rather than tearing raw meat, and a weaker jaw commensurate with our decreased need to chew tough foods. Compared with most other animals, we have a relatively poor sense of smell, because our highly developed brain has given us the ability to identify and evaluate food visually and through customs. But our taste faculties are refined. We can taste and enjoy a very wide range of foods.

Still, for the most part, we ate salt opportunistically. With hunted meats and a range of plant foods providing us with sufficient minerals to survive, we had only infrequent physiological impetus to consume more salt than our diet naturally provided.

That all began to change about 12,000 years ago with the end of the last great ice age. For the first time in thousands of years, people could live in one place amid a relative abundance of food. Staying put gave us an opportunity to experiment and observe. It wasn't long before we discovered that plants didn't appear from nowhere but came from seed, and that some animals could be tamed. Archeologists have found domesticated figs dating to 9400 BCE; figs may have beaten the domestication of grains by a full thousand years. Next came the domestication of sheep, at around 8000 BCE; sometime around 7000 BCE, cattle and pigs were domesticated. We learned to cultivate barley, wheat, and legumes, built homes out of strong timbers and stone, and settled down.

These changes shifted our traditional supply of salt. Before, most of our salt came from the meat of animals caught in the wild, and to a lesser degree from foraged vegetables, roots, and fruits. Growing crops repeatedly in the same fields depleted the natural salinity of the soil, and we found our appetite for added salt growing. Without a ranging habitat, our livestock also needed an external source of salt. Modern milk cows may require as much as 80 pounds of salt per year, though Neolithic cattle likely needed closer to 6.6 pounds. Salt springs drew the first herdsmen and stockbreeders to settle in previously inhospitable lands. In addition to needing salt and arable land, the settlement pattern of the Neolithic age was determined in part by the availability of salt.

The Neolithic period is sometimes thought of as a time of relative calm, a dark age before the advent of the grand cultures of the ancient world. On the contrary, the millennia spanning about 15000 BCE to 5000 BCE were times of intense economic and cultural development. Our species was embracing a radically different lifestyle, adapting from a world where everything was found or hunted to one where by dint of foresight and labor we could provide for ourselves. Now we needed not just access to land, but ownership of land. We needed social conventions and laws that protected our work and property against greedy or needy neighbors, and politics and armies to protect against outsiders. Living on the same plot of land for years, generations, centuries, we optimized our farming practices, and nascent trade with others accelerated the development of new technologies.

During the Neolithic period, salt rapidly took on vital importance—for feeding ourselves and our livestock, and possibly for curing and preserving foods, tanning hides, producing dyes and other chemicals, and medicine. We evolved with a physiological requirement for salt; our culture was born from it. Access to salt became essential to survival. Salt localized groups of people. It was the first distinctively local food. It was also the first exotic one.

THE SALT TRADE

Each man calls barbarism what is not his own practice, for indeed it seems we have no other test of truth and reason than the example and pattern of the opinions and customs of the country we live in.
—Michel de Montaigne

Farming and raising animals provided more food than we had previously known. Populations increased and people lived closer together. With the ability to produce food in abundance, we traded more. It became apparent that some groups could make things better and more easily than other groups. The specialization that started as individual artisanship within a village led to the specialization of entire villages. Some would make wool and cheese in the mountains; some would market fish from the sea and products from other shores. Developing and exploiting saltworks became a specialty for some people.

The phoenix-like Cucuteni culture in the Carpathian Mountains of Romania, famous for periodically burning their own villages to the ground only to rebuild them again from the ashes, spawned some of the first artisans to specialize in salt making—or at least they were among the first to leave ample evidence of their industry. Shards of pottery used to evaporate brines from a salt spring in the Carpathians date to 6000 BCE, and salt is credited with supporting the growth and expansion of the Cucuteni people. Neolithic settlements with

evidence of salt production have been discovered in Thailand, Philippines, Iran, and Egypt.

The Phoenicians established the port city of Tyre in 2750 BCE (according to Herodotus), in what is now Lebanon, and from there they built a powerful, decentralized network of culturally linked city-states based on trade. They were a maritime society with legendary seafaring skills, rumored to have made the first crossing of the Atlantic some 2,000 years before Columbus. Saltworks were one of the chief features of their settlements in Lebanon, Tunisia, Egypt, Turkey, Cyprus, Crete, and Sicily. By 1110 BCE, they had founded Gadir, now Cádiz, in Spain, linking trade operations with Allis Ubbo, now called Lisbon, where Phoenicians may have traded since 1200 BCE. Both settlements boasted saltworks.

Phoenician ships may have spread salt-making technologies as far north as England. The great warehouses of Tyre stocked goods from as far east as India, and it is not unlikely that the Phoenicians promoted salt making across the

WHEEL OF FORTUNE

The sale of salt—and its use as currency—is legend. The technical challenges to administering a salt-based economy are less known. Moving around vast amounts of a granular commodity and exchanging it at a more or less fixed rate for another commodity means packing it in barrels or leather sacks, weighing it out for the customer, then packing the measured quantity in barrels or sacks. All of this packing, unpacking, measuring, and repacking is expensive. Drying wet salt in molds in an

oven provides standardized, easy-to-handle pucks of salt that can be traded at a standardized price. The *queijo de sal* ("cheese wheel of salt") made at the Rio Maior saltworks in Portugal is possibly the last remaining example of this once-common style of currency. Located twenty miles from the sea, Rio Maior is also among the only inland salt farm still active in Europe. Its salt pans are fed by a briny spring that is seven times more saline than the sea. Salt has been made at Rio Maior since time immemorial. In 1177, Pedro d'Aragon and his bride, Sancha Smith, sold a portion of the saltworks at Rio Maior to the Knights Templar, who may have used salt sales to help fund the Third Crusade. In my estimation, the queijo de sal pictured here, a gift from the impassioned Dr. Loïc Ménanteau, an expert in European salt marshes at the University of Nantes, is priceless. ■

Middle East. Assyrians, Byzantines, Persians, Romans, and Celts all took over Phoenician settlements, many of them becoming strategic saltworks.

The growing importance of salt was not a phenomenon confined to the Mediterranean world. The Chinese were making salt on a large scale for at least six millennia before Christ was born. One technology they developed—the process of using bamboo pipes to move brine from wells to iron pans where it was boiled off—was in continuous use at least since 450 BCE until the twentieth century. Prior to that, earthenware vessels were used. A site on the Ganjing River has known salt production more or less continually from the third millennium BC until modern times. The practice of raising revenue through a salt tribute may have started in the Xia Dynasty (2070 BCE to 1600 BCE). Subsequently, entire dynasties rose and fell as a result of wars fought to control salt production, such as the fighting during the Spring and Autumn Period (770 BCE to 476 BCE) between the Ba, Chu, Shu, and Qin. China maintained a monopoly on salt from 221 BCE to 1911 CE, and at one time, more than half of the Chinese imperial budget was raised through the taxation of salt.

Japan did not make the transition from hunter-gatherer to agrarian society until the very end of the Neolithic period, when, around 2200 BCE, successive waves of immigrants from the Korean Peninsula and China brought rice cultivation to the islands. It was only thereafter that the first salts were regularly produced in Japan, using fire to evaporate seawater or brine-soaked sand or kelp in earthenware vessels. The Japanese archipelago has no rock salt deposits of

its own, and its damp, relatively cool climate is inhospitable to the production of sea salt. Salt, the cornerstone of cultures built on farming and raising animals, was essential to the stability of Neolithic economies, and Japan's lack of local salt may well have been the stumbling block that kept Japanese tribes from settling down into agrarian societies thousands of years earlier.

Ancient India had access to voluminous supplies of rock salt from deposits such as the Salt Range just south of the Himalayas, in addition to sea salt from the Rann of Kutch, a marshy region on the west coast, and hundreds of other sites along the subcontinent's vast, often arid coastlines. The *rishis*, divine poets and scribes of Hindu lore, sang of the rock salt *kala namak*. Today, kala namak is a staple of northern Indian cuisine and a favorite of traditional ayurvedic healers, who claim that it possesses therapeutic qualities.

Salt production has been ubiquitous for millennia along the coasts of eastern Africa, where salt is scraped from the mud or boiled from the sand of tidal marshes. One of the most famous routes ever to be used for the salt trade was the path crossing the Sahel to link the salt mines of northern Mali's Sahara Desert to customers in the heavily populated, salt-poor regions of sub-Saharan West Africa. It was here that in ancient times Tuareg and Berber traders transported salt to be exchanged for gold. This trade would become the foundation of three great African empires: the Songhay, the Ghana, and the Mali.

The Mali Empire prospered as much from its salt mines as for its vast supplies of gold. Pound for pound, salt was worth as much as the precious metal or more. Salt, like gold, was taxed across the board, and often exchanged directly as currency. The famous Arab traveler Ibn Battuta visited Mali in 1352 and reported on the city of Taghaza, the home of the largest salt mine in the Mali Empire. Today both city and mine have been swallowed by the desert, and not a trace of either remains, though salt continues to be mined in Taoudenni, a city that drifts like the sands of the Sahara as the mining population follows the veins of salt ribboned across that desiccated landscape.

In Mesoamerica, archeological investigations have uncovered evidence of solar evaporated salt production dating back to the second millennium BCE, and evidence of fire evaporated brine from the second half of the first millennium BCE. An estimated two million people inhabited the Guatemalan and Mexican highlands at the height of the Mayan Empire, around 700 CE, and great saltworks on the Yucatan Peninsula's coastal salt lagoons and along the coasts of Central America may have manufactured thirty tons of salt or more a day to feed them. Incan salt was both mined and evaporated in the Andes; and in highland Ecuador, before the arrival of Europeans, salt was widely produced by boiling saline spring water. Where possible, salt production appears to have been performed on a household scale throughout the New World. North American tribes taught European settlers their salt-making techniques. Among their pupils was Daniel Boone, who needed salt to treat beaver pelts.

For most of history, the story has been much the same wherever salt was produced: whoever controlled salt making had the economic upper hand. Salt became not just a means to achieve power, but a symbol of it. During the Renaissance, European nobility regarded salt as a symbol of status, often storing it in boxes, or cellars, that were crafted from gold and studded with jewels. It was a lust that was matched by connoisseurship—royal tables were supplied with the finest French fleur de sel.

Nations and monarchs have often taxed salt in order to raise revenue. At various stages in the 2,000 years of salt tax codification, these monies provided a major source of funding for the Great Wall of China, built between the fifth century BCE and the sixteenth century CE to protect the Chinese Empire against rivals to the north.

Jo Haemer salt cellar, hand chased, solid sterling silver with 24 karat gold inlay and accompanying scallion salt spoon.

Salt's role in creating prosperity for nations has been rivaled by its role in destabilizing or even breaking them. France's *gabelle* (from the Latin *gabulum*, or tax) was a direct salt tax levied by the king, first initiated in 1286. It gave the monarchy a monopoly over the distribution of salt, and actually forced every French citizen to buy a certain amount of salt per week at a price fixed by the government. At its worst, the purchase cost of salt could reach as high as one month's wages for an average family every year. (In 2010 dollars that amounts to over $3,800 annually spent on salt for an average household!) Violent outbursts of mass civil disobedience were common in France by the early seventeenth century, and one common manifestation was the killing of the agents of tax farmers hired to enforce the gabelle, which had become a potent symbol of inequality.

As the tax rate varied by region, smuggling between regions with lower tax rates and those with higher ones was also rife. Those caught unarmed with contraband salt on them would be sent to the galleys for a year or two for a first offense, six years for the second. Those caught armed in the same predicament were sentenced to death. During the years of the gabelle, 2,300 men, 2,800 women, and 6,600 youths were imprisoned for possession of illegal salt.

In India, the British East India Company began taxing salt in the late eighteenth century, a practice that received government support in 1835. In 1885, the first Indian National Congress in Bombay protested the taxation on salt, and Gandhi used popular opposition to the salt tax to launch his famous Salt Satyagraha in 1930—the first organized campaign of nonviolent opposition to British Rule in India's struggle for independence.

THE RISE OF BIG SALT

Goods are neutral; they can be used as fences or bridges. —Mary Douglass

From the Neolithic period until the invention of the Gutenberg printing press, most human communication outside of the household revolved around the exchange of goods and services. In fact, commerce has always been one of the most powerful ways to transmit culture across distances—for thousands of years, it has been both a dominant mode of communication and the substance of that communication.

Where salt was made, how it was made, and by whom determined the value and meaning of the salt. Was it made near a trade route or deep in a range of jagged mountains? Were the salt makers mercantile and predictable or imperialistic and hostile or neighborly and generous? Was the salt made by solar evaporation and available only seasonally, or by boiling brine over fire that required a constant supply of wood, or both; or was it mined from deposits, dependent on the vicissitudes of human labor as much as geology?

Salt making on a regional basis reached its peak worldwide in the mid 1800s. At the time, the saltworks of Guérande employed in the neighborhood of 900 salt workers. In the late 1850s, mechanization came to the salt-making regions of the Mediterranean, where the topography and climate were conducive to much larger scale production than traditional practices allowed. Salt crystallizing pans that once measured a few hundred square feet were expanded to dozens of acres. Water was pumped mechanically where gravity used to do the job, and mechanical combines replaced hand-held rakes. Rail transportation and steamships brought the resulting low-cost salt to markets across the country, across the continent, and across the oceans.

The sophisticated artisanal techniques developed over millennia to cope with the considerable topographic and climatologic constraints of northern Europe were no match for such economies of scale. By the end of the 1800s, artisan salt making was in rapid decline in Europe; by the 1960s, mechanized salt producers had obliterated most small-scale saltworks around the globe. In 1857, the three primary salt-making centers of western France produced 208,000 metric tons of salt—half of all French sea salt. The other half came from the Mediterranean saltworks of Aigues-Mortes and Salin-de-Giraud in the Camargue, and from inland salt deposits in eastern France. The mechanized salt-making operations of Camargue and elsewhere soon flooded the market in cheap salt, and, by 1949, salt production in western France had fallen to 90,000 metric tons. Salt produced by traditional means reached its nadir in 1987, when the small handful of remaining salt makers produced 7,000 metric tons.

The story was much the same for salt makers elsewhere in the world. Wealthier countries transitioned first, either shutting down small-scale saltworks while expanding those with the greatest potential or turning to cheap imports and abandoning salt making altogether. Artisan salt makers in poorer countries struggled against the vast white wave of cheap salt from the industrialized producers. Sometimes they rallied. More often they vanished. In the span of the last century, tens of thousands of small salt makers around the world found themselves out of business. Efficiency was the name of the game. From the time of the civil war to today, the number of salt workers in the United States tripled—but salt production increased one hundred–fold.

Yet mechanized manufacturing and transportation of salt was outpaced by new industrial demand. In 1861, the Belgian chemist Ernest Solvay invented a process for making soda ash (sodium carbonate) from salt brine. By applying heat to limestone, which contains calcium carbonate, the process released carbon dioxide. Combined with ammonia and sodium chloride, this made one of the major chemical feedstocks of the industrial revolution. Used to make glass and as a precursor for a host of other chemical manufacturing processes, the world produces about 90 billion pounds of soda ash a year, or about 13.5 pounds for every man, woman, and child on earth.

Soon the chloralkali process emerged as an even larger industry using salt. When electricity is passed through salt brine (often with the aid of mercury), two major chemical products are produced: caustic soda (sodium hydroxide) and chlorine. Today, chloralkali processing is the largest single consumer of salt. Rayon, explosives, cosmetics and pharmaceuticals, shampoos, soaps, skin lotions, dry bleach, surgical cautery, gasoline refining—about fourteen thousand other products and processes all require these chemicals or the chemicals made from them. Between the Solvay and chloralkali processes, salt is the second biggest chemical feedstock after petroleum.

In the 1950s, the United States and other industrial countries began building freeways, and then needed salt to keep them clear of ice. Industrial salt found another megamarket, demanding many millions of tons of salt a year.

Food uses for salt have also increased exponentially over the last century and a half. Even as the reliance on salt for preserving foods fell with the advent of refrigeration and high-speed transportation, demand for salt for food manufacture grew. Modern transportation and food-processing technologies allowed single companies to funnel the agricultural productions of entire regions through consolidated processing centers—canning, pickling, and curing everything from peas to pigs. Ironically, the same industrial revolution that brought fresh seafood a thousand miles inland also converted modern people into consumers of more salt-processed foods than ever before

> *In a revolution, as in a novel, the most difficult part to invent is the end.*
> —Alexis de Tocqueville

An estimated 97 percent of the salt produced globally is not consumed in food. In 2008, Morton Salt reported 42 percent of its sales were deicing salt, 34 percent industrial salt, and just 22 percent food salt, with the remainder going to chemical uses. But Morton, like many other salt companies, is actually a division of the much bigger fertilizer chemical and salt company K+S, which surpassed industry titan China National Salt Industry Corporation as the world's largest when it purchased Morton from Dow Chemical.

Big salt companies serve enormous markets and crank out mind-numbing quantities of mined and evaporated salt. K+S had a production capacity of 30 million tons of salt in 2009. China National Salt had a 19 million ton capacity. Compass Minerals and Cargill each have a capacity of about 14 million tons. The other biggies, Dampier Salt (9 million tons), Artyomsol (7.5 million tons), Exportadora de Sal (7 million tons), Südsalz (5.3 million tons), the Salins Group (4.1 million tons), Mitsui & Co. (3.8 million tons), and AkzoNobel (3.6 million tons), all split their sales among road, industrial/pharmaceutical, chemical, and food sectors. The production from just the top ten salt manufacturers would be enough to fill 1,475,714 railway cars, which would form a train 14,000 miles long. More industrial salt is on the way, with a new salt field on Lake Assal in Djibouti—which has a salinity of 34.8 percent salt, ten times that of the ocean, and is considered the largest undeveloped salt reserve in the world—slated

to produce 4 million tons per year starting in 2012. The solution mining of salt, which involves pumping water into an underground salt deposit to make a brine, is an equally huge business, and makes up the bulk of salts used in chemical manufacturing, bringing the total annual output worldwide to about 260 million tons, enough to fill a train that would circle the planet one and a half times.

Small producers focusing exclusively on culinary salt are few and far between. Guérande, once a pillar of the global salt trade, now makes less than 0.005 percent of the world's salt.

Any business that deals in hundreds of thousands of tons of a raw material must be attentive to consistency, purity, and cost. The salt industry is no different. Industrial solar evaporated sea salt costs about $67 per metric ton, or six cents a pound. Production is geared toward yield of pure, commercially valuable sodium chloride. Everything else present in natural salt is viewed as a contaminant. Industrial salt makers regularly achieve 99.7 percent or higher sodium chloride purity. Culinary salt is usually refined even further, removing pollutants introduced by mechanized handling or by the industrialized surroundings, and often adding a host of chemicals to ready it for mass markets. Salts, once nearly infinitely varied, are today standardized into a handful of products. The salt most modern people sprinkle in their food, even home cooks and chefs who pride themselves on using only wholesome natural ingredients, is an artificially uniform cocktail of refined NaCl (sodium chloride) marketed as table salt, kosher salt, sea salt, or rock salt. The takeover of salt by industry was inevitable, and many aspects of the modern economy would not have been possible without it. NaCl is, in that sense, a celebration of industrialism.

But regardless of industrial demand, the salt we put on our food would never have changed so much without a fundamental shift in cultural values. The nineteenth century brought an increased fascination with all things refined and manufactured. Something made by a machine was better than something made by hand. This logic viewed all irregularities (whether nutritional, social, or regional) as undesirable, hailed economies of scale as egalitarian and cost reductive, and promoted manmade things as superior to naturally created things. Salt, for so many millennia an inescapably unique and regionally specific food, vanished. In its place we adopted the NaCl proffered by industry. Thousands of years of salt history were abruptly whited out.

RETURN OF THE ARTISANS

All men are prepared to accomplish the incredible if their ideals are threatened. —Maya Angelou

A shift in consumer values has begun to reverse the dominance—or at least the unquestioned allure—of industrialized salt. The shift is occurring as part of a much larger movement in food awareness. Whole foods are gaining appeal over packaged foods. Produce grown with fertilizers and insecticides is avoided in favor of organically grown options. We pay attention to the types of feed our livestock is raised on. Local food is appreciated for its freshness and for the regional character of the varieties grown. By extension, farmers are again seen as important members of the community. We even think of the environmental impacts of monoculture farming, packaging, refrigeration, and long-distance transport.

Salt was a latecomer to this renaissance. In the West, interest in artisan salt was sparked by the revival of artisan salt making in France, a revival that began in Guérande. Sensing that there would soon be nobody left to continue the ancestral ways of salt making (and also desperate to fend off the imminent destruction of sensitive, culturally unique marine wetlands by real estate developers), a small group of artisans in the almost completely abandoned salt marshes of Guérande banded together. Their idea was to promote salt just like wine: call attention to its *terroir* and *meroir* (the special taste of sea in the area); celebrate its artisan roots; and make it an icon symbolizing the rejection of industrialized food production.

In 1972, these artisans formed Le Groupement des Producteurs de Sel, or the Salt Producers' Group; in 1979, they established a center to train new salt makers. Taking the economic operations of their collaboration into their own hands, they formed an agricultural cooperative in 1988 that buys the salt produced by its members according to a price the workers themselves establish at the beginning of the season. Other traditional salt-making centers along France's west coast rallied as well, and today Ile de Noirmoutier and Ile de Ré, to the south, are major producers of artisan salt. Untold acres of coastal wetlands were preserved in the process. The entire region has become a haven for bicycling ecotourists seeking a summer of birdwatching, oyster eating, and wine drinking.

The Guérande cooperative did more than just elevate and promote artisan salt, it brought international attention to the merits of reviving ancestral salt fields; salt making could preserve cultural heritage, provide a noble and rewarding occupation, promote the natural beauty of a region, catalyze new economic activity through tourism, and offer a viable alternative to destroying natural coastlines. Salt makers in central and southern Portugal, in Spain, in Italy, in Africa, and elsewhere have applied both the salt-making expertise and the business strategies of the Guérande cooperative to their own salt fields.

A similar story took place in the Land of the Rising Sun. The Japanese government placed a monopoly on salt production after 1905 in order to offset the costs of the Russo-Japanese War and pump money into its industrial salt infrastructure. In 1971, the already constrictive reign of the government monopoly delivered a devastating gut check to artisan salt makers by banning production on all coastal salt fields. Ancient saltworks were bulldozed for development. The government mandated production standards, and a process called ion exchange membrane electrodialysis was instituted, more or less at a national level. Ion exchange membrane electrodialysis concentrates and extracts sodium and chlorine atoms in seawater or from brine discharged from a reverse osmosis seawater desalination plant, forming a salt in excess of 99.5 percent NaCl purity. This salt was advertised as safer than traditionally produced salts thanks to the elimination of contaminants, which, ironically, were the result of the industrial effluent polluting coastal waters.

The Japanese point out that beyond the basic differences in the level of salinity, the mineral content of seawater and of human body fluids are closely correlated, and believe natural salts are an important source of the sea's bioavailable minerals. A movement to revive natural salt was founded with the establishment in 1972 of the Investigation on Dietary Salt as a nonprofit research group. Following a wave of popular sentiment in favor of whole, unrefined salt, the government repealed the salt monopoly in 1997. Since then there has been an explosion in artisan salt production in Japan, with more than 700 Japanese salt producers marketing more than 1,500 varieties of salt. The Japanese example testifies to the ability of the marketplace and popular opinion to reconstitute an artisan economy out of seawater.

Guérande remains a bridge from the most distant past to the present: a financially profitable, environmentally sustainable industry that produces one of the most widely celebrated foods in the world. Several saltworks reputedly dating from the Carolingian dynasty (mid-eighth to late tenth century) are still making salt in Guérande.

In 1840, 2,350 *paludiers* (salt workers) of Guérande cultivated 255,577 salt crystallizing pans, called *oeillets,* in a great network of interlinked channels and ponds. By 1934, just 370 workers remained, operating 19,907 oeillets. By 1980, just 8,476 oeillets remained and only 202 paludiers were still at work. By 1994, the salt fields had shrunk to just 5,650 oeillets, but the century-and-a-half-long decline in the number of paludiers had stopped, with 215 men and women tending the marshes. Today about 300 paludiers work some 20,000 oeillets in the Guérandais salt marshes. Our resurgent appetite for food tied to a land, a sea, a people; for food bound with strong and vibrant ties to our common and personal heritages; for a quality of food that tastes great, has resuscitated artisan salt. Salt has emerged once again as a food uniquely representative of its era.

SCIENCE: MIND, BODY, SALT, OCEAN

He who modeled us, considering these things, mixed earth with fire and water and blended them; and making a ferment of acid and salt, he mingled it with them and formed soft and succulent flesh. —Plato

For hundreds of thousands of years, salt has been the glittering, often elusive object of our desire. Its powers bordered on the mystical. It nourished. It healed. It purified. It preserved. And it tasted fantastic. Then, about two hundred years ago, we began to analyze those powers.

THE ORIGIN OF SALT

First, we described salt's chemical components: primarily an electrically neutral crystalline substance produced by the reaction of a base—sodium—and an acid—chloride. Technically, salt is any compound formed when a cation (a positively charged ion) combines with an anion (a negative ion) to become electrically neutral. A salt dissolved in water is called an electrolyte because it conducts electricity. Salts come in every imaginable color, and indeed are often used as pigments. Manganese dioxide is a bottomless black. Ferric hexacyanoferrate is Prussian blue. Potassium dichromate is a brilliant orange-red.

The sea is the biggest repository of salts. Its untold trillions of tons of salt water are 3.5 percent salts. Of that 3.5 percent, sulfate ions make up 7.68 percent, magnesium 3.68 percent, calcium 1.18 percent, potassium 1.11 percent, bicarbonate 0.41 percent, bromide 0.19 percent, and 0.13 percent are other ions. But most of the salts in the ocean are chloride (55.03 percent) and sodium (30.59 percent), which crystallize into the salt sodium chloride ($NaCl$).

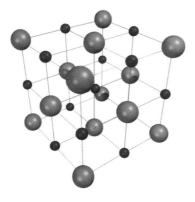

Once humans started researching the way salt performed its myriad roles, we began manufacturing its chemical components on an industrial scale. Pure sodium chloride soon became the primary feedstock of a budding chemical industry and a commodity on store shelves. We grew to think of it as an industrially manufactured chemical. By the time supermarkets came along in the 1920s, industrial salt had become commonplace. To paraphrase the dictionary open on my desk, salt has become "a white or colorless crystalline solid of sodium chloride."

We think we know what salt is. But whenever we try to simplify something in nature, we inevitably get it wrong. The character of an individual salt is determined by the unfathomably complex interactions of sea, land, and climate. Salt crystals offer as many variations of mineral composition, shape, size, and color as there are forms of snowflakes. Every salt bears encoded within it the human and natural environments from which it was born, and through it we can trace the lineaments of the human condition.

Salt started on earth about 5 billion years ago, when the molten planet cooled enough to support liquid water. Falling rain collected vast quantities of soluble minerals from the soil and atmosphere, slowly salting the ocean. Meanwhile, volcanic islands and undersea eruptions spewed clouds of ash into the atmosphere, where lightning bolts fried them into amino acids, the basic building blocks of proteins, and these gradually accumulated on the sea floor. Drying sea beds, tectonic and volcanic activity, sun, and rain—all churned and cooked the earth's crust, ocean, and atmosphere for millions upon millions upon millions of years. All the while, meteors were slamming into the planet, vaporizing water and earth and salt, and low-flying comets hailed down frozen water and carbon dioxide, methane, and ammonia amid fireballs of rock and dirt. Rain washed all of it—protein, ash, meteor dust, noxious gases, everything—into the ocean, which, as you may imagine, became a very complicated place.

Some scientists believe that salts in the primordial ocean provided the organic precursors for the development of life. They think that primordial salts, superheated by volcanic activity, formed pyrroles, which are compounds found in chlorophyll (which converts sunlight to sugar in plants), and hemoglobin (which transports oxygen through blood). Without salt, there may never have been life at all. Over the course of hundreds and hundreds of millions of years of increasingly complex interactions between the sea, sun, atmosphere, and earth, molecules gained the ability to harvest light and something sprang to life. Eventually we had blueprints for life encoded in the complex molecules called DNA; eukaryotic cells formed; and a few billion years later, we have you.

Today's oceans retain much of their primordial vitality. Every element in the earth's crust and in its atmosphere is present in seawater. Eight elements make up ninety-nine percent of the ocean: oxygen, hydrogen, chlorine, and sodium, with considerable amounts of magnesium, sulfur, calcium, and potassium. But a laundry list of another 76 or more minerals follows, from argon to zirconium—the crystalline image of earth's ancient, violent past.

The overall volume of dissolved matter in the ocean is staggering, enough to enrobe the entire planet in a 150-foot-thick blanket of salt, or to cover the entire land mass of the earth 500 feet deep.

THE ELEMENTS OF SEAWATER

Seawater contains virtually every element in the earth's crust. Nine of the top eleven elements in our bodies are among the top eleven elements of the sea.

WATER	Oxygen	85.700%
	Hydrogen	10.800%
TRACE MINERALS	Chlorine	1.900%
	Sodium	1.050%
	Magnesium	0.135%
	Sulfur	0.089%
	Calcium	0.040%
	Potassium	0.038%
	Bromine	0.007%
	Carbon	0.003%
	~74 others	0.239%
TOTAL		100%

SALT IN THE BODY

The cure for anything is salt water—sweat, tears, or the sea. —Isak Dinesen

Chemically, our bodies are about 99 percent oxygen, carbon, hydrogen, nitrogen, calcium, and phosphorus, and the remaining 1 percent is made up of potassium, sulfur, sodium, chlorine, magnesium, and iron, and trace amounts of dozens of other elements.

One of the biggest differences between us and the ocean is that we contain only about two-thirds water by weight, with much of the remaining third built out of carbon, nitrogen, and calcium. Also, our bodies are not as saline as the ocean, so the host of ions found in seawater are not as dominant in us. Blood is about 0.9 percent salt, 77 percent of which is sodium chloride, with lesser amounts of bicarbonate, potassium, and calcium. This holds true not just for humans, but for all vertebrate animals—from fish to reptiles to mammals. But the similarities between our bodies and the ocean are otherwise striking.

You can eliminate almost any single food or group of foods from your diet and still survive. Abstain from apples, and you will live. Abstain from all fruit, and you will live. Abstain from all plants, for that matter, and you will live. Or eat no meat and no animal by-products, and you will still live. But you cannot live without salt.

Dissolved in the water of your body, dietary salt exists as sodium and chlorine ions (chloride). For every ten grams of salt you eat, four grams are sodium and six are chloride. We use the sodium in salt to regulate how water functions within our bodies and, not coincidentally, we use water to regulate the body's concentration of salt. The human body boasts three distinct fluid systems: blood plasma, extracellular fluid, and lymphatic fluid—all salted. The concentration of sodium ions in the blood is directly related to the regulation of all these bodily fluid levels. Sodium performs dozens of functions in the body, mainly to do with fluid regulation, nerve and muscle function, and digestion; it carries water and nutrients into and out of cells; it helps regulate blood pressure and fluid volume; it helps with the function of blood vessels and other membranes.

Salt and water form a system that supports innumerable physiological processes; they're bound together as intimately and mysteriously as life itself. Even our thoughts are made of salt. The 100 billion neurons in your brain each contain about a million chemical pumps, each of which is capable of transporting hundreds of positively charged sodium and potassium ions per second to maintain higher concentrations of potassium ions inside the cells and higher levels of sodium outside. Specialized channels allow potassium to leak out of the cells at a slightly faster rate than sodium leaks in. This polarizes the membrane of the nerve cell, giving it a negative electrical potential, which in turn encourages sodium ions to enter the cell. When the ions are allowed in, the cell is depolarized; this cycle repeats every two milliseconds (0.002 seconds). The transition between the influx and efflux of sodium and potassium ions is called the action potential of the neuron—and makes up the electrical activity of your brain and the rest of your nervous system.

In the body, sodium works in tandem with potassium, the two major cations (positively charged ions) making up the body's salts. Sodium mainly permeates the fluid between cells (plasma) and the blood, providing the saline bath and nutrition necessary for the cells to thrive. Potassium, on the other hand, is retained mainly within the cells (in the intracellular fluid). There are about 157 potassium ions and just 14 sodium ions in intracellular fluid compared to 143 sodium and 4 potassium in interstitial fluids (blood) and 152 sodium and

5 potassium in plasma. (The major intercellular anions, or negatively charged ions, are phosphate and protein. The major anion in blood and plasma is chloride.) The body expends a tremendous amount of energy maintaining the balance of potassium and sodium inside and outside of the cells—recall the sodium and potassium pumps powering the electrical activity of our nerves. The presence of both in their proper balance supports nerve function and muscle contraction and relaxation, and regulates the permeability of the cell membrane, affecting how nutrients, water, and waste are transported to and from cells. Deficiency of one or the other compromises this process and hurts the cell. We regularly lose sodium through the excretion of urine, through our skin when we sweat, and in the production of stomach acid (hydrochloric acid). If we don't eat enough sodium every day, we will rapidly run low.

If you have too little sodium in your body, you are in trouble. Sodium deficiency, or hyponatremia, can cause headache, nausea and vomiting, muscle spasms and seizures, heart arrhythmia, decreased consciousness, or coma. Sodium deficiency among people with high blood pressure increases the risk of heart attack. One of the most serious possible effects of hyponatremia is swelling of the brain, which can lead to death: a healthy twenty-eight-year-old woman died after the 2002 Boston Marathon, not from dehydration as one might expect, but probably from drinking too much water, diluting the sodium level in her blood and causing hyponatremia. Additionally, if your body's sodium level falls below 0.85 percent, you lose the ability to regulate microbe growth, putting your internal organs at the mercy of yeasts, molds, bacteria, and viruses.

The opposite of hyponatremia is hypernatremia, an excess of sodium in the blood. This is caused not by excessive sodium in the body (though drinking seawater can cause it), but by an insufficient amount of water for your body to use to regulate itself. The slightest elevation of sodium levels in the body triggers powerful thirst sensations, making hypernatremia extremely uncommon. It occurs most often among the elderly, who lack the ability to get water when thirsty, or less commonly among infants, the severely mentally impaired, or people taking diuretics. Fatigue and confusion are followed by coma and death if hypernatremia is not treated.

Like sodium, the element chlorine is essential to your body. Chloride (an ion of chlorine) is the primary negatively charged ion in extracellular fluid, and sodium the main positively charged ion. Chloride, like sodium, serves the body as an electrolyte, enabling the electrical signals that allow muscle and nerve tissues to function. It also regulates the blood's ability to carry carbon dioxide out

SODIUM AND CHLORINE: THE DYNAMIC DUO

The two most abundant elements in salt are chlorine and sodium. Sodium is the sixth most abundant element in the earth's crust. It is an odorless metal with a rather luscious, light silvery sheen to it, and it is strangely pliant—in fact, soft as butter. Its chemical symbol is Na, after its Latin name, *natrium*. On the surface it seems pleasant enough, but it's really one of the most terrifying substances imaginable.

While you could cut metallic sodium with a butter knife, you would be very unwise to spread it on bread and eat it. Elemental sodium is incredibly reactive, and some of the substances it reacts most violently with are acids, alcohols, oxygen, carbon dioxide, and water. We are mostly water.

If you were to touch sodium, it would cause severe burns in reaction to the moisture on your skin; it could even ignite, causing a very serious deep tissue injury. If you were to swallow it, it would react with the water in your saliva and possibly explode. And it can cause severe respiratory trauma if inhaled.

Sodium catches fire when exposed to moisture and oxygen in the air. Once burning, it can burn violently enough to explode. Due to sodium's low melting point (about 208°F), sodium explosions tend to be accompanied by the spattering of molten sodium. If you were to attempt to douse burning sodium with water, highly explosive hydrogen gas would result.

Metallic sodium is used to prepare organic compounds and is essential for manufacturing esters—fruity compounds used in many artificially flavored foods and synthetic fragrances. It is part of sodium hydroxide (also called caustic soda or lye), which is in most industrial soaps, dyes, and cleaning agents and is commonly used to neutralize acids.

Chlorine is even more dangerous. Chlorine's chemical symbol is Cl; it exists normally as the gas Cl_2. At high concentrations, chlorine is corrosive and irritating to all body tissues. Inhalation can cause inflammation and breathing difficulty, known as chemical pneumonitis, and pulmonary edema, or fluid collecting in the lungs.

Chlorine reacts with water, yielding hydrochloric acid, which burns the skin and mucus membranes. You can smell chlorine in very minute quantities of just 3.5 parts per million (ppm). It causes throat irritation at 15 ppm, coughing at 30 ppm, and will kill you in a few deep breaths at 1,000 ppm. The German military used chlorine gas as a chemical weapon early in World War I; hence, it has the inglorious distinction of being among the first fatal chemical gases used in modern warfare.

Chlorine and sodium are both so reactive that they're never found in their elemental form in nature. Instead, most sodium and chlorine exist as sodium chloride, in crystalline form in salts and in ionic form in brines. Brine is a major feedstock for the chemical industry, which uses the chloralkali process of passing electricity through a brine to produce chlorine and sodium hydroxide, the two agents at the heart of the modern chemical industry. The chloralkali process accounts for about half of the salt consumption worldwide, supplying chemicals used in making everything from paper to medicine. ■

of the cells and out of the body through respiration. It helps the blood maintain a healthy pH balance and is essential to neurotransmitter function in the brain; chlorine plays a role in protein digestion, as a component of pepsin.

Chlorine is an essential component in the manufacture of the sanitizing agents the body uses to protect itself from contamination. This includes hydrochloric acid, which is the fluid in our stomach that plays a primary role in sterilizing and breaking down the food we eat. Chlorine also allows the body to produce hypochlorite, a disinfectant that the immune system relies on to battle infections.

SALT IN FOOD

Thou hadst better eat salt with the Philosophers of Greece, than sugar with the Courtiers of Italy. —Benjamin Franklin

Ideally, we would get all the salt we need from natural, whole foods. However, all animals, humans included, have always had to compete for food. Since animals first left the sea (where the balance in the ancient salt water they swam in was almost identical to the saltiness of their bodies) to walk the earth, they have had to seek outside sources for salt as a supplement.

There are just two ways to get enough salt in your diet to survive: eat animal flesh or eat some salt. A 120-gram serving of stewed rabbit contains about 20 milligrams of sodium, the equivalent of 50 milligrams of salt. The same size portion of beef sirloin contains 55 milligrams. There is barely any salt at all in plants. Edible forms of both meat and salt take considerable effort to procure. Perhaps, because the availability of salt in nature is so sporadic, and its importance to our survival is so constant and absolute, we have developed these intense physiological salt cravings and such sophisticated taste receptors for recognizing salt.

For these same reasons, our bodies are very good at regulating sodium levels. In fact, the systems regulating water and sodium levels in our bodies are perhaps biology's most well-developed and effective systems. With a compromised immune system, we may get sick. With a compromised endocrine system, our body fails to manage metabolism and tissue function. With a compromised sodium/water regulatory system, all the functions of our body—including immune, endocrine, nervous, and digestive systems—simply stop working.

Physiologically speaking, too much salt is not as severe a problem as too little, and it's highly unlikely to occur on a diet of unprocessed foods. Our bodies have several mechanisms to deal with a spike in salinity. One way is to increase water intake to dilute the level of sodium in our bodily fluids. (Conversely, decreasing the amount of water in our bodies raises sodium levels and triggers a sense of thirst, prompting us to take in water to bring our sodium levels back in balance.) Our kidneys are also incredibly efficient at eliminating sodium; some research has suggested that healthy kidneys supported with enough water can eliminate as much as three pounds of salt in a day. If your body has too much sodium, it will do a very good job of bringing things back into balance quickly.

SIFTING SALT FROM THE SEA

Mankind can live without gold . . . but not without salt. —Cassiodorus

All salt originates in the sea, where it swirls around in a solution of many dozens of ionized minerals and compounds. Chloride and sodium are the major ions giving the sea its salinity, which is the generic term for the concentration of dissolved salts in seawater. Because this is the primary salt we eat, we call sodium chloride "dietary salt." But there are other ions as well, such as sulfate, magnesium, calcium, potassium, bicarbonate, bromide, borate, and strontium. When water is evaporated out of the sea, the positive ions connect to the negative ones and, voila: salt.

Theoretically, if you filled a hundred-foot-tall cylinder with ocean water and let it evaporate, you would end up with a three-foot-thick layer of crystallized sodium chloride sandwiched between two thinner layers of other crystallized salts and trace minerals—mostly magnesium and potassium salts (which precipitate last) on the top and calcium salts (which precipitate first) on the bottom. This occurs because the different minerals in seawater crystallize at different concentrations. (This is why nearly pure sodium chloride can be mined from rock: it is taken from the massive middle layer formed by the evaporation of ancient seas.)

At a salinity of about 70 grams per liter, the first mineral to crystallize from seawater is calcium carbonate ($CaCO_3$), which forms limestone, chalk, and other types of rock. It is also the main component of seashells, eggshells, pearls, and over-the-counter antacids. It is followed by calcium sulfate, then sodium chloride, then magnesium sulfate. If you let the salt dry for long enough, a small amount of magnesium chloride, commonly called bittern, will develop as well. Artisan salt manufacturers tinker with, observe, adjust, and obsess over the process of evaporating salt water in order to achieve the mineral content they determine is most desirable. In Japan, they may even slow-heat the brine in order to ensure that the sodium chloride crystals take up extra bittern, which is tasty, and which they commonly believe to be beneficial to human health and well-being.

THE PHYSIOLOGY OF TASTING SALT

The role of taste is to help you separate what is good to eat from what is bad. Sweetness indicates a food that is high in energy, umami is the flavor of proteins, and our perception of salt insures that we will get the amount of electrolytes we need. Sour and bitter tastes warn us of potential harm, indicating the possible presence of toxins and contaminants in our food. Taste is just one part of our flavor-perception system—the part that's received in the mouth through taste receptors in taste buds. Together with aroma, received through olfactory receptors deep inside the nose, and tactile sensations of texture and temperature, we get all the information we need to perceive flavor—myriad sensations that provide us with much of the pleasure of eating.

Understanding the mechanisms in our bodies responsible for taste sensation has been the objective of intense scientific research, yet we are only just cracking the code for how it works. Taste buds are made up of bunches of taste receptor cells, each with distinct abilities to respond to different taste stimuli. Contrary to what many of us were taught, there are no distinct areas of the tongue more attuned to one taste or another: we detect all flavors in all the areas of the tongue where tasting occurs, and we gain vital information about the characteristics of our food from the other surfaces of our mouth as well.

While we understand a good deal about taste perception, we do not completely understand the most fundamental mechanisms for sensing salt in our mouth, whether it comes through the taste receptor cells or a combination of these and other structures. Salt dissolves into ions of sodium and chloride on our food and in our mouths. The mouth starts to buzz. If you taste salt by itself, you will know what I mean. The overpowering generalized cellular reaction to sodium makes it harder for scientists to isolate what is happening in salt-receiving taste receptors that is different from what is happening in any cell. It is chemically possible that saltiness stimulates virtually all the tissues of the mouth. The best evidence suggests that a special form of voltage-gated sodium channel is involved but pinning this down has proved difficult because all cells, not just those engaged in taste, have voltage-gated sodium channels.

Also a mystery and a subject of great interest is salt's impact on the sensation of other flavors. Add salt to something bitter or sour, and the bitterness or sourness is diminished. Add it to something sweet or umami, and those flavors can be accentuated. Salt not only tastes good in its own right, but it also improves the flavors of foods we need but might be less inclined to eat. Broccoli tastes better with salt. Mackerel tastes better. We may never fully unravel the billions of years of engineering that have resulted in a mouth that can receive so much pleasure from a single essential mineral. ■

Crystallization occurs as water evaporates. At a certain point (the solubility threshold), there is not enough water to hold the salt-forming ions in solution, and they begin to bond together into crystals. This happens in two stages: primary nucleation and secondary nucleation. During primary nucleation, the first seed crystals form in a solution. When there are too few water molecules to effectively hold all of the ions, the excess ions are attracted to one another more than to the water around them and they start coming together into tiny crystals. These microscopic crystals form the seed nuclei upon which secondary nucleation builds. A brine can be gently stirred or otherwise agitated at the start of secondary nucleation to promote the development of larger salt crystals around the seed nuclei. Some salts form only when the wind gives a light ruffle to the brines they come from.

Secondary nucleation makes up the bulk of the crystallization process, and is the only part of the process that you can see happening. It can be initiated through contact with almost any solid foundation, like a seed crystal, a speck of some other material, or the side of a container. Many salt makers believe the halobacteria that live in solar salt ponds help crystal formation, attributing their purplish color (which appears red, pink, or orange in water) with trapping more of the sun's heat and thus encouraging evaporation. Others believe the bacteria themselves may help in secondary nucleation—the salt-crystallizing equivalent of seeding clouds.

SEA SALT, INDUSTRIAL STYLE

I believe in looking reality straight in the eye and denying it.
—Garrison Keillor

Industrial salt making aims for two things: low cost and purity of sodium chloride. Forty-eight percent of all salt produced in the United States in 2007 was in brine, according to the U.S. Geological Survey. Brine is the least expensive salt; it mostly feeds the chemical industry.

Rock salt makes up 34 percent of production. Rock salt is mined from the earth, usually using diesel-powered equipment, dynamite, and grinders in vast underground chambers. Rock salts are the residue of ancient, receding oceans and can be as pure as 99.5 percent sodium chloride. Minable inland rock deposits come in two primary forms: bedded salt and salt domes. Salt domes occur when stratified salt deposits are subjected to pressures that cause them to extend upward and downward vertically, sometimes more than 20,000 feet. Unlike salt domes, bedded salt is not very deep, but can extend horizontally over great distances. Most rock salt is used for road deicing, with some also going toward feedstock for animals. A small percentage is refined for use as food salt.

The purest salts are made by vacuum pan evaporation (they are sometimes called evaporated salts), in which a brine (produced by pumping water into underground salt deposits to dissolve the salt buried in the rock) is pumped back up to the surface. The water is processed with chemicals such as carbon dioxide and sodium hydroxide to precipitate out unwanted calcium and magnesium salts and any other minerals. The refined brine is then boiled off in series vacuum evaporators until salt crystals form. Crystals forming within the brine will generally be tiny, cubic, identical, and up to 99.99 percent pure sodium chloride. The condensed brine can also be pumped to open pans to allow flakier crystals to form on the surface. The salt crystals may then be milled or rolled to create various particle shapes and sizes. This is where the common free-flowing, kosher, and other food-manufacturing salts come from. Vacuum evaporated salts account for about 10 percent of industrial salt production.

Solar salt fields in the United States made up about 8 percent of the total U.S. salt production in 2007, but this number doesn't take into account several of the largest solar salt farms in the world, located just outside the country. Mega salt farms, like Morton's Inagua salt fields in the Bahamas, produce upward of 2 million tons of solar evaporated salt each year. There are even bigger farms in Mexico, like Exportadora de Sal in Baja California, which can yield up to 7 million tons a year. Still more industrial sea salt is imported from overseas.

To keep production up and costs down, industrial solar evaporation relies on two key processes—pure sodium chloride crystallization and mechanized harvesting. The nutritional potential of the natural salt is disregarded. Industrially produced solar salt is made by evaporating water until the calcium carbonate and other unwanted salts crystallize and precipitate out. The remaining water is transferred to ponds where the sodium chloride is crystallized. Then, at about 75 percent salinity, before any of the magnesium or potassium salts begin to crystallize, all of the remaining dissolved salts are pumped out. The salt crystals are often rinsed in brine to remove any lingering magnesium salts. The resulting salt is about 99.7 percent sodium chloride. For example, California sea salt, manufactured by Cargill in the San Francisco Bay, is 99.83 percent sodium chloride.

Sea salt is harvested by bulldozers that scrape it from the pond beds in 350-ton loads. Thousands of tons are produced in a single day. Industrially produced solar salt sells for about $60 a ton, or about 3 cents a pound. The culinary or dietary benefits that might be gained from capturing calcium, magnesium, and potassium salts and the host of other minerals in the natural source water are not a consideration, because the majority of the product is not meant for the table. Most solar evaporated sodium chloride is used industrially, where chemical purity trumps flavor, crystal structure, and mineral content. However, some of this salt is washed to remove the residue of industrial handling and other environmental pollutants and purified so that it can be marketed as "sea salt."

Traditional salt makers shift their brine from evaporating ponds to crystallization pans when the concentration reaches about 170 grams of salts per liter of water, and allow it to remain there until some or all potassium and magnesium salt crystallization is complete, thus capturing a much broader swath of the sea's natural mineral spectrum. It is true, however, that industrialized crystallization and harvesting techniques do not, in theory, have to be used solely to optimize sodium chloride yield. They could also be employed to create salts with a more diverse mineral content.

Industrial salt production can be damaging to the environment. Industrial solar evaporated salt is commonly produced in salt marshes and lakes that are sensitive ecosystems: they are often essential locations on the migratory paths of birds and are the habitat of flora and fauna that are extremely sensitive to changes in the salinity of the water. Coastal salt marshes can play an important role as a storm buffer. Industrial operations generate significant waste, such as highly salinated bittern, which, if released into the surrounding ecosystem, can prove lethal to aquatic life not adapted to high salinity.

Not that industrial salt makers are indifferent to the ecological imbalances created by improperly managed salt making. Scientists believe that not only does a healthy salt pond ecology support native wildlife, it also contributes to the productivity of the crystallizing pans. Bad salt pan ecology can be disastrous. For example, Ghana's 12,500-acre Songor Salt Project—which would, it was hoped, exemplify the economic benefits of industrialized salt production in Africa—ended in catastrophe as salt production fell from 120,000 tons annually in 2002 to just 15,000 tons in 2008 after the ponds were overridden by "a slimy green jelly substance" that prevented crystallization.

Industrial manufacturing depletes salt of most of its natural minerals. And yet, chemical engineers have managed to bulk up industrial salt with plenty of

BEHIND THE IODIZED CURTAIN

Adults need about 150μg of iodine per day, which totals up to one teaspoon in a 120-year lifetime. Ideally, we receive sufficient iodine from the food we eat. It is abundant in all seafood and is also present in vegetables, except where soils are naturally low in iodine, such as in the Himalayas, the Andes, and the Great Lakes region of the United States. The World Health Organization estimates that 740 million people in the world suffer from iodine deficiency disorders (IDD): mostly preschool children and pregnant women in low-income countries. IDDs include goiter, stillbirth, and thyroid problems. The most common disorder is mental retardation in children. One study found IQ scores in iodine-deficient communities to be ten to fifteen points lower than iodine-replete ones. The addition of iodine to salt in the form of potassium iodide, potassium iodate, sodium iodide, or sodium iodate has proven highly effective in the prevention of iodine deficiency.

The push for mass iodization of salt is not the result of iodine being stripped from natural salt. Rather, it is because salt has been selected as a preferred delivery vehicle for iodine supplementation. Advocates of salt iodization argue that it costs merely pennies to iodize the salt for a single person for a whole year, making it a miraculously inexpensive (about $0.05 per person per year) way to improve public health. Any food could be artificially iodized (iodized bread, milk, and water were common in the twentieth century), but salt was chosen because everyone consumes it, levels of consumption are more or less the same across populations, iodization techniques for salt are inexpensive, and salt production is consolidated in the hands of just a few producers, making it easy to implement. That said, salt is hardly a perfect vehicle for artificial iodization. Humidity volatizes iodine in stored salt, and iodine content has been found to vary threefold from one container or brand to another.

Iodization does not harm salt, but it has incited a sense in some people that their health may be at risk without iodized salt. Iodide is found in trace amounts in unrefined salts, but generally not in nutritionally sufficient quantities. But iodine never was a significant nutrient in salt. Fixating on its absence as a health risk distracts us from the real nutritional depletion done to industrial harvested salt during its production and processing, and it has aided and abetted in the standardization of salt as a food. Iodized salt may indeed have its place as a strategy for improving health in various parts of the world, but the wholesale embrace of iodization ignores the broad negative impact on global health of promoting centralized, industrialized food production.

Those with access to fresh and frozen foods can satisfy their needs for dietary iodine by eating two servings of seafood a week. Kelp is particularly rich in iodine, as are vegetables grown in many parts of the world. Iodized salt is also used in many prepared and processed foods. Those wishing to supplement their diet without resorting to iodized salt can take a natural kelp-based supplement such as Liqui-Kelp or Liqui-Duls, which costs only a penny a day. ■

additives. Most important from a manufacturing standpoint, refined salts have all the moisture taken out of them, which makes them thirsty and gives them the tendency to clump as they pull moisture from the atmosphere. To combat clumping, anticaking agents are added. These agents are often aluminum-based

THE YIN AND YANG OF SALT

While scientists advancing Western medicine scramble to come to terms with the role of salt in nutrition, the far more ancient medical practices of the East offer a different understanding. Balance is the key, as represented in the concept of yin yang. Yin and yang cannot be separated, and indeed are continually interchanging with one another, like the crests and troughs of water rippling after a stone is thrown.

Salt in its unrefined form has the most yin of any substance that is used as food. This means it is grounding, and affects the descending, inward activities of the body and mind. Salt directs the energy of the body inward, and is thus more appropriate to be eaten in the cooler months, in order to concentrate the warmth of the body in the yin, or interior and lower body areas. It is believed to contribute to the secretions of hydrochloric acid in the stomach, strengthening digestion and supporting optimal absorption of proteins and of vitamin B12 and other essential vitamins and minerals (all corroborated in the annals of Western medicine, as well). In Chinese medicine, salt used in moderation is believed to support mental clarity as it strengthens the heart and the mind.

Holding with the balance of yin and yang, overconsumption of salt is regarded as similarly harmful. Just as appropriate salt usage enhances calcium absorption and nutrient utilization in general, excess salt consumption has a demineralizing effect on the body, leaching calcium from the bones. It can also injure the kidneys or promote fluid retention.

One of the fundamental properties of salt is its power to alkalize the blood, a useful quality considering many disease processes (not to mention the use of pharmaceutical drugs, intoxicants, and highly processed foods) promote an acidic blood condition. Thus salt can in some cases be used therapeutically in various Eastern medical traditions to neutralize and detoxify blood that is overly acidic.

According to Chinese medicine theory, salt stimulates the kidneys. This promotes fluid metabolism and has a moistening effect that can counteract dryness in the body. Salt softens hardness and masses and is used in many Chinese herbal formulas for cancer and/or other tumors or cysts. It also promotes bowel movements, drawing water into the bowels by its osmotic action.

In Ayurvedic medicine, the traditional medicine of India, salt in small amounts is thought to markedly strengthen one's energy by building reserves and crystallizing direction and action. Kala namak, or black salt, is a common salt in northern India, where in addition to its culinary benefits as a cooling spice, it is considered a digestive aid. ∎

compounds, either sodium aluminosilicate or sodium ferrocyanide (yellow prussi-ate of soda) in quantities as high as 13 parts per million. Aluminum compounds have been found to be adverse to human health, and have been linked to conditions such as Alzheimer's. Anticaking agents can also make the salt difficult for the body to properly process, as they inhibit the absorbability of the salt. In addition to anticaking agents, corn syrup is often added to refined salt in the United States as a binder for iodine and possibly also to cut the bitterness that refined food-grade salt naturally possesses. Often, about 0.04 percent of industrially refined iodized table salt is in fact dextrose. Substances such as calcium oxide and calcium carbonate can also be added to table salt to increase its whiteness.

Koshering salt (also known as kosher salt) is usually not fortified with potassium iodate or iodide. However, a variety of additives such as sodium ferrocyanide can be added to koshering salt. Kosher certification relates to food-handling conformance to *kashrut*, or Jewish dietary law. It has nothing to do with a salt's intrinsic healthiness. On the contrary, the major brands of koshering salt available on the market are entirely refined and in no way resemble the natural salts eaten in the days of Jonah, Abraham, and Moses.

SALT AND PUBLIC HEALTH POLICY

> *It is difficult to get a man to understand something when his job depends on not understanding it.* —Upton Sinclair

Salt is food, and like any food, it is an object of our obsession with health. To say that industrialized populations have a love-hate relationship with salt would be an understatement. Salt has become the subject of intense debate among health experts and the American public at large. There are different sides to the salt health debate: first and foremost, there's the antisalt camp, which seeks to change the consumption through public health policy. In reaction to this camp's calls for a salt-restricted world, there is also a camp that argues that a public health policy focus on salt reduction cannot make us healthier.

The antisalt camp asserts that eating too much salt leads to or exacerbates high blood pressure (hypertension), and thus increases the risk of heart disease. They summarize the current body of scientific research as follows: High blood pressure is a major risk factor associated with heart disease. If you consume a lot of salt, your blood pressure will go up anywhere from 1 to 5 millimeters of mercury (mm/Hg) before returning to its presalt level. If you consume a lot of salt, and then keep on consuming a lot of salt, your blood pressure may remain elevated. Therefore, if you consume too much salt on an ongoing basis, you are at increased risk for high blood pressure and, by extension, for heart disease.

Some health organizations are recommending hypertensives and normotensives alike consume less than 1,500 milligrams of sodium per day, which translates to 3.8 grams (or 3/4 teaspoon) of refined table salt. At present, Americans consume between 4,000 and 5,000 milligrams of sodium per day, 77 percent of which comes from food processing and restaurants. Twelve percent is naturally occurring in food. Eleven percent is discretionary, added during cooking (6 percent) and at the table (5 percent). In other words, if we stopped eating all restaurant and processed foods and doubled the amount of other foods we ate, we'd consume somewhere around half the salt we eat today.

Some medical experts believe sodium has been singled out unnecessarily. Dr. Miles Hassell, Medical Director of the Integrative Medicine Program at Providence Health & Services, says, "Salt intake in moderate amounts can be perfectly healthy. Total salt intake appears to be less critical in the setting of a high potassium (and probably magnesium) intake, such as when a whole food diet is consumed." Other research, such as a Harvard study of 60,000 nurses, suggests calcium may play a key role in lowering blood pressure. Yet other studies focus on the importance of magnesium.

Dr. David A. McCarron, who was Director of the Hypertension Program at Oregon Health Sciences University in Portland, Oregon, before becoming Adjunct Professor with the Department of Nutrition at the University of California, Davis, argues against reducing the heart health debate to a question of sodium consumption. "Sodium is but one factor in the complex interplay of multiple, inextricably related regulatory systems of which hypertension is the end result. A rise in blood pressure means you need to add minerals to your diet, not cut back on salt. Tragically, the idea that salt is bad for your blood pressure is one of the most generally accepted notions out there."

Most research papers that are cited in support of salt reduction do not actually show a measurable improvement in health outcomes as a result of lowering salt intake. Instead, they focus on statistical models extrapolated from many sets of scientific data to determine the probability of reduced cases of high blood pressure that *would* result from widespread dramatic reduction in salt intake. For example, there is some scientific consensus on data to support the idea that limiting sodium intake to 1,500 milligrams per day could lower the systolic blood pressure in hypertensives by 4 to 5 mm/Hg, and by 2 mm/Hg in people with normal blood pressure. But consider that "optimal normal" systolic blood pressure is 120 mm/Hg. Moderate hypertension starts at 20 mm/Hg above normal and severe hypertension starts at 60mm/Hg above normal. If a person with blood pressure of 160 mm/Hg were to cut salt consumption by two-thirds, from 4,500 milligrams per day to 1,500 milligrams, she could hope to see her systolic blood pressure drop to 150 or 155 mm/Hg. In other words, even the most successful campaign against salt imaginable would not lower the blood pressure of patients with high blood pressure down to a normal range. (And the impact that a sweeping reduction in sodium intake might have on our intake of other minerals like potassium, magnesium, and calcium has not been studied.) There are vast pools of data that suggest even the modest improvement above might not actually come to pass. The Intersalt study, which evaluated 10,079 men and women age 20 to 59 sampled from 52 populations around the world, found no correlation between average salt intake levels and average blood pressures. In fact, those who consumed the most (Tianjin China, 14 grams a day) had a median blood pressure of 119/70 mmHg, while those who consumed the least (an African-American community in Chicago, 6 grams a day) had a similar median blood pressure of 119/76 mmHg.

The entire argument may be beside the point. So long as the salt debate centers on sodium, it will fail to describe the importance of salt in our lives. In 1850, if you wanted to eat chicken you would raise one on grains and whatever bugs and seeds the bird could forage in your yard. You would cook it, and then sprinkle a few precious grains of handmade, mineral-rich sea salt on top. In 2000, you ordered a bag of fried nuggets made with a corn-fed chicken injected with refined sodium chloride solution to make it plumper, battered with a host of ingredients you can't even pronounce, and then sprinkled with more refined sodium chloride on top. Our food has evolved into something strange and abstract, and it has become inundated with sodium chloride to help make it economical and palatable.

The easy way to gain clarity on the subject of salt and health is to focus on eating food intelligently. To paraphrase the writer Michael Pollan, buy only the foods your grandma would recognize. Or, in the case of salt, your great-grandma. Throw away the frozen poultry nuggets and, as far as I'm concerned, throw away the artificially refined koshering, table, and sea salts while you're at it.

CRAFT: ARTISAN SALT MAKING

Let there be work, bread, water, and salt for all. — Nelson Mandela

There are two types of salt; rock and evaporative. Rock salts are mined from salt deposits in the earth. Evaporative salts are crystallized from saltwater seas, lakes, or springs. From these two basic sources come countless varieties of salt. The vast majority of artisan salts are evaporative salts, each a manifestation of the unique circumstances inspiring and constraining its production. Some salts are born with the scantest of interventions from man, crystallizing whenever the sun so much as bats an eyelash. Other salts crystallize grudgingly after months and years of back-breaking labor—of painstakingly collecting, sequestering, and monitoring seawater. Some crystals may never form at all in the open air, and so are born only under cover in a greenhouse. Others must wait for fire built under a boiling vat to bring them to life. Some need both.

And human intervention is just a small part of the story. Nature seems at times bent on defying its own laws, making the strangest things happen at the strangest times and for the strangest reasons, or sometimes for no discernible reason at all. Salt crystals in cooler climates may blossom unexpectedly on the surface of water only on the rarest of days when a light, warm breeze tickles the surface of a salt pan. In warmer climates, the crystals may vanish with the first breath of wind, lingering long enough to be harvested only in the cool calm of early morning.

Defined by the crystalline structure of their dominant mineral, sodium chloride, salt crystals often resolve themselves into tidy cubes. Industrial salt manufacturers have capitalized on this to create refined salts with perfect uniformity. But in nature, crystals are anything but uniform. Nature is the prodigal mathematician, riffing tirelessly on geometry as it assembles salt crystals from the attraction of a dozen kinds of ions amid the playful disruptiveness of scores of trace minerals, responding to the infinite variability of the environment. Salt crystals can be jumbles of cubes, or jumbles of jumbles of cubes. Or they may form into a few huge, fractured cubes that are then stuck together to form even larger cubes. Or the cubes could be arranged neatly into larger pyramidal or box-shaped structures, or into massive incoherent wads. Or they may not be cubes at all, but unruly bursts of spines and fronds.

When salt water is evaporated in a boiling vat or under the protection of a greenhouse, crystals may form into tall, hollow pyramids, pointy as arrowheads; or into squat pyramids, flat as Chinese throwing stars. Some crystals are shaped by the wind blowing them snowball style into little ball bearings. Some crystals are feathered, fine as owl down, so dainty around the edges they flicker in and out of visibility.

Crystallographic variation contributes much of an individual salt's character, but the mineral makeup and moisture content engendered by different salt-making practices are also important. Source water for evaporative salts might be collected effortlessly from the shores of a salt marsh or it could be laboriously pumped from 3,000 feet beneath the surface of the sea. It could come from a salt lake at the edge of a desert or from a salt spring high in the mountains. The weather could be hot and arid or cool and humid. Each environment, each geography, informs the mineral makeup, crystallization, flavor, and color of its salt.

ARTISAN METHODS FOR MAKING SALT									
Most descriptions are generalizations, and do not account for a variety of exceptions to the rules.									
TYPE	SOLAR EVAPORATED SALT					FIRE EVAPORATED SALT			MINED
SOURCE	Oceans, lakes, springs/aquifers					Oceans, lakes, springs/aquifers			Halite deposits
CLIMATE	Dry, temperate to hot			Rainy, temperate		Rainy, cool	Rainy, cool to temperate		n/a
EVAPORATION	Open air			Greenhouse		Fire only	Hybrid (solar evaporation, fire crystallizing)		n/a
SALTS	Fleur de sel	Sel gris	Traditional	Flake	Traditional	Flake	Shio	Flake	Rock
DRYING	Sun	Sun	Sun	Kiln	Sun or kiln	Kiln	Sun	Kiln	None
MOISTURE CONTENT	High	Very high	Low to moderate	Low	High	Low	Moderate	Low	None

Salts can be mined in deep, 600-million-year-old veins clear as Waterford crystal or cut from surface deposits in fuzzy white blocks brittle as sandstone, or it may appear as a marbled mixture of both. The salt could be pink from a little iron or blood red from lots of iron. On the other hand, salts with an abundance of trace minerals can be perfectly transparent, as can salt with virtually no trace minerals at all. Salt is also naturally found in whites, grays, yellows and oranges. Once in a blue moon, a blue salt appears, or a green one, or a violet one.

SOLAR SALT

Salt is born of the purest of parents: the sun and the sea. —Pythagoras

There are two ways to make evaporative salt. Brine can be circulated through ponds and solar-evaporated by the sun and wind until crystals form, or it can be heated in a vessel over fire to achieve the same thing. Both methods are ancient. Solar evaporation is the most widely practiced artisanal method.

Four types of salt are produced by solar methods. *Fleur de sel*, the finest and most delicate crystals, are skimmed or netted from the top of a pond shortly after forming. *Sel gris* (also called *bay salt*), comprising coarser and usually moister crystals, may form first on the top of the salt pan and drop to the bottom, or it may simply grow on the bottom. Sel gris is raked off daily or every few days. Salt makers can let the salt accumulate for anywhere from several days to several months into a thick cake lying on the bottom of the pan. This very coarse salt is called *traditional salt*, and it often needs to be ground up. In regions lucky enough to be graced by just the right hot, dry, windless climate (or a greenhouse), pyramid-shaped salt crystals may form on the surface of the evaporating pan in the place of more granular fleur de sel. These delicate crystals often break into flakes when raked off, and are consequently called *flake salts*.

Most solar salts are evaporated, crystallized, and harvested outdoors in a process called *winning*. In some cases, greenhouses are used. The precise techniques used in each stage of the process differ enormously based on a variety of factors, such as the salinity of the source water (generally, the ocean, a salt lake, or salt spring), geology, tradition, economics, and the salt maker's preference. The most important factor is climate. Where it can take more than forty days for salt water to evaporate enough to precipitate crystallization in cool, damp climates of France, it can take less than five days in hot, dry climates of

Australia. The techniques used from region to region have more in common than they do differences, however, and the most advanced are highly efficient, making optimal use of sun, wind, and tide.

There are no better exemplars of the absolute mastery of salt making than the *paludiers* (salt makers) south of Brittany, who have developed exquisitely refined techniques to maximize the quality of salt production in their climate. Perfected more than a thousand years ago, Breton salt making has been practiced continuously and in the same way since at least medieval times, using four sources of renewable energy—none of them mechanical—to convert seawater into salt: sun, wind, moon, and human labor. The layout of the Breton salt pans on France's Atlantic coast exhibits astonishingly sophisticated hydraulic engineering. A series of holding ponds, evaporating basins, and crystallization pans are dug into a salt marsh, each arranged slightly lower than the next, so that water is fed by gravity from collection pond to evaporation basin to crystallizing pan. The first holding pond is at an elevation just below sea level at high tide. The last is set just above sea level at low tide.

The twice-daily surge and retreat of the tides irrigate the natural salt marsh with salt water via a manmade canal called an *étier*. Twice each month, there's an especially high tide known as the fortnightly tide. When a fortnightly tide occurs during the salt-making season, the paludier opens a trap and lets water flow from the étier into a large decanting pond called the *vasière,* or silt-pond. The trap is closed before the tide goes out, leaving the salt maker with a large pond of water at the highest elevation of the saltworks. The vasière thus frees the salt maker of the need to wait for high tides to replenish the source water. Vasières are typically a few feet deep, and the water temperature will usually reach about 72°F. The salinity of the water will rise a little while it's in the vasière, from about 3.5 percent to about 4 percent.

All of the evaporating basins in the *saline*, or salt field, have names specific to western France's salt-making traditions—*cobiers, fares, adernes, oeillets*—with some terms in this lexicon varying from town to town. Each basin provides a carefully calibrated ratio of volume to surface area to allow for the proper rate of evaporation.

As the name *vasière* implies (*vas* means "muck" or "mud"), part of the function of a vasière is to allow organic and inorganic matter to settle out of the seawater as it sits. After the water has stood for several days, the salt maker opens a gate to allow the water to flow into the first of a series of specially designed basins that make up the salt field.

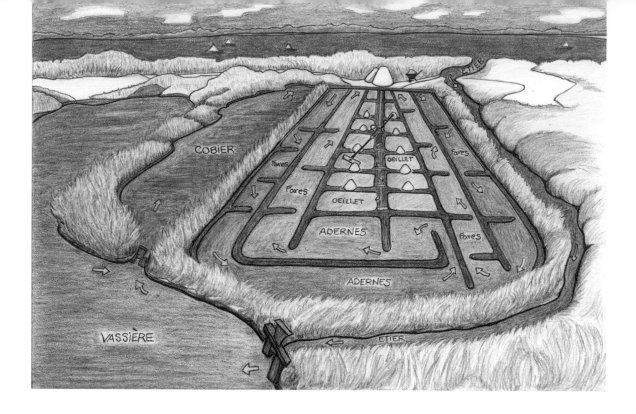

The water from the vasière flows down slowly into a succession of four types of basins linked to it. The first of these is the cobier. While the vasière is basically a pond dug from the surrounding marsh, the cobier and all subsequent basins are meticulously excavated from the magnificent pale gray porcelain clay bottoms of the region's marshes. The number and size of the cobiers in a saltworks are dependent on the salinity and temperature of the water. About 20 percent of the water will evaporate here. Salinity will reach about 5 percent and the water will warm to about 77°F. Brine is defined as saltwater that has greater than fifty parts per thousand salt, so it's at this point the seawater officially becomes brine, or *saumure.*

Next, in the fares, most evaporation occurs. Fares can take up half or more of the total area of the salt farm. The fares are cut by a number of *talus,* the banks and borders fashioned from clay that define the basins and channels of the salt farm. The talus in the fares form *chicanes*—tight switchback turns—so that the water meanders from one fare to the next, circulating slowly in a highly controlled manner. By this time, the water temperature is about 82°F and salinity has climbed to 20 percent. It's here that the calcium salts calcium carbonate and calcium sulfate form, precipitating out of the brine as they crystallize. These are the first of several salts that form naturally from evaporating seawater. They are removed as part of the maintenance of the salt pans; these salts are not used by most artisan salt makers, though in many big mechanized salt fields they are sold to a variety of industrial markets.

The brine then passes to the adernes, the final evaporating basins before crystallization. The adernes often comprise the largest surface area of the evaporating basins after the fares, each measuring about 50 by 80 feet. More calcium salts may crystallize here. The adernes are very shallow, allowing the water to heat and evaporate rapidly. Here, water can reach 86 to 95°F, and salinity will reach 25 percent.

When the brine is virtually saturated with salt, it is passed into the most meticulously crafted basins of all, the oeillets, or crystallizing pans. The pale porcelain *argile* clay from which the salt pans are formed provides a perfect, effectively hermetic environment for the production of salt. In addition to being highly malleable, the clay has good refractory properties, maximizing the amount of heat captured from the sun.

The oeillets vary in size depending on the salt maker's preferences and local tradition, but are often about 30 feet square; many are rectangular, with dimensions more like 20 by 30 feet. Because one cannot wade into the pans without disturbing the delicate porcelain clay bottom, the oeillet's dimensions are restricted by the length of the rake that can be handled to reach halfway across it. The water level in these pans is as shallow as 1/4 inch and salinity reaches 30 percent. Here, finally, salt crystals form. Sel gris and traditional salt will form throughout the salt-making season. On the Atlantic coast, fleur de sel only comes on warm, sunny days, when a light wind ruffles the water. When it does appear, each oeillet will produce 4.5 to 6.6 pounds of fleur de sel in a day, compared to 90 to 165 pounds of sel gris.

The wind plays a vital role in crystallization by increasing the amount of water vapor that can be carried away from the surface of the water. Lack of wind can be just as serious a problem in a salt field as rain. The Trapani salt fields of Sicily have been known to suffer radical drops in salt production due to occasional calms that descend on western Sicily in the summer.

The Camargue on the Mediterranean coast of France is one of Europe's most productive salt-producing regions. In addition to long, dry summers, the region is buffeted by two different winds: the moist tramontane descending from the Pyrenees and the drier mistral emanating from the Alps to the northeast. The combination of strong sun and multiple winds (not to mention mechanization) helps make the solar salt fields of the Camargue the most productive in Europe.

A major difference between industrial salt makers and most artisans is the salinity level at which the brine is admitted to the crystallizers, and its finished

THE MINERAL BODY OF THE SEA

The sea (and many other saltwater bodies) are generally 3.2 percent to 4 percent saline. Salt springs can be much higher in salinity, as can some isolated inland seas; the Dead Sea is 33.5 percent saline and Lake Assal in Djibouti is 34.8 percent. At 40 percent, Lake Don Juan in Antarctica is the most saline body of water in the world, remaining liquid at temperatures below -22°F. The ocean has a 3.5 percent average salinity. About 99 percent of the salts that make up this 3.5 percent salinity are made from just eleven ions. Salt-making techniques are designed to concentrate the optimum balance and combination of these and other ions to achieve the desired salt. In the case of industrially made sea salts, this can be 99.8 percent or higher sodium chloride. In a traditional sea salt, the number could be 85 percent sodium chloride or lower. Minerals of the salt are, in a sense, the unique imprint of the techniques with which a salt is made and the minerals of the sea from which it is born. ■

salinity when it is evacuated. Different minerals will crystallize from brine at different levels of salinity based on their solubility in water. Some minerals, like calcium, are far less soluble than sodium, and so they crystallize and precipitate out of the brine earlier. Others, like magnesium and potassium, are more soluble, so they crystallize later. Artisans may admit water into crystallizers at 15 to 17° Baumé (a measure of the density of the water, and hence of its salt concentration), which is early enough to allow for considerable amounts of low-solubility salts and trace minerals to crystallize along with the sodium chloride. Industrial producers, keen on capturing pure NaCl, wait until 24° Baumé. Artisan salt makers may also wait longer to evacuate the dense brine left over after most of the sodium chloride crystallization has occurred, allowing more of the magnesium and potassium salts that remain to crystallize, along with many other trace minerals that either crystallize as salts (such as magnesium chloride) or are just captured within and on the surface of the salt crystals (such as gold). A good artisan solar salt can capture upward of eighty-four minerals from the sea.

THE HARVEST

The type of solar salt produced is determined by harvesting techniques. Regardless of type, however, a chief benefit of salts made using patient, quality-oriented techniques is a high degree of heterogeneity of crystal formation. Within a single pinch is a universe of specks, cubes, flakey hoppers (flat, scale-like crystals), layered hoppers, pyramids, and fused conglomerates. Each minute crystal has an immense surface area, with crannies and crevasses harboring moisture and minerals. These variations in size and structure, combined with characteristic moisture levels and mineral contents, are the hallmarks of an excellent culinary salt.

Most artisan salts are harvested using only human labor and highly specialized wooden tools designed centuries ago. Bare feet are the traditional footwear of the salt harvester. Sel gris, fleur de sel, and flake salts can be harvested daily, while the harvest of traditional salt is more flexible: depending on conditions and the desired output, traditional salts can be harvested every several days, every several weeks, or perhaps just once per season.

Sel Gris

In general, sel gris is harvested by standing on the edge of a salt pan and pushing and/or pulling the salt toward the edge with a wooden rake, and then raking or shoveling the crystals out of the pan into a pile on the *ladure* to allow any lingering water to drain. The specific techniques for harvesting sel gris vary depending on the land from which the salt fields are made, the climate in which the salt takes form, and the design of the salt farm itself. The basalt-, sand-, or concrete-lined salt pans of the Mediterranean are very different from Brittany's clay-lined pans. In the Philippines, a tile floor is laid over the rich, dark mud of the salt fields, and after a few good days' harvests, salt crystals actually cement the tiles together to provide a hermetic barrier between salt and silt that makes raking a piece of cake (except for the fact that it's well over 100°F under the blazing sun and each of the pans is producing hundreds of pounds of salt per day).

In Guérande and the other western France salt marshes, the silt and mud that naturally accrete there are removed until the beautiful porcelain clay beneath is exposed. Harvesting the heavy layer of sel gris crystallized on this clay bottom is delicate work. Tremendous precision is required to avoid disturbing the bottom or, worse, gouging it, and dirtying the salt. Standing barefoot on the *galpont,* the clay border of the salt pan, the paludier moves with balletic fluidity, raking the crystals to a round platform in the middle called the *ladure,* where the day's harvest is collected. The paleness of sel gris will vary somewhat from maker to maker, but most agree that while a certain amount of grayness is part of the character, quality, and romance of the salt, too much can make the salt dirty and unappealing.

This is heavy work. A single pass of the salt rake can gather several pounds of coarse sel gris crystals that have to be pushed and pulled across the twenty-foot floor of the salt pans, lifted into piles, drained, then shoveled and transported to consolidated piles, dried to the desired degree, and finally protected and stored for sale later.

Though not as physically strenuous, harvesting fleur de sel requires more skill, as well as vigilance. When the weather is warm enough and a light breeze tousles the shimmering waters of the oeillet in the afternoon, a frail bloom of salt appears on the surface. Fleur de sel should be a beautiful silvery pink when first harvested, and contain virtually no particulate clay. Harvesting it involves very gently lifting the crystals from the surface of the pan without disturbing the bottom. The distance separating the fleur de sel at the surface of the pan and the gray clay at the bottom is less than $3/8$ inch, and one slip of the rake will disturb the gray porcelain clay at the bottom, ruining the fleur de sel.

Making matters more difficult, the time during which fleur de sel can be harvested is fleeting. Fleur de sel appears at different times in different climates. Some salt makers in very accommodating climates can allow fleur de sel to form all afternoon and all evening, and then harvest a thick crust of it from the surface in the morning. In Europe, the best fleur de sel generally must be

THE FEMININE ART OF SALT HARVESTING

The role of women in the traditional household of northern France's salt-making communities is as diverse and integral as anywhere. In the past, women not only attended to the needs of family and community, they also were the primary workers in the small gardens and farms that brought in much of the food. But the skills attributed to women were needed in the salt fields as well.

Fleur de sel was and is an essential cash crop for the salt maker, fetching about ten times the price of sel gris, and for the paludiers its quality is also a point of pride. In addition to the usual brute physical strength required to harvest salt, the harvest of fleur de sel holds at least one additional requisite: precision.

Harvesting without disturbing the bottom involves very gently lifting the crystals from the surface of the pan. In the closely knit community of the traditional Brittany paludiers, this precision labor was provided by women. Many modern-day paludiers recognize this, acknowledging that women can be faster and more precise than men in the harvest of fleur de sel. Women continue to work in the salt fields of northern France, providing a unique bridge to a time when women managed both economic and domestic responsibilities as a traditional way of life. ■

harvested in the afternoon, because by the following morning it will have settled to the bottom of the pan and transformed to sel gris. And the following day may fail to bring the fleur de sel at all. The paludiers must rush to the fields and try to harvest it all before night falls. Fleur de sel harvesting is sort of like picking peaches before a freeze: every moment counts, but any clumsiness will ruin the effort. To see a salt harvester rake fleur de sel is to witness in action a superb physical exactitude combined with endurance and composure.

Traditional Salt

Traditional salt is similar to sel gris in its formation, but because it is allowed to accumulate for a longer period of time, far more of it is harvested at a time. The crust of traditional salt, rich in magnesium and trace minerals, called "cake," can be several inches thick lying on the bottom of the crystallization pans. Harvesting it is the equivalent of removing the topsoil from an entire farm, by hand. It is heavy work, and some artisan salt makers do use mechanical help for the harvest, dragging a plow from the edge of the crystallizers with a winch or tractor or, in less developed countries, a mule or an ox. In most regions, from Sicily to Vietnam to Ghana, traditional salts are still raked and shoveled laboriously by hand—sometimes without so much as a rake or shovel.

Because the crystals in traditional salts have formed over a long period of time, they are generally conglomerated into a thick muddle of haphazard chunks. Such salts must be ground mechanically to size—to anywhere from a coarse jumble resembling *sel gris* to very fine grains and shards.

THE OFF-SEASON

During a good year in northern France, the salt-harvesting season lasts from June to September, though it can be cut short by foul weather. These are months of intense work, as every day the paludier must gather the salt to make way for the following day's harvest. Any loss of work means a loss of income. Still, while the romance of salt making may focus on the harvest, much of the work on a salt farm is done during the spring, fall, and winter months—the off-season. There is considerable work to do maintaining, repairing, and preparing for the next year.

Establishing a salt field can take years, even decades, of excavating ponds, trenching canals, and shaping borders, embankments, and levees from shifting

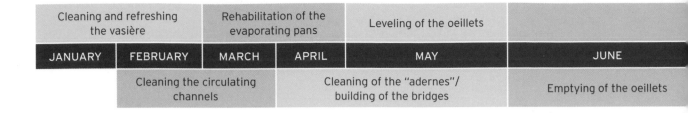

Cleaning and refreshing the vasière		Rehabilitation of the evaporating pans		Leveling of the oeillets		
JANUARY	FEBRUARY	MARCH	APRIL	MAY		JUNE
	Cleaning the circulating channels		Cleaning of the "adernes"/ building of the bridges			Emptying of the oeillets

and flood-prone expanses of silt, clay, and vegetation. Maintaining salt pans is no easier, with the majority of the year spent actively rehabilitating salt fields in preparation for the harvest season. All of this requires the integrity and skill of an artisan, the knowledge and wisdom of a farmer, and the strength and fortitude of a pack mule. Work in the saltworks is effectively 10 percent hydraulic engineer, 10 percent meteorologist, and 80 percent human bulldozer.

Before any work can be done on the salt fields, the year's harvest must be dealt with. This means hauling thousands of pounds of salt from the side of the salt pans; piling it in a protected, central location; and covering it against the rain. In France, sel gris and traditional salt are usually left outdoors, covered with a tarp, while fleur de sel is brought indoors for safekeeping. In other places, such as Sicily, salt mounds are still made traditionaly, with salt makers meticulously covering each mound with terra-cotta tiles to shield the salt from rain while allowing the moisture in the salt to continue to evaporate.

Every few years, following the harvest, comes some of the heaviest work: draining and cleaning the large vasière. After a year or several years of receiving seawater and holding it for use in salt making, these large ponds can be lively communities of sea life; they can also be laden with silt that has settled from the ocean water. In a step called the *poissonnage,* which can start as early as October and last through February, the water in the vasière is channeled into the *rai* (a trench dug around the vasière), where it is allowed to drain and evaporate until little is left, making for a quick harvest of sea breams, mullets, and eels to supplement the paludier's income as well as his diet.

When the vasière is dried, it is dredged and redug as needed. Staunch traditionalists do all of this by hand. But it's increasingly common to bring in a mechanical shovel of some sort to do some of the work. Salt makers are intensely proud of their traditional work, and only grudgingly turn to mechanization of any kind. Most that do use machinery insist that it not be allowed inside the ponds themselves, but instead only reach into the ponds with the shovel, avoiding contamination from the machinery.

Next, the *rayage* involves drying and redigging the vasière and its peripheral channels. There is also the *curage de la bondre:* the cleaning of

The harvest			Rest, marketing	Special works	
JULY	AUGUST	SEPTEMBER	OCTOBER	NOVEMBER	DECEMBER
Bird watching		Loading and stocking of the salt		Two months off	

the labyrinth of inlet trenches, inlet ponds, and precrystallizing pans, where the mineral and excess clay deposits collect. A rake called a *boutoué* is used to remove deposits, a manual dredging implement called a *lousse à ponter* to lift the deposits onto preexisting structural bridges separating ponds *(gal-ponts)*, and a shovel called a *boyette* to move them from the galponts to shore. Whether as part of the poissonnage or on its own, the rayage must be done every year to remove mud and vegetation accumulated over the previous year and from winter rains.

These same tools are employed for the next work. The *habillage de la saline* is essentially hydraulic engineering, landscaping, and sculpting of the earth to restore the elaborate features of a salt field. The salt marshes from which salt fields are formed are natural wonderlands of grasses, reeds, wildflowers, shrubs, and trees that flourish in the pristine marine environment. This plant life is essential to reducing wave and tidal forces on the salt marshes, and to cleaning and keeping in balance the waters used in salt making. Some plants, such as *Salicornia* and other small shrubs, prevent erosion of the clay banks that define the salt fields. Every year this abundant plant life must be kept from encroaching into the salt pans. During the habillage, unwanted vegetation is removed from the borders and channels of the salt fields, earth at the sides is compacted, and the various ponds are leveled and their respective elevations reestablished.

Pascal Dufour is a paludier on Ile de Ré. He is a lean, strikingly handsome man with sharp blue eyes and tousled hair the color of drying marsh grass. He pauses for a moment to talk to a visitor, balancing the handle of a *simouche*, a long-handled wooden rake like one that might have been used by a Celtic salt maker 1,500 years ago.

Watching Dufour work is mesmerizing. Standing at the edge of a pan, he gently pulls the long pole of the wooden tool toward him. As the dark, mocha-colored mud lifts up, clear water swirls behind it. With just the right amount of pressure—which appears to be, more or less, no pressure at all—streaks of a paler, grayish, blue-green color appear from the darkness.

For several weeks, Dufour will continue the *aplanissement,* the masterful craft of leveling the bottom of the crystallizing pans with the simouche. With a sculptor's sure hand and a farmer's enduring strength, he carefully rakes off the

thin layer of dark mud that develops over the winter, exposing the hard, pale *argile* beneath. During salt making, the condensed brine in the oeillets may be less than 3/8 inch deep. Even the slightest variation in depth across the twenty-foot expanse of the pan would result in dry spots or deeper pools, reducing the efficiency and rate of salt crystallization. The raked-off mud is left to settle on the side of the oeillets for a day or two to allow the water to drain off. In a process called *graissage,* the mud is raked and plastered onto the clay-and-mud dikes between the oeillets to redefine them.

"There, you see," Dufour exclaims as if he has just struck gold. "That is the argile." He continues across the width of the pan. The progression of work can be seen by looking at the pans Dufour has just completed. The two pans next to him contain banks of goopy dark mud at their borders. Beyond that, the mud has been shoveled from the pans and sculpted with the expertise of a plaster worker onto the levees and banks, which glisten with the dark color of freshly tempered chocolate. Past that, the mud-plaster has dried to the color of graphite, and beyond that it has begun to develop fine cracks as it contracts under the sun. Rainfall, or just the passage of time, will necessitate undertaking this process repeatedly within a single season.

The result of all this exertion is a salt field that appears quite literally clean enough to eat from. In fact, the pans are actually made of the same porcelain clay used in many ceramics (though grayer than the most sought after China porcelain). You have the impression that you should take off your shoes before setting foot there. And sure enough, that is more or less the way the salt maker approaches it.

Staring out at the procession of more than sixty pans making up the salt fields, one wonders: how many people work a salt field like this? The answer: just one. "What I love about this work is its purity," says Dufour, who began working in the salt fields in 2000. "It is just the sea, the sun, the wind—and my work. From these things, salt is created."

GREENHOUSE EVAPORATED SALTS

In rainy climates where open-air solar evaporation is not possible, greenhouses can be used to help evaporation and shield from rain. In the calm air of a greenhouse, crystals are free to follow their hearts. Some will form as fleur de sel. Left undisturbed, this small grain may create a dimple in the water as it grows, clinging by surface tension to the water's surface. Along the outer edge of this dimple, more crystals form, until the salt becomes a small inverted pyramid, floating like an ice cream cone in the water. Skimming the crystals from the water at this point produces flake salt. If crystals continue to grow along the rim until they sink, the flakes continue to grow until eventually sel gris results; if crystallization is allowed to continue for some time, a thick crust will form and traditional salt can be harvested.

The principles for making salt in greenhouses are much the same, but space constraints dictate very different shapes and sizes of evaporating pans. Some salts are evaporated and crystallized in the same pan, in batches. Others are made using one or a series of evaporators before the water is passed to the crystallizing pans. Such techniques generally employ mechanical pumps to move brine from one pan to the next.

Some salt makers argue that greenhouse evaporated salts are actually purer and cleaner than open-air salts. Naturally occurring pollens, leaves, and insects can be excluded from the salt-making process by taking the whole affair indoors. Greenhouse evaporators can also be used to shield against acid rain or airborne pollution in vulnerable areas.

Some salt makers take advantage of the environment of the greenhouse to purify the water using more advanced technologies than those of the traditional method of holding seawater in a vasière. Reverse osmosis processes are used by some. Ultraviolet light is used by others. However, because these salts can be fed through evaporators and crystallizers made of metal or plastic, they lack the clay and other mineral solubles that can characterize open-air solar salts.

Some greenhouse techniques don't use pans at all. The Japanese, for example, have developed vertical evaporators. One example of this involves hanging bamboo mats from the ceiling of a greenhouse, spraying seawater on them, and letting the water drip down, evaporating as it falls. The brine is then collected from the bottom and again sprayed on the mats. This process is repeated until the brine is saturated and crystallization takes place. Other saltworks feature towers. Bamboo branches may be suspended from the ceiling to increase the surface area, and the brine is pumped to the top of the tower, allowed to trickle down the branches to the bottom, and then pumped back to the top. Holes in the walls to allow wind to blow through, evaporating the brine within.

THE LEGACY OF SALT

It is the most unlikely juxtaposition imaginable: uninspired, barren apartment buildings hunching over narrow, hastily constructed roads and weeds growing between buckled concrete—just across the road from well-maintained saltworks from the Roman era. Saltmaking is a unique economic force for the preservation of sensitive natural environments. The salt fields of San Fernando, near the ancient Phoenician seaport of Cádiz in modern-day Andalusia, Spain, have seen dramatic changes brought on by nature and man's agricultural activities for tens of centuries. Legend has it that the Greek dynamo Hercules founded Cádiz after completing his tenth labor, slaying the three-bodied monster Geryon.

The city is considered the oldest continuously inhabited settlement on the Iberian peninsula, originally founded by those intrepid salt wheelers and dealers, the Phoenicians, in 1100 BCE. At the time, there was nothing but open bay, some tidal marshes, and reefs made of shells and sandstone. The Romans knew a good thing when they saw it, and set up a number of saltworks throughout the bay in about 500 CE. The region flourished, with small towns like San Fernando prospering from the salt trade. For a dozen centuries, a symbiosis existed between the environment from which salt was made and the civilization that profited from it.

Just a few hundred years ago, San Fernando was still a small town perched on a rocky outcropping overlooking the Bay of Cádiz. In the 1700s, the number of active saltworks in the estuary was greatly expanded. In the ensuing centuries, engineers cut through the meanders of the San Pedro River, drained marshes in the pursuit of agriculture (a failed effort), and constructed fortifications, wharfs, industrial areas, and urban developments. The great bay was being filled in. But, for the most part, the conditions necessary for the production of salt from the sea were preserved, and the inhabitants of the area were raised with a respect—a veneration even—for their ancestral ways. But these changes, no matter how dramatic, pale in comparison to the impact of the industrialization of salt production in the late twentieth century. Salt was devalued, and the economic interests of the salt workers—who had previously insured the preservation of the wetlands as a precious natural resource—largely vanished.

San Fernando is now entirely surrounded by land, silted in by constantly shifting tidal estuaries. Saltworks that produced salt for more than a millennium were filled with rubble and waste, and then paved over to make room for apartment buildings. An aerial view of the region tells the story. The vast tidal estuary near Cádiz is mottled with salt fields. Encroaching on all sides is housing and industrial development. Where development has not yet succeeded in making use of the land, many salt fields are nonetheless abandoned, victims of the collapse of the salt market over the last hundred years.

A tremendous number of birds still live here—more than 150 species by most accounts. The pigeon and shelduck spend their winters there, as do the Limicolae (shore birds). Migratory birds use the area as a staging ground en route between Africa and Europe. Black-winged stilt, plover, redshank, pratincole, avocet, and little tern nest there. Flamingos, the ever present salt-marsh connoisseurs, live there year round. In addition, the area serves as a reserve for birds displaced during periods of drought elsewhere. All of this wildlife is now threatened by development infill, as are the salt pans of San Fernando, Chiclana de la Frontera, and Puerto Real. Modernity has not been kind to the area.

But all is not lost. The saltmakers of San Fernando are keenly aware of the importance and uniqueness of their trade, which is brought into sharp relief by the tension between the ancient methods by which they work the salt marshes and the pressures of modernity that threaten them on every side. Of the two hundred-odd salt makers in the Cádiz region, six still follow the salt-making practices established by the Romans in 500 CE. Visit one of those six salt makers and you will see ponds whose borders have not been altered in over a millennium, except with minor modifications to allow for trucks to haul salt where just decades ago donkeys and boats were used.

Salt making is one of the few economic interests remaining in the region with a voice against encroachment. Moreover, the very practices that harness a salt marsh to produce salt preserve and invigorate the marsh's natural ecology. A traditional salt farm uses no mechanization, and introduces no pollutants. The plants and animals that live there contribute to the stability of the shifting waterways and tides. The natural ecological diversity of salt ponds also aids in the efficient evaporation of seawater and therefore the productivity of the saltworks. Preserving the fragile ecology preserves the saltworks, and vice versa. Incredibly, you can still taste, buy, cook with, and eat salt that has been made in the manner of the ancient Romans. And, most beautifully of all, you can still walk up to a man at work by the side of a salt barn, strike up a conversation, and listen raptly as he tells of the struggle, achievement, and pride still to be had in the making of salt from the sea. ∎

FIRE EVAPORATED SALTS

In places where rough terrain makes solar evaporation impractical, or where inhospitable climate makes it impossible, fire can be enlisted to accelerate the evaporation of water. A tremendous variety of salts can be made by fire evaporation. Coarse granular traditional salts are possible, but often as not the salt maker takes advantage of the highly controlled environment to make something more unusual.

Rapid boiling produces large, parchment-fine flakes. Slower simmering produces *shio,* the fine-grained salt mastered by the Japanese. Shio crystals are the most delicate of all salt crystals, perfected by continuous, carefully studied stirring.

The gentle agitation of brine densely saturated with sodium and magnesium salts induces downy tufts of salt so fine they seem made up of single molecules. A few artisan salt makers crystallize their salt in a mold, drying it completely to yield a puck or ingot reminiscent of the salts made using *briquetage,* pottery shards, hundreds of years ago.

Collecting seawater or brine from a salt spring and boiling off over a wood fire is a common and ancient form of salt making. It is also the best documented. Pottery shards found in large quantities at many Neolithic settlements across Europe and Asia, once thought simply to be discarded ceramics, are now believed to be broken *briquetage* pots used in the boiling off of brine to make salt.

Modern artisan methods for evaporating salt have not changed much, though certain conveniences have been adopted, such as the filtering and/or purifying of seawater beforehand. Some very creative, high-tech evaporators have harnessed geothermal energy. Salt makers in some countries avoid heat altogether in favor of electricity-based techniques like ion-membrane separation. But such

This salt was tinted a copper-oxide blue from the unlined pots used to evaporate the salt. The original expedition would have had zinced or tinned pots to make a salt described by Lewis as "excellent, fine, strong, and white."

A salt maker re-creating a Lewis and Clark salt-making camp, Seaside, Oregon. Every year, the Lewis and Clark Museum in Seaside, reenacts the explorers' salt-making enterprise, undertaken to provision the party for the long return voyage to the eastern states.

methods generally yield salt that has been robbed of its soul, its ties to nature severed. It is difficult to think of such salts as artisan, regardless of the salt maker's intentions.

Artisan or otherwise, salts made with fire require considerable input of natural resources. It can take as much as two tons of liquid fuel to make one ton of salt. The huge industrial solar saltworks at Rio Tinto in Australia produce 6.1 million metric tons of salt a year by evaporating 1.1 million metric tons of saltwater (290 million gallons, enough to fill 18,000 residential swimming pools) every day. The company estimates 14 million tons of coal would be required daily to achieve the same result. As outlandish as that may sound, consider that seawater is just 3 percent sodium chloride, so more than 30 tons of water must be boiled or simmered off to make that ton of salt. Nonetheless, fire evaporation has a long and distinguished place in our history, and the fire evaporated salts that have survived the industrialization and subsequent hyper devaluation of salt can achieve extraordinary culinary heights. Like a fluffy chocolate mousse, a blazing

Cyril Osborne making Maldon salt with his son Clive.

INDUSTRIAL FIRE EVAPORATED SALT

In industrial settings, vacuum evaporators—and some artisanal ones—are used to improve fuel efficiency. Water is boiled in a closed vat and the air above is vacuumed out, dramatically decreasing the boiling temperature of the brine. Vacuum vessels are arranged in sequence, so steam emerging from one vessel heats a subsequent vessel, and so on, until the brine is condensed sufficiently to permit crystallization. A variety of crystallization methods can be used. Brine can be sprayed onto a heated plate of stainless steel, or it can be sprayed into the air of a kiln to allow the crystals to form and dry midair. Such salts attain 99.9 percent NaCl, a level of purity not found in nature. ∎

flambée, or an architectural salad, our awareness of the food is heightened despite the artificiality of the process—or indeed because of it. Turning your back on fire evaporated salt would be like turning your back on gin or hamburgers or pasteurized milk: they all require fuel to produce, and yet their deliciousness makes them indispensable.

SOLAR-FIRE HYBRID SALTS

One way to decrease the amount of fuel needed to evaporate salts is to preconcentrate the brine by solar evaporation. Because many fire crystallized salts are made in damp, cool climates, a greenhouse is usually used in lieu of open air evaporators, and then the concentrated brine is crystallized in a vat over fire. The solar pans, whether indoors or out, concentrate the brine to precipitate out unwanted salts and minerals such as the sulfates and carbonates, then the brine is further concentrated until it has the mineral profile desired by the salt maker. This conditioned brine is then fed into open cauldrons or pans and heated very slowly, usually by wood fire, to assist the formation of crystals. Many such salts are hand stirred—or even hand massaged! (see Temomi Tenpien Enmusubi, page 103)—to aid in the uptake of magnesium and potassium (the salts that remain after the crystallization of NaCl, known as *nigari*) into the crystals of sodium chloride and other salts. Many of the great Japanese artisan salts are made this way.

What was probably the most common and ancient way to create a condensed brine was to extract it from sand or dirt. Sands or soils in salt estuaries or swamps that drain seasonally or with the tides can be scraped up and mixed with any available water. Ocean water could be sprayed or poured over clean beach sand and evaporated in the sun, then washed out with more salt water. Inland soils naturally high in salt can be soaked in fresh water. These brines can then be filtered and boiled off over a fire to crystallize salt.

For most of human history this was probably the method practiced across the widest variety of geographical domains. Today, it is mostly the salt of last resort practiced in the most impoverished parts of the world, though Okunoto Endenmura is an ancient salt still made in Japan made the process of *"shio maki,"* casting sea water over the sand covered salt fields and *"kama taki,"* boling down the brine in a kama or pot to achieve optimal concentration and crystallization. The result is a magnificent artisan salt that communicates a samurai's fury and discipline.

FLAKE SALTS

Pure sodium chloride crystallizes in sharp, defined faces, which, in a perfect environment, grow into dauntingly large, sharp-edged cubes. The more uniform the salt crystal, the harder it is. A jumbled, highly irregular crystal has a much more pleasant crunch than a uniform crystal. A moist crystal is more yielding than a dry one. The softest crystals of all, such as fleur de sel and sel gris, are both jumbled and moist, and can seem downright unctuous. But salt's natural tendency to form in cubes can produce an entirely different category of crunchable salts: flake salts. Instead of granular, irregular crystals, flake salts have plate-like (lamellous) crystals that are dry, thin, and brittle—so brittle that even the largest flake salt seems to pop into a million pieces if you so much as look at it the wrong way.

Flake salts are basically the skeletons of much larger crystals that form when the faces of the crystals have a different growth rate than the edges. This can occur for a variety of reasons, and can result in crystals like pyramids or extraordinary hollow-faced boxes. I have found pyramidal crystals larger than a silver dollar. Many of these hollow crystals are crushed during crystallizing, harvesting, and packaging, resulting in flakes.

Salt can form into flakes in carefully regulated boiling water, or in the sheltered calm of a greenhouse-enclosed solar evaporator, or even in the open air. Water temperature, evaporation rates, salinity, atmospheric conditions (both natural and manmade), and a variety of other factors will influence the shape, size, and the thickness of the resulting flakes. By varying the conditions, flake salts can actually end up looking not so flakey. Instead of flakes radiating ever outward, flakes can be made to assemble one over another, resulting in a laminated structure reminiscent of potato chips that got stuck together in the fryer. Many flake salt manufacturers are highly secretive about their techniques.

QUARRIED SALTS

The first question I ask myself when something doesn't seem to be beautiful is why do I think it's not beautiful. And very shortly you discover that there is no reason. — John Cage

Salt in its mineral or rock form is called halite, which derives from *halos*, the Greek word for "salt," combined with *lithos*, meaning "rock." Luckily for us, salt even in its purest form is soft, with a Mohs hardness of just 2.5 (about the hardness of a fingernail), compared to, say a hardness of 100 for quartz or 1,600 for diamonds. We can crush a salt crystal with our teeth provided it is small enough. Still, a solid crystal is fairly hard in biting terms. Rock salt deposits have been mined for far longer than we are ever likely to know. However, mining was probably the least common way of acquiring salt for most of human history. Most rock salt mines were likely discovered by hunters pursuing wildlife that had congregated around salt springs. The hunters would have had an easier time getting their salt by evaporating the spring water than by digging through solid rock to access underground deposits. The Hallein salt mines in present-day Austria were the site of salt-winning from salt springs using briquetase for 4,000 years before organized rock salt mining began there, around 600 BCE.

Mining for rock salt was nasty, dangerous work. Every hundred years or so, the salt mines at Hallein yield the salt-cured body of a brightly clad Celtic man who worked thousands of feet beneath the earth many centuries ago. (Salt is an amazing preservative. Scientists recently found strands of 419 million-year-old DNA from a bacteria inside an ancient salt deposit.) The

THE BITTERN TRUTH

Bittern, referred to in Japanese as *nigari* (as with the English bittern, nigari is derived from the Japanese word for bitter), is what is left over after all the water is evaporated from a seawater brine and most of the major sodium and calcium salts are crystallized. Bittern contains magnesium compounds and a variety of trace minerals. In nature, it occurs as thin flakes of mostly magnesium chloride, with some magnesium sulfate and other trace elements. Since it is highly water soluble, it often appears in nature as a very viscous liquid or a paste.

Bittern is an important coagulant used in the preparation of tofu from soy milk, and it is also an ingredient in baby formula; these are its two primary industrial uses. In Japan, however, bittern has become the subject of a health-food craze that developed from the perceived nutritional benefit of bittern in salt. Bittern is sold as a white powder and also marketed in *nigarisui*, a popular Japanese version of mineral water with bittern added. It is believed to have one of three effects, depending on how it is used. If taken on an empty stomach or after exercise, it replenishes the body with minerals, especially if taken with citric acid. If taken during a meal, it limits the appetite. If sprayed on the skin, it cleans and softens, and reduces wrinkling while it's at it.

Some believe bittern mutes our ability to taste sodium chloride and monosodium glutamate (MSG). It may also decrease our biological craving for salt, and perhaps MSG.

Evaporated bittern usually accounts for 7 to 9 percent of the original brine (sodium chloride accounts for 19 to 21 percent).

Japanese salt makers often slow-cook a brine in order to intentionally fuse the bittern into the developing salt crystals. Japanese salts are inclined to be very rich in trace minerals, largely because they include a relatively large proportion of bittern to the other salts: minerals commonly found in bittern besides magnesium are calcium, sulfur, potassium, iron, phosphorus, boron, silicon, lithium, and iodine. ■

discovery of bodies in mines is an excellent way to determine when salt mining took place in a particular location and who did the mining, as the bodies are preserved so perfectly that even their stomach contents can be analyzed and carbon-dated. But such finds are rare. For most of history, rock salt mines were small and their exploitation opportunistic, providing for local needs on a modest scale. Mining rock salt was rarely worth the effort.

Most traditionally harvested rock salts rely on manual labor to carve them from their mountain redoubts, employing the room-and-pillar strategy, whereby rooms supported by salt pillars and connected by tunnels are slowly extended deeper and deeper into salt deposits. Mines in Poland, Austria, and Detroit are famous for their ambitious scale, boasting entire cities underground. Pack animals would be lowered down into the mines and then spend the rest of their lives in underground stables. Elaborately carved chapels were dug directly into the stone to attend to the miners' spiritual needs in the gloom.

One example of artisan rock salt mining occurs in the Salt Range, a hill system in the Punjab province of Pakistan. The range runs along the northern portion of the province from the Jhelum to the Indus Rivers. Although salt mined here is called Himalayan salt, the range is actually separated from the Himalayas by nearly 200 miles. The mines have been used since their discovery in 326 BCE, and there is evidence to suggest that salt was being mined prior to that.

People had set up small, opencast mines to glean salt from the surface, but it wasn't until 1872 that the first tunnels were built at ground level to access the salt layers inside the hills. A room-and-pillar mining strategy was implemented to preserve the structure of the mountain; this allowed production to be increased dramatically, and it is still in use today.

In some of the mines, the use of this technique has been taken to another level. The Khewra salt mine, located at the foothills of the Salt Range about 100 miles south of Islamabad, is said to be the second largest salt mine in the world because of its extensive reserves—an estimated 220 million tons. The mine head buildings have nineteen stories, eighteen of which are underground. The salt itself occurs in an irregular domelike structure, varies in color from white to pink to deep red, and is from 97 to 99 percent pure sodium chloride.

The Khewra mine has become a major tourist destination in Pakistan. Deep in its nearly two-mile-long tunnels winding about over seventeen levels, large chambers have been excavated where rock salt artisans have been permitted to carve large and elaborate salt structures. Among them is a 350-foot-tall assembly hall with 300 narrow stairs of salt; a 3,000-square-foot mosque that was constructed over the course of half a century; and a salt bridge known as the Pull Sarat, or bridge of trial. It is twenty-five feet long, with no supporting pillars, spanning a subterranean saline pond. Other items include miniature versions of the Great Wall of China, the Eiffel Tower, and two Pakistani landmarks, Chaghi Mountain and Lahore's Minar-e-Pakistan. Because the salt they are made from is of different purities, the sculptures come in various hues of red, pink, and white.

On the surface, it may seem difficult to categorize a mined salt as "artisan." Salt deposits are made by nature, so the workmanship involved relates more to the extraction of the salt from the mountain than to the making of salt. But artisan or otherwise, the contrast between a salt mined by traditional methods and one mined industrially can be stark. Most obviously, there is a difference in scale dictated by the availability of investment and technology; the regional economics of salt making; the formation of the salt deposits; and, more often than not, the broader cultural landscape with all its attendant values about nature, work, money, and food. The larger of these traditional salt mines, such as the Khewra mine, operate on a much smaller scale than a large industrial mine. Khewra produces 300,000 tons per year, whereas a good-sized industrial salt mine might produce ten times that amount or more.

The tools used to produce the salt differ in each context as well. Traditionally mined salt relies primarily on hand labor, employing only a light-rail system for the removal of the ore from the mountains. Industrial salts are thoroughly polluted by the diesel-powered heavy machinery used in mining, and therefore require refining if they are to be sold for culinary use.

There is a last consideration, one that applies to all salts, be they solar-evaporated, fire-evaporated, or mined. Art historians use the term *aura* to describe the intangible but nonetheless profound sense of an object's unique identity in the world—you know the feeling. There is the electrifying impression of genius, the existential tug of history, the sense of presence. Great cuisine does this for us, too. Traditional salts represent some of the greatest achievements in human ingenuity, are born of the most ancient traditions, and resonate with a diamond's mineral splendor. They are the crown jewels of great food.

SALT GUIDE

THE TAXONOMY OF SALT

He La I ka pa´akai ´ole, He la mana´ona´o no!
A day without salt is a dreadful day indeed! —Hawaiian saying

Historically, the categorization of salts has been haphazard. Some, such as fleur de sel and sel gris, started out as regionally specific salts and have evolved into universal categories. Others, such as flake salt, have emerged as artisan salt makers introduced sophisticated crystals to increasingly interested markets. Yet others have been misclassified. It is not uncommon for a sea salt in the shape of a pebble to be called "rock salt." Conversely, marketers rather disingenuously use the term "sea salt" for rock salts mined from the earth, based on the argument that mined salt deposits are residues of ancient seas. To be useful, descriptions of our one crystalline food must both encompass the limitless creativity of nature and make it accessible to cuisine.

Artisan salts fit into seven classes: fleur de sel, sel gris, traditional, flake, shio, rock, and unconventional. There are two additional classes outside this scheme: "Modified salt" is defined as any of the above classes of salt that is altered after its formation, including flavored and smoked salts. Last are the "industrial salts," which are classified separately.

The boundaries between classes are not crystal clear, nor even is the distinction between artisan and industrial salts—some industrial salt makers skillfully produce wonderfully interesting salts. The grains of the most delicate sel gris can be finer than the most ungainly fleur de sel. Some flake salts are so crumbly they might also be described as granular traditional salts. In the context of this book, when the classification is a particularly close call, I will assign the class that helps us best understand how to use the salt and what to expect of it.

Guides such as this one are inherently incomplete. I learn about two or three new salts a week—even in a slow week—and it is not uncommon for me to encounter entire new vistas of salt when I least expect it. When I am translating foreign language publications, or when I have them translated for me, sometimes dozens of obscure or forgotten salts emerge. Most agreeably, sometimes a beautiful person will walk into the shop, eyes gleaming with mischief, and place into my hands something sparkly just hauled back from the Mongolian steppes, or a bay in Alaska, or an encampment on the dunes of the Sahara. And the marketplace for salt is moving fast. Everyone interested in salt has something different to share. Some salts are named, renamed, and branded in countless ways.

Codifying a subject as deep and unknowable as the sea, as vast as the earth, and as inspired and quixotic as humanity is an exercise in humility. The salt profiles later in this section describe the most interesting, illuminating, and useful salts I have encountered so far. They are grouped by type and listed alphabetically. I will continue to share new salts and new insights on the website of The Meadow, www.atthemeadow.com, and on my blog, www.saltnews.com.

FLEUR DE SEL

Fleur de sel is a solar harvested salt made by evaporating saline water in open pans with energy from the sun and wind, then using rakes to harvest the fine crystals that blossom on the surface of the brine. The salt is characterized by highly irregular, relatively fine crystals and typically contains a considerable amount of residual moisture. The gustatory sensations of fleur de sel border on the mystical, yet the characteristics that give it these powers are not difficult to understand. Irregularly sized and unevenly shaped crystals are key to fleur de sel's behavior on food and in the mouth. Smaller crystals dissolve quickly, pouring out a surge of intense salinity that subsides almost as quickly; then larger crystals break apart and dissolve, providing another wave of sensation, then another, then another—a sort of modulated flavor experience.

Upwards of 10 percent residual moisture is locked in fleur de sel crystals. Because the salt already has moisture in it, the crystals have the power to resist dissolving when they come in contact with food, allowing them to maintain their integrity on moist or steaming foods. The residual moisture also preserves the suppleness of the crystals, lending them a delicate but satisfying crunch. The resulting sensation is one of constantly shifting between acceleration and deceleration of flavor as the salt, the food, and your palate race to integrate into something cohesive.

Last, fleur de sel is loaded with trace minerals that deepen food's flavor and round out the flavor of the salt itself. Rich in minerals, high in moisture, and complex in form, fleur de sel is the munificent king of salts, perfectly suited for all subtle foods, from fried eggs to steamed vegetables to fried fish to caramels. Fleur de sel is an elegant and practical choice as an all-around finishing salt for the kitchen and the table. In a kinder world, fleur de sel would glisten from a small dish on table of every restaurant on the planet.

QUICK-REFERENCE GUIDE TO ARTISAN SALTS

FLEUR DE SEL

■ **MANUFACTURE:** Solar evaporated sea, lake, or spring salt with fine, irregular, moist, mineral-rich crystals made by raking the crystals that blossom on the surface of a crystallizing pan. ■ **IMPACT:** Commingles gently with food, adding a mild, delicate crunch. ■ **USES:** Finishing salt for subtle foods. Cooking salt for specialty dishes. ■ **EXAMPLES:** fleur de sel de Guérande (page 90), flor de sal do Algarve (page 90), flor de sal de Manzanillo (page 90).

SEL GRIS

■ **MANUFACTURE:** Solar evaporated sea, lake, or spring salt with coarse, irregular, moist, mineral-rich crystals made by raking crystals that accumulate on the bottom of a crystallizing pan, soon after they form. ■ **IMPACT:** Deep, mineral crunch with enough moisture to ensure lasting power on the heartiest and moistest of foods. ■ **USES:** Finishing salt for steaks, chops, or roasts and bean, root, or hearty vegetable dishes. Ideal all-around cooking salt. ■ **EXAMPLES:** sel gris de l'Ile de Ré (page 101), grigio di Cervia (page 91), The Meadow Sel Gris (page 94).

TRADITIONAL SALT

■ **MANUFACTURE:** Catch-all category for solar and fire evaporated salt made by periodically or seasonally harvesting crystals accumulated on the bottom of a crystallizing pan. Harvest might employ large plows drawn across a salt pan in Vietnam or spatulas scooping from a kettle in Denmark. ■ **IMPACT:** Varies widely from salt to salt, though often hard and brittle to the tooth and bright and intense on the palate. ■ **USES:** Finishing salt taking advantage of dramatic color and crystal formation and diverse cultural associations. Many traditional salts make good all-around cooking salts. ■ **EXAMPLES:** Trapani (page 104), alaea volcanic (page 85), Maine coast (page 95).

FLAKE SALT

■ **MANUFACTURE:** Solar or fire evaporated salt with pyramidal, flake, or layered parchmentlike crystals. ■ **IMPACT:** Crispy snap of intense but fleeting flavor. ■ **USES:** Fresh vegetables; green salads; any dish where the full experience of salt's most flamboyant texture or sensation is desired. ■ **EXAMPLES:** Maldon (page 95), Marlborough flakey (page 95), Halen Môn (page 91), Hana flake (page 92).

SHIO

■ **MANUFACTURE:** Seawater evaporated over fire, in a greenhouse, or other ways, then crystallized over fire to form exceptionally fine granular crystals. ■ **IMPACT:** Complex, clean taste that bursts instantly from the crystals. ■ **USES:** The small crystals don't call attention to themselves, so use with any food where the ingredients should stay front and center but the fullest wealth and complexity of flavor is desired. ■ **EXAMPLES:** Shinkai deep sea (page 102), amabito no moshio (page 86), sara-shio (page 101).

ROCK SALT

■ **MANUFACTURE:** Mined from the earth and ground to a desired size. ■ **IMPACT:** Hard crystals with constant, relatively homogeneous delivery of flavor. ■ **USES:** In salt mill when the desired effect is dissolving the salt on the surface of moist food, left whole and then grated with rock salt shaver when a fine "mist" of salt is desired on dryer or fattier foods, and in large blocks as cooking or serving utensils for many types of food. ■ **EXAMPLES:** Himalayan pink (page 92), Andes mountain rose (page 87), Jurassic (page 93).

UNCONVENTIONAL SALT

■ **MANUFACTURE:** Salts that fall outside the defining criteria of other evaporative salts. May be made using unusual, generally high-tech processes such as sequence vacuum evaporation or ion-exchange membrane concentration, and/or salts with unusual naturally or artificially formed crystals. ■ **EXAMPLES:** South African pearl (page 102), Icelandic Hot Springs (page 92).

MODIFIED SALT

■ **MANUFACTURE:** A sub-classification for any class of salt that is altered in some way after its creation, such as by smoking, infusing, blending, or roasting. ■ **EXAMPLE:** Halen Môn oak smoked (page 91), black truffle (page 87), 7 salt (page 102), China Sea parched salt (page 88).

SEL GRIS

The name *sel gris*, or "gray salt," comes from the French, who popularized it not only in Europe, but around the world. The name is also a shortened form of *gros sel gris,* or "coarse gray salt," so sel gris is by definition a coarse, granular crystal. Sel gris is very rich in trace minerals; its namesake gray color comes not from minerals, but from small amounts of porcelain clay raked up from the bottom of the salt pan. Fleur de sel, which is made in the same pans as sel gris, lacks this gray color because it is harvested directly from the surface of the brine and never comes in contact with the clay. Some makers of sel gris—especially those in regions where the natural soil of the marsh is a mud or silt that would not be desirable in salt—allow a layer of salt to form on the bottom of the pan and then rake their sel gris from that layer. Such sels gris are not gray at all, or their grayness is barely discernible.

Sel gris provides enormous benefits over most other salts as an all-around culinary salt. First, it brings mineral depth to every food when dissolved during cooking. Second, its moist crystals do not overly dehydrate other ingredients in grilled, roasted, or baked dishes. Third, it lends a hearty crunch when used as a finishing salt. A few pinches of sel gris is the perfect amount for sauces (the pale sel gris varieties lack any deposits that might cloud the thoughts of the most perfidious chefs or the color of the whitest sauces), and a handful or two should be added to water for boiling pasta or blanching, brining, or pickling vegetables. Used to prepare foods for cooking, sel gris draws a small amount of moisture from the surface of food, but this moisture has nowhere to go because the salt crystals are already saturated with moisture (13 percent residual moisture is typical of many sels gris), so there the moisture stays, glistening on the surface of the food until the heat of an oven or grill sets to work browning it to a golden, crunchy crust. Kosher salt, or many other sea salts, tend to absorb all of this moisture into the salt crystal itself, dehydrating the food and doing little to brown it. Sel gris is the most natural and cost-effective choice for anyone looking to replace artificially refined salts such as table salt, koshering salt, or mass-produced sea salt.

Sel gris is also an excellent finishing salt. While the crystals are large and can be intimidating, the moisture in them makes them supple, each one yielding with a tantalizing, unctuous bite. With its ample moisture and toothsome crunch, sel gris is the ultimate salt for finishing hearty foods like steak, lamb, veal, roasted poultry, and root vegetables. Some sels gris can be mild enough for finishing subtly flavored foods like eggs, steamed vegetables, and fruit.

TRADITIONAL SALT

Traditional salt is the broadest category of salt, and is proportionately resistant to generalization. The most conventional examples are solar evaporated sea salts that are harvested only one or two times a year after they collect in a thick layer along the floor of the crystallizing pans. The resulting coarse salt is then dried and ground to a usable consistency. Some traditional salts are rocky, but others can be delicately crunchy and, when finely ground, even silky. Many traditional salts make excellent all-around cooking salts.

The difference between sel gris and traditional salt is that sel gris is harvested more or less daily, and its crystals are left in the shape and structure formed naturally during the time between harvests. Sel gris that is ground to a fine texture is referred to simply as *sel marin,* or sea salt, and is classified as a traditional salt.

FLAKE SALT

Flake salt is a very different animal from the more or less granular, mineral-rich, and often moist salts like fleur de sel, sel gris, and traditional salt. Some flakes form in thin, sculpted shavings, as if the ocean were frozen in time and then spun on a lathe. Others are pyramidal in shape, crystalline representations of life's molecular soul.

Flake salts are lower in trace minerals than most other salts, which can make them more pungent and bold. Thin crystals have a large surface area and low mass, so they snap into bright sparks in the mouth, then dissolve almost completely, vanishing as quickly they appeared.

The taste sensation of flake salt is interesting: rather than chat amicably with the flavors in your mouth like the urbane fleur de sel or the powerful but good-natured sel gris, a flake salt jolts your tongue with all the subtlety of a frayed wire yanked from an electrical socket. When in league with fresh vegetables, herbed seafood, or chocolate mousse, flake salt provides voltage that illuminates other flavors with contrast and dazzle.

THE POETRY OF DESCRIBING SALT

CRYSTAL: The class of salt is the primary determinant of its crystal. For example, fleur de sel is almost always granular. For this reason, I would not bother to describe a fleur de sel as granular unless there was something characteristic about the granularity. The irregularity of crystallization is the opposite of homogeneity. It is usually desirable for crystals to be heterogeneous rather than homogeneous because crystals of different sizes and shapes contribute in different ways to the flavor dynamics between food, salt, and mouth. Irregularly-shaped and -sized crystals are good. On the other hand, a "fractured" salt that is too irregular will have an unappealing broken-upness that prevents it from resolving to a particular purpose. This is a salt that has no sweet spot where it contributes something special.

COLOR: Perfect salt crystals are transparent, but most salts are not perfect crystals, and it is the imperfections that make each salt unique. Qualities that help in describing the whiteness of salt include brightness (the amount of light it reflects); hue (tonal variation from pure white); and translucency (the amount of light that passes through the crystal or is refracted within it). The aesthetic determination of a salt is predicated on there being some way to turn its color to the benefit of a dish or the stimulation of an appetite: "grayish chalk" is not particularly appealing; "halogen-lit aquarium" is. Because we have about ten words for white, and those don't tell us much, descriptions of many salt colors rely on a certain degree of imagination on both our parts—mine as the writer, yours as the reader.

BODY: The feel of salt as it dissolves in the mouth and the way it crunches between the teeth or grazes the palate comes from its body. Salt can penetrate sharply into your tongue, or just float around warmly. The concept of body also relates to a salt's staying power. If the salt has the wherewithal to stick around and do good things as it interacts with your food and your palate, it has body. When we talk about the body of salt, we are talking about how it feels physically. A salt that is dry and dusty may have little or no body. A salt that is moist and chunky probably has a lot of body. Moisture is the most potent force lending body to a salt, though mineral content and crystal structure also contribute.

TASTE: We don't normally eat salt by itself, so talking about the taste of a salt involves physical and psychological gymnastics, like talking about loneliness while you're pressing your lips against someone's warm neck. Making matters more difficult, the physics of salt on the tongue—whether smacking rudely or simmering tantalizingly or sizzling painfully or whispering caressingly or bubbling gleefully or gushing excitedly or hiding coyly—is more than just flavor. Salts have behaviors. Combined with food, these behaviors translate into something societal, with varying degrees and styles of manners and social verisimilitude. But all that said, any talk of a salt's taste should place the emphasis on mineral balance—the combination of flavors produced by the unique chords struck by minerals as they strum your mouth. From there, we imagine and experiment our way toward understanding how these subtler characteristics will play out against its texture and other qualities, and how all this will unite in support of the pleasure of eating.

MEROIR: Whenever something of the sea's character is revealed in a salt, we call that character *meroir*. An adaptation of the French word *terroir* (used to describe a wine's mineral inheritance from the earth), "meroir" is also used to describe variations in the briny flavors of seafood, such as oysters. Like the earth, the sea comes in different flavors. The salinity of seawater can vary considerably. The Mediterranean Sea, for example, has about 3.8 percent salinity compared to the open Atlantic, which has about 3.5 percent. Moreover, the salts themselves vary from place to place. The salts of the Dead Sea are primarily magnesium chloride, compared with sodium chloride in the Atlantic and Pacific.

	OCEANS	MEDITERRANEAN SEA	DEAD SEA
SALINITY	3.5 percent	3.8 percent	33.5 percent
CHLORIDE	19,400	23,000	224,000
SODIUM	10,800	12,700	40,100
MAGNESIUM	1,300	1,500	44,000
CALCIUM	416	470	17,200
POTASSIUM	390	470	7,650
BROMIDE	66	76	5,300

In addition to the proportions of various minerals making up salt water, ecology also plays a role in determining merior. Most seas support myriad micro- and macroorganisms that contribute organic and inorganic nutrients to the water. Shrimp in a salt pond contribute carotene to the water, and microscopic halophytes produce a host of amino acids that find themselves in the source water for salt. The roles that all of these elements play in the characteristics of a salt are vast and complex, and can be as vital to the salt's character as the soil of a vineyard is to a wine.

COST: I don't talk about the cost of salt. It is hard to find examples of where it is relevant. Finishing salt is the most effective, most natural, and least expensive way to improve the flavor of your food. A meal for two seasoned with a hefty two-grams (1/14 ounce, or six two-finger pinches) of the most expensive salts in the world costs about twenty cents. Americans spend 9.5 percent of their annual income on food—less than anyone in history. The French and Italians, by comparison, spend between 15 percent and 17 percent. If you are what you eat, good salt is a bargain investment no matter where you live.

Making valuations based solely on price is an exercise in false assumptions. Is a vintage 1960 Alfa Romeo Duetto Spider for $40,000 a better deal than a new Bugatti Veyron 16.4 Grand Sport for $2 million? I suppose it costs less, but is it a better deal? Both cars stir our passions, but in different ways. The beauty of salt is that at $0.001 to $0.05 per serving, you can own all the Bugattis and Alfa Romeos you want and experience whichever one strikes your fancy at the moment, whether it's scrambling eggs in your villa in Monaco or making a midnight snack of foie gras and caviar with your roommates in college. ■

塩 SHIO

Shios are usually fire evaporated salts with near microscopic crystals that resemble miniaturized fleur de sel or flake salt. They are generally high in trace minerals—magnesium in particular—in keeping with the Japanese taste for a full-blown yet refined bitter-sweet flavor balance.

The superfine crystal structure of shios is both the constraint and the imperative for their use. When shio is sprinkled on dry foods like popcorn or food with low surface moisture like edamame, the palate experiences something akin to dream-walking through snow—a quietly falling softness on bare skin—as the minute crystals alight and vanish with every bite. On moist foods, shios dissolve instantly and completely, consummate collaborators lending perfect mineral balance to the subtlest facets of a food's personality. Shios are all about subtlety—except when they're not. On fatty or firm foods such as avocado, crab, raw fish, and fried foods, the crystal merges with the food and then shines forth miraculously from within.

ROCK SALT

Rock salts are extracted from deposits in the earth rather than evaporated from the sea. Rock salt deposits are the remnants of ancient evaporated seas, but because they have been buried for anywhere from a few million to hundreds of millions of years, usually very deep in the earth, they are densely compacted into monolithic crystals. These solid, hard crystals contain no moisture, and they must be ground or dissolved to make them edible. They contain anywhere from a small to a moderate amount of trace minerals, depending on the source, and the resulting flavors range from spicy-hot to floral-sweet. Beyond these subtle distinctions of flavor, the primary allure of rock salts is their otherworldly beauty. They are the only gemstones we eat.

Rock salts make very good grinder salts. They don't contain moisture to gum up the works of a salt mill, and they don't have nooks or cavities where moisture can collect from the air. Rock salt can also be grated into a superfine powder with a rock salt shaver. However, mechanically ground rock salt can rarely rival a naturally formed sea salt. Exceptions are when a hard, tooth-defying experience might be desirable, such as on a loaf of crusty bread. Among the best uses for rock salts is to cut them into blocks and use them as a cooking surface or a natural platter for serving food (see Cooking on Salt, page 267).

UNCONVENTIONAL SALT

Some salts are not easily categorized. The salt might be visibly or structurally odd, or the methods used to make the salt are mysterious (every manufacturer keeps secrets), or the flavor or texture of a salt may resist fitting in with the characteristics of other salt types. Varieties include man-made spherical salts, powdered salts, high-mineral salts, and liquid salts, also known as brine products.

MODIFIED SALT

A salt from any class can be modified after it has been crystallized or mined to add totally new qualities not naturally present in the salt when it emerged from the sea or earth. Techniques for modifying salt include: cold or hot smoking with hardwoods or other botanicals; baking in an oven or firing in a kiln to impregnate with flavors and/or develop texture; melting salt into a liquid form to crystallize anew as it solidifies; saturating salt with a flavorful liquid such as wine or essential oils; and blending salt with flavorful and aromatic ingredients.

Smoking is the most ancient method of modifying salt. It probably started as an accident when salts evaporated over an open fire and took on flavors from their smoky surroundings. Some doubtless found this smoked salt—perhaps sprinkled on raw fish or bland vegetables—to their liking.

Baking and melting salt are quintessentially Asian techniques. The Koreans, Chinese, Japanese, and others in the region heat sea salt to temperatures approaching or exceeding its melting point, 1,474°F, in the presence of clays or botanicals that catalyze reactions between the salt and its surroundings, resulting in new flavors and textures.

Salt blends are the most common modified salts. In fact, salt blends threaten to overwhelm us. I follow a simple rule when looking at any salt blend: the blend must deliver something more than the sum of its parts, achieving something that cannot be achieved by using the flavoring ingredients and salt separately. This rule is valuable because any salt can be combined with virtually any ingredient. Dried fish eggs and salt? Sure. Chocolate and salt? Yes! Herbs and salt? Absolutely. Salt and salt? Why not? Even by the most stringent criteria, there are a good many excellent salt blends out there. The handful of blended salts included in this guide are either culinarily valuable, strategically important, conceptually interesting, or all three—as are the other modified salts here.

SALT REFERENCE GUIDE

These stones alone will whisper in the midst of general silence.
—Carl Linnaeus

The right salt adds beauty, improved texture, and better taste to your food. It also gives you a deeper connection to your ingredients and to the people who made them. This Salt Reference Guide tracks more than 150 salts. Some of the classifications in this chart, such as the type and origin in the description column, are empirical. Others, like application, flavor, and use, are more subjective.

The flavor of a salt on food is highly interactive, contingent on a host of external considerations like the appearance, aroma, texture, and flavor of the food being seasoned, and how this plays into a salt's unique identity. I've done my best to parse these variables in my flavor analyses, but recognize that my conclusions are necessarily personal. Use, likewise, is a matter of personal taste and whim, and should be considered inspirationally as a leaping off point.

The names of salts are often changed by the company that imports or repackages them. I've tried to note a few of the commonly used names for some of these salts, but it may be necessary to refer to my comments on color, crystal, moisture, and flavor to make a proper identification of a specific salt. Salts in shaded rows have full profiles in this book; follow the cross-references to learn more about them. Still can't find a salt? Try the Index (page 305). If you are looking for a substitute for any salt, reference other salts of the same type first, then go on to match crystal structure, moisture, flavor, and color, in that order.

	NAME(S)	DESCRIPTION	APPLICATION	FLAVOR	USE
	Aguni Koshin Odo, Aguni no shio, Aguni salt (page 154)	Japanese shio; bluish white, superfine, highly irregular, complex crystals; moderate moisture	finishing, cooking	bright, intense up front with lingering sweet, elusive cucumber	rare beef filet; sashimi; raw and barely cooked vegetables such as spring peas
	Akoh Arashio	Japanese traditional salt; translucent, fine-grained crystals; moderate moisture	finishing, cooking	structured, umami, buttermilk	steamed vegetables, vichyssoise; turns butter into crème fraîche
	alaea Hawaiian (coarse), alaea salt (coarse), alaea volcanic (coarse), Hawaiian red (coarse) (page 128)	U.S. traditional and/or industrial salt; brick red, coarse, oblong gravel bits; very low moisture	finishing, cooking, may be ground in a mortar and pestle	oceanic, bright	fish, pork, chicken, rice; a soulmate for fresh fruits; tamales, salsa
	alaea Hawaiian (fine), alaea salt (fine), alaea volcanic (fine), Hawaiian red (fine) (page 130)	U.S. traditional and/or industrial salt; brick red to terra cotta, fine crystals; no moisture	finishing	ferrous, clean, oceanic, faintly hot	mozzarella, corn with lime juice, cocktail rims
	alaea traditional, Bright Alaea, Hawaiian pink salt	U.S. traditional and/or industrial salt; pale, translucent, coarse oblong, gravel bits; very low moisture	finishing, cooking, may be ground in a mortar and pestle	oceanic, bright	traditional Hawaiian dishes such as poke, Kalua pork; hearty Mexican foods; fish
	Alcochete sal grosso, sal de Alcochete, sal de Alcochote, sal marinho tradicional de Alcochete (page 131)	Portuguese sel gris or traditional salt; oxidized steel-colored highly irregular shards; high moisture	finishing, cooking, may be ground in a mortar and pestle	mild mineral, faintly sweet	general-purpose cooking salt; roasted marrow bones, fresh cheeses; ground over tropical fruits; salt crusts
	Amabito no Moshio, moshio, ancient sea salt (page 156)	Japanese shio; tan superfine, complex crystals; low moisture	finishing, cooking	savory, rich, round, minerals	tempura vegetables, scallop sashimi, cucumber sandwiches, ice cream, popcorn
	Amashio	Japanese traditional salt; semi-translucent very fine grains; moderate moisture	cooking	powerfully acrid, bitter	pasta water, batter, seaweed salad dressing

	NAME(S)	DESCRIPTION	APPLICATION	FLAVOR	USE
	Amethyst bamboo salt 9x (page 173)	Korean modified, roasted sel gris; amethyst cracked pebbles; no moisture	finishing, cooking	sulfurous, candied egg, mossy, with rust	medicinally, and sparingly on spicy foods or blended with other salts as all-purpose salt
	Amethyst bamboo salt 9x powder	Korean modified, roasted sel gris; blush-colored soda powder; no moisture	finishing, cooking	sulfurous, candied egg, mossy	medicinally, and sparingly on spicy fried foods, braised pork belly
	Antarctic sea salt, South African traditional salt	South African traditional salt; clouded quartz-colored massive grains; low moisture	finishing, cooking	flat, big, minerals, faint round finish	all-around cooking salt, cracked over thick rare steaks
	Baja salt, Si Salt	Mexican traditional salt; sparkling white fine fragments; moderate moisture	cooking	flat, absent	sidewalks, weeds
	Bali fleur de sel, Bali Reef fleur de sel (page 105)	Balinese fleur de sel; antique white, medium-sized, highly irregular granules and flakes; light moisture	finishing, cooking	balanced, warm	pasta, roast pork, broiled fish, steamed and grilled vegetables, floating atop sauced foods
	Bali Kechil Pyramid, coarse Kechil Balinese salt (page 142)	Balinese flake salt; translucent ice-colored crystals in miniature jewel boxes; low to moderate moisture	finishing	clean, briny, faintly bitter finish	salad, fish, smoked duck, green apple tarte Tatin, homemade pretzels, cold and hot soups, any satay
	Bali Rama Pyramid, coarse Balinese salt (page 143)	Balinese flake salt; barely clouded ice-colored crystals in pyramidal tapers; low to moderate moisture	finishing	clean, briny, faintly bitter mineral finish	salad, grilled vegetables, roasted fruits, oatmeal chocolate chip cookies
	Bamboo Leaf	Hawaiian traditional salt; chopped gravel of illuminated jade green; moderate moisture	finishing	grassy, straw, sassafras, warmth	sushi, rice, squash, sea snails, crustaceans of all kinds

	NAME(S)	DESCRIPTION	APPLICATION	FLAVOR	USE
	Bamboo Jade	U.S. traditional-industrial blend; green-brown cracked gravel; low moisture	finishing, cooking, suitable for milling	lawn, green tea, metallic, faint bitterness	fruit salad, leg of lamb, curry, raita
	Bengal Blue, bay of Bengal salt	Bangladeshi sel gris; sandy white coarse rubble; low moisture	finishing, cooking, may be ground in a mortar and pestle	sharp bite, intense, metallic, very full mouth	grilled fish, beef, fried vegetables
	Bitterman's Chocolate Salt	Oregon modified, infused fleur de sel; chocolate-brown fine, irregular shards and granules; high moisture	finishing, may be ground in a mortar and pestle	hearty, bourbon-sweet, olive-oil finish	cookies, rubs, mole dishes, salted candies, tagines, couscous, cheese soufflé
	Bittern, nigari, *lushui*	various countries, unconventional salt; clear viscous liquid of magnesium chlorides, bromides, iodides	finishing	snake venom; soldering flux; circuit boards	making tofu, baby formula, medicine
	Black Diamond	Cyprus flake salt; massive pyramids of wrought-iron black; no moisture	finishing	tannic, earth, pungent, fluctuations between boldness and subtlety	pork loin, stir fry, grilled and seared fish, biscuits and gravy, fresh goat cheese, tzatziki, pumpkin soup, pumpkin pie
	black truffle salt, truffle salt, sale al tartufo, sel aux truffes (page 174)	Italian (and others) modified, blended traditional salt; flat white with black specked crystals in pulverized granules; very low moisture	finishing, cooking	deeply earthy, dried fruit, woody, garlicky	steak, roast duck, brown butter, roasted vegetables, eggs, mushroom pasta, steak, French fries, popcorn
	Bolivian Rose (coarse), Andes Mountain Rose (page 162)	Bolivian rock salt; cranberry-tangerine rose-quartz gravel; no moisture	finishing, cooking, suitable for milling in grinder or shaving with a grater	mild, mineral, with long sweet-mineral finish	chiles rellenos, fried plantains, pan-fried trout; ground fine for cocktail rims and salt blends
	Bonin, pure Bonin sea salt	Japanese unconventional salt; flat paper white caked powder; low moisture	finishing, cooking	subdued sweetness, bracing vinegar tang, balanced	fresh fruit salads, poultry, braised meats, game birds, pork, coleslaw

	NAME(S)	DESCRIPTION	APPLICATION	FLAVOR	USE
	Brazilian sal grosso, Brazilian sea salt	Brazilian traditional salt; translucent white, very coarse, sea-worn gravel; no moisture	finishing, cooking, suitable for milling in grinder or shaving with a grater	fast onset of clear hotness, clean-hot finish	beef, pork, lamb; ground over steamed vegetables, fish
	Cayman sea salt	Cayman Islands flake salt; translucent white stratified flakes; moderate moisture	finishing	clean, fruity, delicate mouth feel, clean finish	fresh fruits, greens, any fish, fried foods, poultry, pork
	China Sea Parched salt	Korean modified, roasted sel gris; rose-tinted opaque eggshell crystals in irregular medium to large shards; low moisture	finishing, cooking, may be ground in a mortar and pestle	minerally with strong fruity undertones, and chrysanthemum	tea-smoked duck, chow mein, soups
	Cornish Sea Salt (page 144)	English flake salt; icy white crumpled clusters of stratified flakes and pyramids; moderate moisture	finishing	metallic, bright, with mild but faintly bitter finish	savory pies: herbaceous leek with butter and pork lardoons, or steak and kidney; pan-seared calf's liver
	Cyprus black flake salt, Cyprus Black Lava, Turkish Black Pyramid (page 145)	Cyprus flake salt; charcoal-colored large pyramids; no moisture	finishing	tannic, earthy, clean, warm, touch of hotness	grilled asparagus, chevre, duchess potatoes
	Cyprus flake, Cyprus Silver (page 146)	Cyprus flake salt; frost-white massive pyramids and flakes; no moisture	finishing	buttery, bright, seafoam, a dream of lactose and seawater	green salad, summer fruit, olive oil dipping, seeded rolls, shortbread cookies, canapés
	Cyprus hardwood smoked flake	Cyprus modified, smoked flake salt; golden brown massive pyramids and flakes; no moisture	finishing	candied hardwoods	all meats, raw cheeses, potatoes, pasta
	Danish Viking smoked, Viking salt (page 175)	Danish modified, smoked traditional salt; coppery, golden brown crumpled gravel; very low moisture	finishing, cooking, may be ground in a mortar and pestle	beefy, campfire	pastas, mashed potatoes, red meats; transformative with hard cheese

	NAME(S)	DESCRIPTION	APPLICATION	FLAVOR	USE
	El Salvadorian flor de sal, Mayan Sun	El Salvadorian traditional salt; warm white, fine, irregular granules; low to moderate moisture	finishing, cooking	hard, harsh, bitter, dirty finish, good mouthfeel, silty river salt feel	baked potato, fried pork chop, rub
	Fiore di Cervia, fiore di sale di Cervia (page 106)	Italian fleur de sel; blue-silver-white, fine, irregular granules; high moisture	finishing	sweet minerality with clear, slightly hot fruit finish	pasta, popcorn, sautéed fish, beef filet, everything with olive oil, especially olives and artichokes
	fiore di sale di Trapani	Italian fleur de sel or traditional salt; silver-white coarse, irregular, angular clusters; high moisture	finishing, cooking	intense minerality, meaty flavor, lacy mouth feel	grilled fish, fried garlic, herbs and olive oil pasta sauces, pork or lamb chop off the grill, duck breast
	fleur de sel de Camargue, Le Saunier de Camargue Fleur de Sel (page 107)	French fleur de sel; translucent white, semifine, cubic-leaning but irregular granules; moderate moisture	finishing	tangy, bright minerals, balanced	fried eels, game birds, duck, steamed or grilled vegetables, fresh tomatoes, buttered toast, cookies
	fleur de sel de Guérande (page 109)	French fleur de sel; silver-white, fine, highly irregular granules; moderate moisture	finishing	wild horse sweat, mineral clay, briny finish	poultry, fish, steamed vegetables, butter cookies, caramels, butter, tomatoes; the best mozzarella salt
	fleur de sel de l'Ile de Noirmoutier (page 110)	French fleur de sel; silver-white, fine, highly irregular granules; moderate moisture	finishing	floral, briny, wooden barrel	poultry, baguette with butter and a thin slice of ham, poached sole with herbs
	fleur de sel de l'Ile de Ré (page 111)	French fleur de sel; rose-tinged silver-white fine, highly irregular granules; moderate moisture	finishing	minerally, occasional bitter notes, extraordinary mineral balance	duck fat-fried potatoes, fish, small game birds, fresh vegetables, steamed vegetables, butter cookies, butter
	Flor de Delta	various countries, unconventional salt; clear viscous liquid of magnesium chlorides, bromides, iodides	finishing	snake venom; soldering flux; circuit boards	making tofu, baby formula, medicine

	NAME(S)	DESCRIPTION	APPLICATION	FLAVOR	USE
	flor de sal d'Es Trenc (page 112)	Spanish fleur de sel; translucent pink-white, fine, highly irregular granules; moderate moisture	finishing	mild, mineral-backed sweetness	fresh vegetables, seafood salads, all manner of fish, poultry, foie gras, sandwiches
	flor de sal de Manzanillo, Flor Blanca (page 113)	Mexican fleur de sel; silvery white to whitish silver, small to medium granules; moderate moisture	finishing	sweet-sour note, light brine	lightly fried fish, plantains, eggs Benedict, watermelon, garlic shrimp
	flor de sal de Sanlúcar de Barrameda	Spanish fleur de sel; flat white, small, irregular granules; high moisture	finishing, cooking, may be ground in a mortar and pestle	hot, hard, metallic, slightly abrasive	grilled meats, French fries
	flor de sal do Algarve, Portuguese flor de sal (page 114)	Portuguese fleur de sel; lush white, medium, irregular granules and flakes; moderate moisture	finishing	bright, slightly hot, faint bitter aftertaste	Dover sole or blanched skate in white wine butter sauce, poultry, braised pork or beef, rich sauces
	flor de sal do Aveiro, Eduardo Oliveira (page 115)	Portuguese fleur de sel; silver-white, fine, highly irregular granules; moderate moisture	finishing	very floral, green, chlorophyll, cheery, bright, happy, a young pangasinan	grilled octopus, deep-fried eels and sea bream, hearty stews, poached fruit
	Flos Salis (page 117)	Portuguese fleur de sel; translucent white, super-fine, irregular granules and flakes; moderate moisture	finishing	warm, mild note of clean metal	foie gras, salt-crusted sea bass, delicate vegetable dishes such as steamed new potatoes with herbs and butter
	Fumée de Sel, barrique Chardonnay (page 175)	French modified, smoked fleur de sel; gray-brown to golden mossy colored, medium-size, clumped irregular granules; low moisture	finishing, cooking, may be ground in a mortar and pestle	oak with grass and spice	rubs, butter logs, fruit, mushrooms, pasta with butter and crab
	Ghana bay	Ghanaian traditional salt; gray-silver-white coarse rubble; low to moderate moisture	finishing, cooking, may be ground in a mortar and pestle	hot, spicy, full	hearty meat dishes, spicy stews, ground up on rim of gingery cocktails

	NAME(S)	DESCRIPTION	APPLICATION	FLAVOR	USE
	Ghana mahogany smoked	Ghanaian modified, smoked traditional salt; mahogany gem fragments; no moisture	finishing, cooking	cask-strength lowland Scotch, peat, moss, deep jungle hardwoods, deep jungle animal hide	rabbit, quail, all game, steak, chèvre, hearty salty cheeses, apple pie, tarte Tatin, crème brûlée, vanilla ice cream
	grigio di Cervia, Riserva Camillone sea salt (page 121)	Italian sel gris; seagull gray, small to medium crumbled granules; moderate moisture	finishing, cooking, may be ground in a mortar and pestle	warm, briny, round minerals, roundness with a vibration of nectarine	pasta water, veal scallopini, chanterelle omelet, dark chocolate, fresh ricotta
	gros sel de Camargue	French traditional salt; transparent white, coarse, hard, worn, pebbles; low moisture	cooking, may be ground in a mortar and pestle	pleasant resin, sharp high notes, oceanic with chalky, tannic aftertaste	pork, curing pork, fatty meats, bull stew
	Haleakala Ruby, Haleakala Red (chart, page 129)	Hawaiian traditional salt; deep brick-red amalgamation of irregular crystals; moderate moisture	finishing, cooking, may be ground in a mortar and pestle	slightly metallic, buttery body, clay notes	fresh mango or papaya, curries, sticky rice
	Halen Môn oak smoked, Halen Môn gold (page 176)	Welsh modified, smoked flake salt; yellow-amber stratified flakes; moderate moisture	finishing	warm oak, caramel sweetness	vanilla ice cream, turkey, wild duck, grilled vegetables
	Halen Môn, Halen Môn silver (page 147)	Welsh flake salt; lustrous rain-silver stratified flakes; moderate moisture	finishing	really strong butter, mineral freshness	grilled lamb, caprese salad, grated cheddar and popcorn, mixed nuts
	Halen Môn Sea Salt with Taha'a Vanilla, Taha'a Vanilla salt	Welsh modified, infused flake salt; frosted white pyramids with auburn to mahogany specks; low moisture	finishing, cooking	root beer, mulling spice	rabbit with heavy cream sauce, bechamel, green tea ice cream
	Hana Flake, Hana no shio (page 148)	Japanese flake salt; icy white, sharp, flat pyramids; moderate moisture	finishing	light, super fresh Arctic air, very balanced, glass	delicate salad, ceviche, cold snow pea soup, foie gras, poached halibut

	NAME(S)	DESCRIPTION	APPLICATION	FLAVOR	USE
	Hawaiian black lava salt	U.S. industrial and/or traditional salt; clear blackish, medium, irregular granules; low moisture	finishing, cooking, suitable for milling in grinder or shaving with a grater	tannic, earthy, clean, oceanic, faintly hot	grilled seafood, all pork, sweet potatoes, other moderately moist foods from mozzarella to chiles rellenos
	Himalayan pink, Himalayan rock salt, sendha namak (India), Pakistani namak (India) (page 163)	Pakistani rock salt; white to blood-red small pebbles; no moisture	finishing, cooking, suitable for milling in grinder or shaving with a grater	stainless steel, Play-Doh	pasta water, ground up in baking, negroni rim, venison or buffalo steak, shaved over sashimi, salt brittle
	Iburi-Jio Cherry (page 177)	Japanese modified, smoked shio; caramel-colored fine grains; moderate moisture	finishing	proscuitto, caramel, conifer	squid steak, abalone, miso soup, popcorn, beef filet, raw salmon, toast, ice cream sandwiches, bourbon
	Icelandic Hot Springs (page 171)	Icelandic unconventional salt; blue-white fragmented clumps of powder; low moisture	cooking	acridly mineral, hair-raising, sour Altoids, chalkiness	meat rubs, salt-packed fruit
	Ilocano Asin, Pangasinan Star, Philippine fleur de sel (page 118)	Philippine fleur de sel hybrid; pale white, small, hollow cubes and highly irregular granules; moderate moisture	finishing	almost lemon juice, brine, sun-warmed brambles, timothy grass	rare, simply prepared meats: lamb carpaccio with lemon, aged porterhouse with cracked black pepper; every other cooked food
	Ittica d'Or (coarse)	Italian traditional salt; frosted white, coarse, irregular shards; very low moisture	finishing, cooking	bright, clean, neutral, imperfectly balanced with moderate bitterness	lamb, mutton, roast meats, sheep's milk cheese, hearty seafoods, savory pies, olive oil and olives
	Ittica d'Or (fine) (page 132)	Italian traditional salt; translucent white, fine crumbled sand; very low moisture	finishing, cooking	bright, clean, neutral, balanced with touch of bitterness, hard finish	raw cheeses, bread and olive oil, focaccia, pastas, pickled vegetables
	Jade Sands, Lutai Jade	Chinese traditional salt; dirty white, fine, regular crystals; moderate moisture	finishing, cooking	immediate harshness, clay, rocky, brightly salty, slightly bitter, long mild finish, but lacking complexity	rice, steamed vegetables, shellfish

	NAME(S)	DESCRIPTION	APPLICATION	FLAVOR	USE
	Japanese nazuna, nazuna (page 133)	Japanese traditional salt; clusters of translucent white fine pyramids and cubes; high moisture	finishing	balanced, clear	raw beef, salmon, butter
	Jewel of the Ocean, Uni no Houseki (page 134)	Japanese traditional salt; translucent iced-silver, massive flattened boxes; medium-low moisture	finishing	balanced, clear, intense	decoration, garnish
	Jurassic salt, Real Salt (page 164)	Utah rock salt; clear, red, or brown gravel of irregular fine to coarse crystals; no moisture	cooking, suitable for milling in grinder or shaving with a grater	minerals, hot, flat, big, gritty	brining, pasta water
	kala namak (coarse and fine), black salt, Indian black salt, sanchal (page 166)	Indian/Pakistani rock salt; purplish-brown pebbles; no moisture	finishing, cooking, suitable for milling in grinder or shaving with a grater	sulfur, fruit, earth (pine forest dirt-style)	lamb or goat kebabs, tagines and curries, pickled vegetables, chaat, fruit salad
	Kauai guava smoked, guava wood smoked Hawaiian sea salt (page 178)	Hawaiian modified, smoked traditional salt; auburn-brown, small, non-uniform granules; low to moderate moisture	finishing, cooking, may be ground in a mortar and pestle	bacon, cane juice, campfire	ice cream, barbecue, seafood omelet, tropical fruit
	Kilauea black, Kilauea Onyx	Hawaiian traditional salt; jet-black amalgamation of small to large irregular chunks; low moisture	finishing, may be ground in a mortar and pestle	complex wood notes, no smoke, minerals, ashy	rice with coconut milk, fish, mangos
	Kona sea salt, Kona Deep Sea salt	Hawaiian traditional salt; bluish slushy-translucent amalgamation of small to large irregular chunks; moderate moisture	finishing, may be ground in a mortar and pestle	freshly sweet, faint fruit, cleanly mineral	cookies, bread, fish
	Korean bamboo 1x	Korean modified, roasted traditional salt or sel gris; powdered eggshell to gray-black fine grains; no moisture	finishing, cooking	soapy, boiled eggs	curries, kimchi, japchae (sweet potato noodle stir-fry)

	NAME(S)	DESCRIPTION	APPLICATION	FLAVOR	USE
	Korean bamboo 3x	Korean modified, roasted traditional salt or sel gris; powdered eggshell to gray-black fine grains; no moisture	finishing, cooking	bitter-sour, eggs, complex mineral notes	curries, kimchi, japchae (sweet potato noodle stir-fry)
	kosher salt, koshering salt (page 185)	various countries, industrial salt; flat white to translucent fine flecks; no moisture	other (curing, oddball uses)	hot, bright, sometimes metallic and/or faintly acrid	industrial food manufacturing
	Lemon Flake	Cyprus modified, infused flake salt; sunflower-yellow massive pyramids and flakes; no moisture	finishing	bright, pungent, candy-sweet lemon juice, faint bitter lemon oil	yams, green salads, Arctic fish, banana cream pie, lemon mousse
	Lewis & Clark Expeditionary salt	Oregon traditional salt; blue-green-gray fine granules; moderate moisture	cooking, other (curing, oddball uses)	bitter, cuprous, faint acridness	seasoning venison and elk, preserving elk and bear
	maboroshi plum, maboroshi no ume shio (page 179)	Japanese modified, infused shio; cherry blossom-pink fine chunks; low moisture	finishing	sour, sweet, bitter, umebashi	vanilla ice cream, tropical fruit, rice noodle salad, soft-boiled eggs
	Maine alder smoked, Alder Smoked Maine Sea Salt	Maine modified, smoked traditional salt; espresso bean-colored crystals of small to medium aquarium gravel; very low moisture	finishing, cooking	cedar-alder smoke, grill char	rubs, fatty fish
	Maine apple smoked, Apple Smoked Maine Sea Salt (page 180)	Maine modified, smoked traditional salt; espresso bean-colored aquarium gravel; very low moisture	finishing, cooking, may be ground in a mortar and pestle	campfire, piecrust, applewood	rub on wild meat such as boar, elk, goose; grilled cheese sandwich
	Maine hickory smoked, Hickory Smoked Maine Sea Salt	Maine modified, smoked traditional salt; espresso bean-colored aquarium gravel; very low moisture	finishing, cooking	hickory smoke in mist, grill char	rubs, fatty fish

	NAME(S)	DESCRIPTION	APPLICATION	FLAVOR	USE
	Maine mesquite smoked, Mesquite Smoked Maine Sea Salt	Maine modified, smoked traditional salt; espresso bean-colored crystals of small to medium aquarium gravel; very low moisture	finishing, cooking, suitable for milling in grinder or shaving with a grater	charred, sharp, minerally	rubs, barbecue, bacon, duck, chips (homemade)
	Maine Sea Salt, Maine Coast (page 135)	Maine traditional salt; radish-colored, medium shards and granules; moderate moisture	finishing, cooking, may be ground in a mortar and pestle	super salty, sharp, bitter	fried smelts, grilled swordfish, lobster salad and crab cakes, hearty vegetable salads, clam chowder
	Maldon (page 149)	English flake salt; shimmering frosty white pyramids; low moisture	finishing	oceanic, fresh, clean	butter leaf lettuce salad, salsa, cantaloupe
	Maldon smoked	English modified, smoked flake salt; camel-hair colored pyramids; low moisture	finishing	caramel, sheep's wool, turpentine, resin	chocolate ice cream, fatty fish, fresh cheese
	Marlborough flakey (page 151)	New Zealand flake salt; frosted white miniscule pyramids; no moisture	finishing	sweetly sharp with delicate minerals	snowpeas, pasta primavera, baby green salad, chocolate cake
	Masu	Japanese shio; cocaine-colored nano powder; low moisture	finishing, cooking	mouthful of seawater, smooth, warm, incredibly intense but with no harshness	lasagna, starchy foods, raw vegetables, oysters, shellfish
	Matiz Mediterráneo smoked	Spanish modified, smoked/infused traditional salt; ginger-gold fine gravel; moderate moisture	finishing	harsh vinegar, wet burnt logs, biting astringency, acrid, wet ember finish	dynamite-fished carp
	The Meadow Fine Traditional	Korean traditional salt; silver-gray-white, very fine, velvety, grains; low to moderate moisture	finishing, cooking	rich yogurt body, opulent umami bounded by minerals	all-around baking, dissolving, rubbing, finishing chicken dishes with light lemon or caper sauces

	NAME(S)	DESCRIPTION	APPLICATION	FLAVOR	USE
	The Meadow Fleur de Sel	Mexican fleur de sel; silvery translucent irregular, complex granules	finishing	sea, bright, minerally, heating, long clean scotchy oceanic body, rich finish	butter, fatty pork, honeyed toast, banana tart, banana flambée, banana bread, bananas
	The Meadow Flake	Cyprus flake salt; frost-white massive pyramids and flakes; no moisture	finishing	buttery, bright, seafoam	green salad, tabouli or farro salad, tomato salads like Greek or caprese, foie gras, rolls, butter cookies
	The Meadow Sel Gris, Korean sel gris (page 122)	Korean sel gris; opalescent silver large boxes and medium granules; moderate moisture	finishing, cooking, may be ground in a mortar and pestle	lush roundness, with a vibration of nectarine	all meats for cooking and finishing, preserves, wild mushrooms, pasta water, steamed vegetables and butter, caramel
	Molokai Alaea (coarse) (chart, page 129)	Hawaiian traditional-industrial blend; brick red chopped gravel; moderate moisture	finishing, cooking, suitable for milling in grinder or shaving with a grater	ferrous, earthy warm	fish, chicken, pork, sausages, rice, fruit, salsa
	Mongolian Blue Steppes, jamts davs (page 167)	Mongolian rock salt; purple-gray to gray ultramarine blue carved rock forms; no moisture	finishing, cooking, other (curing, oddball uses), may be ground in a mortar and pestle	stainless steel, sucking a knife, dipped in honey	grate over: butter, fresh root vegetables, truffles and pasta, lemon- and salt-crusted chicken, duck confit
	Mongolian Rose	Mongolian rock salt; orange-pink to rosy white carved rock forms; no moisture	finishing, cooking, other (curing, oddball uses), may be ground in a mortar and pestle	sweet, mild, round, gentle, unfermented mares' milk, long, sweet finish	freshwater fish, fresh root vegetables, salad, green beans, custard, chocolate
	Moroccan Atlantic, Moroccan sea salt (page 136)	Moroccan traditional salt; warm white cracked pebbles and grains; low moisture	finishing, cooking, may be ground in a mortar and pestle	hot, bitter, overlaid with richness, warm finish	couscous; lamb stew with harissa; roasted vegetables with cumin; grilled sea bass with caraway, lemon, and cilantro
	muối biển, gros sel de Viêt Nam, Vietnamese sel gris, Vietnamese traditional (page 137)	Vietnamese traditional salt or sel gris; creamy white chunks and clusters of granules; high moisture	finishing, cooking, may be ground in a mortar and pestle	potato chip roundness slaked with flower nectar	omelets, stir-fried anything, spicy beef soup, pan-seared beef with chiles

	NAME(S)	DESCRIPTION	APPLICATION	FLAVOR	USE
	Murray River flake, Murray Darling (page 152)	Australian flake salt; tiny pinkish-apricot pyramids; low moisture	finishing	fruity, pine notes, iron, faint dry bark, hot finish	kangaroo, snake, grilled lamb, moist cheeses, butter cookies
	Nama Shio	Japanese traditional salt; translucent white fine grain; moderate moisture	finishing, cooking	seacove warmth, acidic, lingering vegetal	shellfish, stir-fry, tomatoes, water-melon, seasonal berries, pineapple, pomegranate
	Okinawa shima masu (page 157)	Japanese shio; white-sand-colored cubes; moderate moisture	cooking	harshly salty, brine	fish, soups, braised meats, vegetables, cookies
	Okinawa Snow	Japanese shio; arctic white miniaturized snow; high moisture	finishing	sparkling water, San Francisco mist	delicate white fish, daikon, vinegared fruits, tempura, tea, wasabi ice cream
	Okunoto Endenmura (page 158)	Japanese traditional salt; frosty white, very fine, highly irregular granules; high moisture	finishing, cooking	intense brine with fresh air	any raw or cooked fish, fried vegetables, beef carpaccio, game birds, soft cheeses, rice or noodle dishes
	Oshima Island Blue	Japanese shio; buffed white fine grains; low to moderate moisture	finishing, cooking	citron notes, balanced	yam tempura, seaweed salads, sea urchin
	Oshima Island Red	Japanese shio; snow white superfine grains; moderate moisture	finishing, cooking	sharp and hard up front; astringent, modulated undertones of gruyère	whale blubber, octopus
	Oyster bamboo salt 9x	Korean modified, roasted sel gris or traditional salt; gray-white cracked pebbles; no moisture	finishing, cooking	sulfurous, ocean foam	medicinal, and sparingly on spicy foods or blended with other salts as all-purpose salt

	NAME(S)	DESCRIPTION	APPLICATION	FLAVOR	USE
	Pa'akai, traditional Hawaiian salt, Hanapepe salt	Hawaiian traditional salt or sel gris; cream-colored medium chunks and shards; low to high moisture	finishing, cooking	flat mineral, duskiness, big warm finish	fruit tarts, fruit salsa, pineapple-glazed pork, fried eggs, crispy-fried fish and chicken
	Papohaku white, Papohaku Opal (page 138)	Hawaiian traditional salt; opalescent white amalgamation of small to large irregular chunks; moderate moisture	finishing	sweet, buttery fruit	finely ground on pop-corn, grains, sautéed shrimp with chiles and ginger, sashimi
	Persian blue (page 168)	Iranian rock salt; clear, with lapis specks, irregular oblong gravel; no moisture	finishing	minerally, sweet, silken coolness, mild spice, perfumy body, pretty, sexy sophistication	salads of all kinds, melons, caramels, roasted lamb, parsnip puree, poached perch, pears
	Pinot Noir salt, Burgundy salt, other red wine-infused salts	U.S, French, and Italian, modified, infused fleur de sel or sel gris; burgundy and flamingo, irregular granules; high moisture	finishing, may be ground in a mortar and pestle	wine lees, tamarind-like tart-sweetness	barbecue, roasted and grilled meats and fish, game, fruit reductions and sauces, cheeses, chocolate, ice cream
	Piranske Soline fleur de sel, Soline salt flower, Slovenian fleur de sel	Slovenian fleur de sel; translucent silver-amber fractioned nanoshards and bits	finishing	spectral clarity, taught, athletic mineral body, cleansing spring-water finish	all dairy, all fish, all light meats, all lightly or well cooked fleshy and leafy vegetables, sweets, drinks
	potassium salt, low-sodium salt	various countries, uncon-ventional salt; chalk-colored with crystals like shattered chalk sticks; low moisture	finishing, may be ground in a mortar and pestle	citric acid, blend of metals	ask your physician
	Prague powder #1, pink curing salt, Insta Cure No. 1, selrose (page 186)	various countries, indus-trial salt; pale pink fine cubes; no moisture	other (curing, oddball uses)	n/a	curing only
	Prague powder #2, Insta Cure No. 2 (page 187)	various countries, indus-trial salt; pale pink fine cubes; very low moisture	other (curing, oddball uses)	n/a	curing only

	NAME(S)	DESCRIPTION	APPLICATION	FLAVOR	USE
	queijo de sal, Rio Maior queijo de sal (pictured in ground form)	Portuguese traditional salt; sandy white, oversized hockey pucks of compacted flecks; no moisture	finishing, cooking, suitable for milling in grinder or shaving with a grater	sweet, super mild, rich, complex	grating over fresh fruits and seafoods, caramel-sauced ice cream sundaes
	Ravida	Italian traditional salt; crystalline white small granules; no moisture	finishing	ocean air, mineral water	bread, cheese, tomato dishes, in olive oil sauce
	red clay parched salt	Korean modified, roasted sel gris or traditional salt; pale terra-cotta jagged granules; no moisture	finishing	supple crunch, staying power, slightly sweet, smooth and round, bright mineral complexity	sweets, buttery foods, ice cream, shellfish, paella, fatty tuna, escargot, brioche, salad, fish, hearty squash soup
	roasted salt, parched salt (page 180)	Korean modified, roasted sel gris; chalk-colored, puffed, jagged grains; no moisture	finishing, cooking	firecracker, minerally, mild, light pungency, ferrous, clean granite rocks, vanishes on food	use liberally on pretzels, brioche, tarts, ice cream, radishes and other vegetables, spicy short ribs
	rosemary flake	Cyprus modified flake salt; blue-green massive pyramids and flakes; no moisture	finishing	bright, pungent, rosemary	lamb, savory pies, flourless chocolate cake
	saffron salt (page 181)	various countries, modified. infused traditional salt; bright yellow fine sand grains with red saffron strands; no moisture	finishing, cooking	floral, lightly peppery	paella, salt-crusted sea bass with fennel, Bloody Mary rims, tagine, rice, chocolate ice cream
	sal de gusano, worm salt (page 182)	Mexican modified, blended traditional salt; brick and ochre-colored bits of crust; no moisture	finishing, cooking	savory broth of earth and smoke, fiery finish	ceviche, amazing on tropical fruit, licked from hand or neck with mezcal, cocktail rims
	Sal de Hielo de San Fernando, flor de sal de Cádiz (page 119)	Spanish fleur de sel; snow white very fine to fine granules; moderate moisture	finishing	mild, very balanced, faint sweetness	raw vegetables, pastries, roast pork, veal steaks, skirt steak and pommes frites, grilled sausage

	NAME(S)	DESCRIPTION	APPLICATION	FLAVOR	USE
	sal de tradicion de San Fernando	Spanish traditional salt; pale white, massive, highly irregular shards; moderate moisture	cooking, may be ground in a mortar and pestle	sweet, rich minerals, astringent finish	all-around cooking salt for meats, curing, heavily sauced dishes, stews
	sal marinho tradicional de Aveiro, sal de Aveiro (page 123)	Portuguese sel gris salt or traditional; pale gray medium coarse, irregular blocks; high moisture	finishing, cooking, may be ground in a mortar and pestle	mineral, faintly sweet	thick beef steaks, saucy fish dishes, heavy stews, roasted beets, salt crusts
	sal grosso do Algarve, sal marinho tradicional do Algarve	Portuguese traditional salt; translucent white, coarse, irregular granules; high moisture	finishing, cooking, may be ground in a mortar and pestle	faint bitterness overlaid with warm minerals	saucy fish dishes, heavy stews, salt crusts
	sal marina de Barcelona, sal gruesa	Spanish traditional salt; cloudy small to medium granules; very low moisture	cooking	sour, sore throat, bitter	roasted chicken, pork, fennel root
	sal marinho do Algarve (fine)	Portuguese traditional salt; pale gray, fine, silken grain; low to moderate moisture	cooking	rich minerals, buttery, bitter notes, mineral finish	baking, rub on meats and vegetables for roasting
	sal rosa de Maras, Peruvian pink salt, Peruvian warm spring salt, Inca salt (page 125)	Peruvian sel gris; rosy cream small to medium granules; moderate moisture	finishing	sour, potter's studio dust	roasted potatoes, buttery pasta, roast venison in Burgundy marinade, ceviche, pan-fried trout
	sale di Cervia, dolce di Cervia	Italian traditional salt; shimmery white irregular crystals of all sizes; low moisture	finishing, cooking, may be ground in a mortar and pestle	faint harshness, mineral-sweet undertones, mild	roasts, whole fish, stew, pasta water
	salfiore di Romagna, salfiore di Cervia, Pope's sea salt, il sale dei papi	Italian fleur de sel; metallic-translucent, fine, fairly uniform crystals; no moisture	finishing, cooking	in-your-face intense, hot	seafood, pastas, grilled meats, curing hams and salami

	NAME(S)	DESCRIPTION	APPLICATION	FLAVOR	USE
	Salish alder smoked, red alder smoked (page 183)	U.S., modified, smoked traditional or industrial salt; medium-dark woodsy brown aquarium gravel; low moisture	finishing, cooking, may be ground in a mortar and pestle	grill char, almost burnt pork	venison or elk steaks, bison or ostrich burgers
	saltpeter, saltpetre, potassium nitrate (page 188)	various countries, industrial salt; white, very fine, trained qlobs; no moisture	other (curing, oddball uses)	n/a	curing only
	Salzburg rock salt, Altaussee stone, Hallstatt rock salt, Hallein rock salt, Austrian rock salt (page 169)	Austrian rock salt; mix of pale brown, pink, and transparent gravel bits; no moisture	cooking, suitable for milling in grinder or shaving with a grater	warm to start, milder mineral finish	ground over cheeses and nutmeg spaetzle; coarse over steamed potatoes, buttered dinner rolls
	sara-shio (page 159)	Japanese shio; opaque milk-colored with a powdered milk consistency; very low moisture	finishing, cooking	fruit, aspartame, candy wrapper, lemon taffy, miracle fruit	everything, especially rice, noodles, rice candy
	sea salt, California sea salt, sel de mer, industrial sea salt, chemical feedstock salt, and most widely distributed brands of sea salt (page 189)	various countries, industrial salt; flat white, fine, fairly regular grains; no moisture	other (curing, oddball uses)	sharp flatness	none
	sel gris de Guérande, gray salt, Celtic Sea salt (page 126)	French sel gris; blue-gray small to medium grains; moderate moisture	finishing, cooking, may be ground in a mortar and pestle	chlorophyll, mineral, faint clay	thick grassfed porterhouse grilled over a wood fire, pork, whole fish, pasta water, salt crusts
	sel gris de l'Ile de Noirmoutier (page 127)	French sel gris; gray with silver lining, fine to medium grains; very high moisture	finishing, cooking, may be ground in a mortar and pestle	sweet notes, briny, bitter	roasted and grilled game meats, gingersnap cookies, salt crusts, pasta water
	sel gris de l'Ile de Ré, gray salt	French sel gris; silver-gray small to medium grains; high moisture	finishing, cooking, may be ground in a mortar and pestle	briny, earthy for a sel gris	chicken, pork, steak, pasta water, piecrusts, salt crusts

	NAME(S)	DESCRIPTION	APPLICATION	FLAVOR	USE
	sel marin de Guérande, sel marin moulu, Celtic Sea Salt (fine), Velvet de Guérande	French traditional salt, sel gris; grayish white grains with specks of glitter color, very fine; moderate moisture	cooking	sweet, briny, round, faint bitterness, clean finish	baking, rubbed on meats and vegetables for roasting, dissolved in other foods
	sel marin de l'Ile de Noirmoutier, sel marin moulu	French traditional salt, sel gris; grayish white with specks of glitter, fine to medium grains; moderate moisture	cooking	sweet, briny, faint bitterness, clean finish	baking, rubbed on meats and vegetables for roasting, dissolved in other foods
	7 Salt, Seven Salt	U.S., modified, blend of various salts; calico of hard chunks, hollow pyramids, large flakes, amalgamated granules; moderate moisture	finishing, cooking	simmering-explosive juxtaposition of rich, spicy, peppery, sweet, and smoke	rubs for red meat, pork, fatty fish, roast potatoes, olive oil–drenched chevre
	Shinkai deep sea salt (page 160)	Japanese shio; arctic white superfine clusters and fragments; moderate moisture	finishing, cooking	mineral water freshness, lingering sweetness, freshest primordial ocean water	sashimi, fried fish, kobe beef filet, foie gras, terrines, edamame and other steamed vegetables
	South African caviar	South African unconventional salt; dirty white whittled-down BBs; low moisture	finishing	astringent, mild, faint bitterness, clean finish	sauced meats, fish stews, baked apples, orange ginger mint salad
	South African flake, South African sea salt flakes (page 153)	South African flake salt; cloudy-clear platelets of agglomerated cubes; high moisture	finishing	hot, full, faintly aluminum	dense soups, chili, braised meats
	South African Pearl (page 171)	South African unconventional salt; cream-colored BB-sized pellets; low moisture	finishing	intense, faint dry bark, hot finish	citrus and mint salad, steamed snow peas
	soy salt	Japanese modified, infused unconventional salt; deep chestnut flakes and pumice-like granules; low moisture	finishing	warmly metallic, slightly souring finish, balanced	on rice, in place of soy sauce for texture, in an Asian rub

NAME(S)	DESCRIPTION	APPLICATION	FLAVOR	USE
sugar maple smoked, Maple Smoked Maine Sea Salt	Maine modified, smoked traditional salt; coffee-colored small to medium granules; very low moisture	finishing, cooking, may be ground in a mortar and pestle	campfire, piecrust, applewood	rubs; wild meats like boar, elk, goose; grilled cheese sandwich
Sugpo Asin (page 120)	Philippine fleur de sel hybrid; pale flamingo-colored small, hollow clustered granules; moderate moisture	finishing, cooking	buoyant minerals, hearty, faint heat	fish in a banana leaf, fresh tomatoes, onions, tropical fruit, fire-roasted clams, spit-roasted venison
table salt, iodized free flowing (page 190)	Various countries, industrial salt; gray-white fine homogeneous cubes; no moisture	other	drying spray paint, dirt, fishhooks	none
Taiwan Yes salt	Taiwanese unconventional salt; lush white micro-fine flecks; moderate moisture	finishing, cooking	berries, tartness, electric buzz, flat finish	piranha, water buffalo
Takesumi bamboo (page 184)	Japanese modified, roasted shio; faded black medium-grained rubble; no moisture	finishing	blood, metal, charcoal, fuzzy sweetness	vegan foods where meat flavor is required, lean game meats (venison, ostrich), cod, raw oysters
Temomi Tenpien Enmusubi, hand kneaded shio	Japanese shio; snow white micro-fine granules and clustered flecks; very low moisture	finishing, cooking	massive mouth-feel, balanced bitter-sweetness	raw beef, fish, and vegetables, everything fried
Tidman's Natural Rock (saltmaker changed in 2009)	PRESENT: German traditional salt; frosted, beads; no moisture PAST: Spanish traditional salt; cloud white, smallish granules; no moisture	other	PRESENT: processed fire, flat, hard, bitter, flavorless PAST: sweet, wild-flower, cornmeal, well-balanced	PRESENT: none PAST: bagels, pretzels, lamb, pork, grain salad with vinegar-based dressing, the best prime rib salt on earth
Timbuktu salt, Sahara desert salt, Mali salt, Sel de Azalaï (page 170)	Malian rock salt; white lightbulb-colored crystals in powder-like tailings of dune sand; no moisture	cooking	slightly metallic, with beach aroma undertones, tangy, lack of complexity, faintly floral	couscous, eel, curries and tagines, cured lemons, mummifica-tion, and, weirdly, sushi and fresh fruit

	NAME(S)	DESCRIPTION	APPLICATION	FLAVOR	USE
	Trapani, sale marino di Trapani, Trapani e Marsala salt, Sicilian salt (page 139)	Italian traditional salt; cloudy white, irregular, small to tiny grains; no moisture	finishing, cooking, other (curing, oddball uses)	bright, briny	olive oil-glazed pasta, snail bruschetta, gamey cheese, homemade yogurt, olives and pickled mushrooms
	Uminosei Yakishio Syokutakubin	Japanese shio; luminescent white slightly clumpy powder; very low moisture	finishing, cooking	exceptionally sweet, mild, with vanishing aftertaste, sugar orangey-tangerine, softness, buttery, alkaline	butter, cheese, steak, cheeseburgers, popcorn, rice, fish, tempura, raw vegetables, classical French dessert tarts
	Vietnamese pearl, Vietnamese traditional (page 141)	Vietnamese traditional salt; very pearl white, large, irregular, pyramidal and cubic shards; high moisture	finishing, cooking	nine-volt battery, minerally, touch of raw egg	yams and pumpkin, butternut squash, spicy soups, char-grilled whole fish
	white truffle salt, sale al tartufo bianco, sel a la truffe blanche	various origins, modified, blended traditional or industrial salt; white pulverized granules with greenish white flakes; no moisture	finishing, cooking	2,4-dithiapentane, noxious paint, mold	none
	Wieliczka rock salt	Polish rock salt; white, purple, and orange-pink sandy gravel; no moisture	cooking, suitable for milling in grinder or shaving with a grater	bright, minerally, faint hotness	stews, soups, slow-cooked meats

FLEUR DE SEL

Bali Fleur de Sel

■ **ALTERNATE NAME(S):** Bali Reef fleur de sel ■ **MAKER(S):** n/a ■ **TYPE:** fleur de sel ■ **CRYSTAL:** medium-to large-grained; soft; fluffy; irregular ■ **COLOR:** slightly antiqued white ■ **FLAVOR:** balanced; mild warmth of melon without sweetness ■ **MOISTURE:** light ■ **ORIGINS:** Bali, Indonesia ■ **SUBSTITUTE(S):** ilocano asin; fleur de sel de Guérande; fleur de sel de Camargue ■ **BEST WITH:** sauced food, because the dry, fluffy crystals stay afloat

The cleanness of a Brittany fleur de sel, the sharpness of a Trapani, the warmth of an Ilocano Asin, or the fruitiness of a Cervia is lacking here. Bali fleur de sel instead presents a pleasantly professional persona. Think of it as a maitre d' for your mouth: "Welcome, may I help you? Yes, please, would you like a glass of Champagne while you wait—oh, I do insist, and perhaps something to nibble? Oh, never mind, your table is ready; right this way." Bali fleur de sel offers service with a smile.

Bali fleur de sel is made during the dry summer months, when artisan salt makers wade into calm blue waters in the early morning, gathering seawater in buckets made from native lontar palm. The water is carried by hand and poured into salt pans dug in black coastal sands. After an elaborate process of solar evaporation, the concentrated brine is transferred into troughs made of palm trunks for crystallization. After sifting, a moist, complex salt emerges.

The medium-large crystal structure, nuanced color, and rich mineral diversity make this an elegant multipurpose finishing salt, excellent on anything from broiled fish to roasted pork. Despite its lower moisture content, it's good scattered over a sauce or a moist food. Moister varieties of fleur de sel maintain their shape and texture in sauces, but Bali fleur de sel has the weird ability to float on the surface of viscous liquid, like crystalline buoys on a sea of cream.

Because Bali fleur de sel is drier than other types of fleur de sel, being left out on a table all day does little to diminish its natural charm. Its slightly larger than normal granular crystals provide a salt-crunch that calls attention to itself, helping to make sure that restaurateurs get credit for serving quality salt. Also, it plays intriguingly with light, its flat white crystals absorbing light so that a salt cellar of Bali fleur de sel sitting on a table seems to glow rather than sparkle.

Fiore di Cervia

■ **ALTERNATE NAME(S):** fiore di Sale di Cervia ■ **MAKER(S):** n/a ■ **TYPE:** fleur de sel ■ **CRYSTAL:** fine; irregular granules ■ **COLOR:** hints of translucent blue in silvered whiteness ■ **FLAVOR:** sweet; bright; Froot Loops ■ **MOISTURE:** high ■ **ORIGIN:** Italy ■ **SUBSTITUTE(S):** fiore di sale di Trapani; fleur de sel de Guérande; fleur de sel de Camargue ■ **BEST WITH:** pasta, where its smaller crystals don't compete with the silky glide of noodles; oily foods like olives, pickled mushrooms, and artichoke hearts where it only partially dissolves; and delicate preparations of small, tender fish

Fiore di Cervia provides a luscious and tingling pleasure not unlike diving into the scary, blue, fish-infested waters off Cinque Terre in northwestern Italy; and it is entirely possible that the fresh lemon-marinated anchovies you eat as the brine dries on your shoulders will be salted with it. The salt is in fact harvested from the placid salt pans of the happy blue Adriatic on the other side of the country by amiable Italian blokes who wield wooden rakes in precisely the fashion that their ancestors did, way back when wily, lethal Etruscans roamed the Mediterranean.

The flavors of Fiore di Cervia capture the celebratory spirit of central Italy—fruit sugars and spring water dance off the palate with an utter lack of pretense. The transparent, inscrutably fine crystals shimmer with moisture, imparting the mouthfeel of an excellent Prosecco. On the right food, at the right time, the sensation of Fiore di Cervia is innocently voluptuous, like lucking into a busy day with its agenda unexpectedly dropped.

Fiore di Cervia is a private-label salt made in the ancient salt-making region of Cervia, in central Italy. Fiore di Cervia is much like a great Brittany fleur de sel, but warmer and less briny. The absence of this fresh saltwater edge can be either a good thing—if you are open to this salt's subtly sweet innocence— or a bad thing—if you are accustomed to a lucid, firm mineral foundation to the flavors of your food. Another great contrast is with the rare fleurs de sel of Trapani, Sicily, which are coarser, with cleaner, brighter flavors.

TEN REASONS WHY CUCUMBERS ARE GREAT FOR SALT TASTING

A cucumber, sliced into rounds and then halved, provides the perfect little half-moon surface for tasting salt. The basic cucumber, *Cucumis sativus,* is a classic high-potassium food with 80 milligrams per 100-gram serving, and so is always nice to pair with salt from a nutritional standpoint. It's also high in vitamin C, vitamin A, manganese, and other great things like molybdenum, dietary fiber, and folate. But that's not why I love serving cucumbers for salt tasting. There are more tangible reasons:

1. Cucumbers are moist, providing a nice example of how the moisture of a typical food will interact with the salt, and vice versa.
2. Nobody feels guilty eating a cucumber.
3. Cucumber slices are pretty.
4. Cucumbers are cheap.
5. Cucumbers are easy to prepare.
6. Cucumbers keep well.
7. Cucumbers are old school.
8. People bring me cucumbers from their gardens.
9. Everybody likes a cucumber.
10. Cucumbers taste better with salt.

Fleur de Sel de Camargue

- **ALTERNATE NAME(S):** Le Saunier de Camargue Fleur de Sel ■ **MAKER(S):** Le Saunier de Camargue; Salins Group
- **TYPE:** fleur de sel ■ **CRYSTAL:** semifine; highly irregular
- **COLOR:** silvery white ■ **FLAVOR:** balanced mineral; briny
- **MOISTURE:** moderate ■ **ORIGIN:** France ■ **SUBSTITUTE(S):** fleur de sel de l'Ile de Ré; Fiore de Cervia ■ **BEST WITH:** duck; fried eels; grilled eggplant; Mediterranean salad of rice and fresh vegetables; buttered toast; caramels

The quality of Camargue's light captivated the painter Vincent van Gogh, who spent the most productive period of his career in nearby Arles. Stop for a moment at a produce stand by the side of the road and let the warm, humid, faintly briny breeze caress your face; look up at the flocks of birds pinwheeling in the pale sky; breathe in the many subtle fragrances of the fields—and you will prepare yourself for the pleasures that fleur de sel de Camargue will bring to your table.

Fleur de sel de Camargue radiates with Lucite translucency, clearer and whiter than most other types of fleur de sel, like snow that has briefly melted and then partially refrozen. If you look at the crystals closely, it's apparent that each is more cubical—more blocklike—than many of the best examples of fleur de sel, as if the crystals were molded rather than formed. In fact, up close, some of the crystals bear an unsettling similarity to certain mass-produced salts. On the other hand, the heterogeneity of the crystals' sizes is very good. Some are virtually microscopic, others measure about half a millimeter across. The few rogue grains closer to two millimeters in size are infrequent, and do not pose a threat to subtler dishes.

Fleur de sel de Camargue contains slightly less moisture than many other types of fleur de sel due to a combination of factors, the first being that it is very hot in Camargue during the salt-making season, so the salt has ample opportunity to shed some of its moisture. The second factor is that the salt's crystals generally lack the typical jumbled composition, and so offer fewer nooks and crannies for moisture to hide in.

Brazenly clear, blocky crystals aside, fleur de sel de Camargue settles on the tongue with a bashfulness that contrasts seductively with its persistence. There is no hint of the harsh or abrasive quality of some other southern European examples of fleur de sel, and you can't help but admire its easygoing nature. The salt is happy to be with you: it doesn't say much, just gently brushes your bare skin now and then with the beguiling absentmindedness of a hummingbird choosing you as a roost.

Our eyes set upon Aigues-Mortes . . . a jewel carefully set in a case of stone. —Alexandre Dumas

DEATH OVER DEAD WATERS

During the Hundred Years War, the inhabitants of the great fortified city of Aigues-Mortes ("Dead Waters" in the Occitan dialect of southern France), Camargue's salt-making center, put salt to a novel use. After being forced outside of the city's protective walls by attacking Burgundians, Charles de Bourbon led a force of Armagnacs to retake the town. A long siege ensued—one that included some of the earliest uses of a cannon. Then, one night in 1421, the Baron Vauverde led a force made up of the city's evicted inhabitants on a surprise attack. Killing the gatekeepers, the baron proceeded to slaughter the entire Burgundian force, with no quarter given. There were so many Burgundian corpses that the villagers now feared pestilence. The solution? Stack the bodies under piles of salt in the southwest tower of the city. To this day the battlement bears the name Burgundy Tower. Children in the countryside are put to bed with an eerie lullaby about salted Burgundians. ■

Fleur de Sel de Guérande

■ **ALTERNATE NAME(S):** none ■ **MAKER(S):** cooperative; independent ■ **TYPE:** fleur de sel ■ **CRYSTAL:** fine; highly irregular ■ **COLOR:** silvery clouded ice ■ **FLAVOR:** balanced mineral; briny; wild horses ■ **MOISTURE:** moderate ■ **ORIGIN:** France ■ **SUBSTITUTE(S):** fleur de sel de l'Ile de Ré; fleur de sel de l'Ile de Noirmoutier; fleur de sel de Camargue ■ **BEST WITH:** fish; steamed or roasted vegetables; fresh tomatoes; it's the best mozzarella salt (sorry, Italy)

Fleur de sel de Guérande is fresh and mineral, with a slight sun-warmed brininess. The salt is marketed by cooperatives owned and operated by a group of producers and also directly by independent producers. While production can vary from salt maker to salt maker, it tends to be slightly more mineral-rich to the tongue than fleur de sel from Guérande's sister regions Ile de Ré and Noirmoutier. The salt it is most likely to be compared to—fleur de sel de Camargue, hailing from the sun-scorched salt flats of Aigues-Mortes—is much whiter, brighter tasting, and generally finer-grained than its Guérandais cousin. Fleur de sel de Guérande emerges from the salt pan a pale pink color, and shifts to its trademark silvery hue as it dries in the sun. Its moist crystals come in a wonderful range of sizes and colors, so that every pinch bears within it all the unpredictable diversity of the natural world.

Fleur de sel de Guérande is one of the most versatile and bulletproof artisan salts. If you are going to have one artisan salt in your life, this is a good choice. Start simple: spread some good unsalted butter on toast and sprinkle with a pinch of fleur de sel de Guérande. Suddenly the butter comes alive, infused with richer, headier dairy flavors than you ever thought possible. The bread reveals a hazelnutty sweetness. With every bite, a fresh, mineral resonance reflects an ever more satisfying spectrum of flavors. This fleur de sel also enhances broiled fish dishes, roasted game birds, and simply prepared vegetables, like blanched carrots, cauliflower, or broccoli with butter or olive oil.

My dream meal for fleur de sel de Guérande would start with a small asparagus and crab tart topped with fleur de sel, then move on to roasted sole on a bed of leeks, and then a small salad of thick slices of mozzarella and tomato. For the finish, I'd have a plate of assorted burnt caramels, some with the fleur de sel mixed in, some with it sprinkled on top, and some with no salt at all but served with a salt dish on the side.

Spread some out in the palm of your hand and observe the jumble of crystals ranging from nearly microscopic flecks to granules the size of sesame seeds. While many contrast with it, and more yet emulate it, fleur de sel de Guérande is the standard for fleur de sel the world around.

Fleur de Sel de l'Ile de Noirmoutier

■ **ALTERNATE NAME(S):** none ■ **MAKER(S):** cooperative; independent ■ **TYPE:** fleur de sel ■ **CRYSTAL:** fine; highly irregular grains and clumps ■ **COLOR:** oyster shell ■ **FLAVOR:** mild brine; lean minerals; hints of grape skin ■ **MOISTURE:** high ■ **ORIGIN:** France ■ **SUBSTITUTE(S):** other French fleurs de sel from the Atlantic ■ **BEST WITH:** potatoes fried in duck fat; baguette slathered in butter with a thin slice of ham

The potato takes us a long way toward understanding fleur de sel de l'Ile de Noirmoutier. In fact, it's difficult to talk about fleur de sel from Ile de Noirmoutier without a discussion of potatoes. *Pommes de terre primeurs* from Noirmoutier are harvested before their maturity, at less than ninety days of age, and must be eaten immediately. Aromatic, beautifully sweet, with a firm texture that nonetheless melts in the mouth, even the sound of their names make you hungry: la Sirtema, la Bonnotte, la Lady Christl, la Charlotte. (Perhaps salt makers will someday bestow upon their prize salts such charming and weirdly timeless names.)

Sprinkled on steamed potatoes cracked open and topped with a little sweet cream butter, the minute granular crystals of Noirmoutier's fleur de sel glimmer with the utmost subtlety against the flaking potato flesh. Atop the same potatoes fried crunchy-rich in duck fat, their flavor somehow exhibit a more pronounced mineral note in proportion to the increased richness of the potato. Now roast the potatoes with olive oil or a beef rib roast, and the salt takes a step back, allowing you to enjoy the caramelized crust of the potato skins with no trace of harshness. Noirmoutier Island's fleur de sel is not the only great fleur de sel, but sprinkled on any number of traditional dishes, it offers as good an example as any of the multifaceted potency of the fleur de sel family.

As with so many salts in the region, fleur de sel de l'Ile de Noirmoutier varies from producer to producer. The salt sold by Coopérative des Producteurs de Sel de l'Ouest, the cooperative on the island, is slightly heartier than the other French Atlantic salts. It has a distinct, slightly metallic mineral flavor, and larger, sometimes more irregular crystals. Independent producers can make salts that are finer.

Fleur de Sel de l'Ile de Ré

■ **ALTERNATE NAME(S):** none ■ **MAKER(S):** cooperative; independent ■ **TYPE:** fleur de sel ■ **CRYSTAL:** fine; highly irregular ■ **COLOR:** blushing silvery white ■ **FLAVOR:** extraordinary mineral balance; mildly briny ■ **MOISTURE:** moderate ■ **ORIGIN:** France ■ **SUBSTITUTE(S):** fleur de sel de Guérande; fleur de sel de Camargue ■ **BEST WITH:** duck fat-fried potatoes; fish; small birds; fresh vegetables; butter cookies; it is amazing churned into sweet cream butter

Extremely delicate to the touch and glittering with a rosy tint, freshly harvested fleur de sel de l'Ile de Ré is possibly the most perfectly crafted artisan salt in the world. The crystals are pristine, like gemstones cut by a master jeweler. The flavor is clear, defined, unashamed, and at the same time mild. Mineral flavors reflect the temperate climate's tendency to evaporate water from the condensing salt brine more slowly than many other places.

The weather on the island is better than the nearby surrounding areas. "We can sometimes see the rainfall over La Rochelle, while we ourselves are working in the sun on the salt pans," laughs one salt maker. In the small town

of Ars-en-Ré, you will find an unusual combination of salt-making cooperatives and small, independent producers working side by side. The best fleurs de sel come from Ile de Ré's many independent producers. Visiting a few of the boutiques set up in shacks around the island by independent salt makers will give you an idea of the subtler charms that emerge when comparing many different salts—like taking a wine tour through Oregon's Willamette river or the France's Rhône. The largest independent producer, Esprit de Sel, produces very good salt and packages it with the care it deserves.

Across from Esprit de Sel's sparkling headquarters is the island's decidedly unsparkly salt-making cooperative, Les Sauniers de l'Ile de Ré. The building itself still retains its flavor as a bare-bones organization, conceived to perform the necessary functions that fall outside the salt makers' domains of expertise, such as quality control of harvested salt, storage, packaging, marketing, sales, and distribution. The salt makers contributing to the cooperative often put just as much care and expertise into their salts as independent salt makers, so virtually any fleur de sel you buy from Ile de Ré is likely to be of very high quality.

What would be the perfect meal for fleur de sel de l'Ile de Ré? As comfortable as this salt is in the most elegant setting, it also has a natural ability to lend a sense of refinement and quiet celebration to everyday life. My choice: mild radishes spread with butter and dipped in fleur de sel de l'Ile de Ré served with a small glass of sweetly floral Pineau des Charentes poured over ice; grouper in a light saffron cream sauce finished with a few fresh herbs and fleur de sel; and a wild berry tart with fleur de sel baked on the crust.

Flor de Sal d'Es Trenc

■ **ALTERNATE NAME(S):** none ■ **MAKER(S):** Gusto Mundial Balearides ■ **TYPE:** fleur de sel ■ **CRYSTAL:** fine; highly irregular ■ **COLOR:** transparent with a faint blush ■ **FLAVOR:** mild; very balanced; warm ■ **MOISTURE:** moderate ■ **ORIGIN:** Spain ■ **SUBSTITUTE(S):** fleur de sel de Camargue ■ **BEST WITH:** saucy fish dishes; vegetable sandwiches; fried green tomatoes

Es Trenc's fleur de sel seems coarser to the eye than some of the finest-grained fleurs de sel. But to the touch and tongue, it is pure elegance, with a crunch and tactfully delivered flavors that are as provocative as eyelashes fluttering against an upturned cheek. The salt flirts with color, each grain seemingly as clear as winter air, yet when piled up, the crystals resonate with hints of warmth. Its crystals are moist and perky enough to dance off pork chops grilled with caramelized figs, and then facile enough to shift gears, light some candles, and commingle devilishly with thick slices of Jonagold apple and Emmental cheese. Or just skip the Emmental.

Flor de sal d'Es Trenc compares easily with fleur de sel de Camargue, which makes sense since its creation was inspired by Camargue salt makers. After becoming enamored of the meditative art of raking salt in southern France, Katja Woehr, the founder of Gusto Mundial Balearides, moved to Mallorca to make fleur de sel, and obtained a license in 2003 to farm salt in the traditional salt fields of Es Trenc, located on the island's southern shore, about 150 miles off the east cost of Spain. The salt is made by passing seawater from Es Trenc Bay along a nearly two-mile route to the crystallizing pans. On a good year, Woehr's company harvests as much as twenty-eight tons of fleur de sel.

Flor de Sal de Manzanillo

- **ALTERNATE NAME(S):** Flor Blanca - **MAKER(S):** cooperative; independent - **TYPE:** fleur de sel
- **CRYSTAL:** medium-fine; obliqued cubes - **COLOR:** silvery white to whitish silver - **FLAVOR:** clear mineral flavor; light brine; evanescent Mai Tai - **MOISTURE:** medium to slightly drier than medium, but balanced - **ORIGIN:** Mexico - **SUBSTITUTE(S):** any Brittany fleur de sel - **BEST WITH:** anything you have been eating with free-flowing iodized salt—eggs Benedict to watermelon, garlic shrimp to alligator steak

Rollicking edgy Mexico, where in my childhood I would sneak sips off the rusted lip of a Tecate can until, puckering and smacking, blinded by lime and acrid iodized salt, my eyes rolling backward toward the egg-yellow sun, I would run off to a dusty lot in search of huge iguanas that would bloat themselves into balls in the dark safety of galvanized irrigation pipes as a defense against my poking. Such a wild, snarly place has no

right to make a balanced nuanced artisan salt, and yet in Manzanillo, on the West coast of Mexico, they do.

Mexico makes loads of salt, most on an industrial scale, but some on a very small human scale. With lots of coastal wetlands and lots of sun, it does both very well. Flor de sal de Manzanillo is a solar evaporated sea salt on a par with the fine artisan fleurs de sel of France. It looks virtually identical to many of the Brittany fleurs de sel, but it brings its own slant on fleur de sel to the table. The crunch is as vibrant and confident as any salt—violent almost—the myriad chasms and pinnacles of its minute crystal clusters exploding between the teeth. Yet the explosion is polite and pleasant—very French. The flavor is super-balanced, though a tendril of sweetness licks at the back of the palate from time to time—fresh spring water emerging at the shore of an ocean.

Flor de Sal do Algarve

▪ **ALTERNATE NAME(S):** Portuguese flor de sal ▪ **MAKER(S):** Necton S.A.; Marisol; others ▪ **TYPE:** fleur de sel ▪ **CRYSTAL:** medium-fine; highly irregular flecks and grains ▪ **COLOR:** lush to calcareous white ▪ **FLAVOR:** sharp front; metallic finish ▪ **MOISTURE:** moderate ▪ **ORIGIN:** Portugal ▪ **SUBSTITUTE(S):** fleur de sel de Guérande; fleur de sel de Camargue ▪ **BEST WITH:** Dover sole, skate, or other rich, mild white fish swimming in white wine, butter, and an abundance of garlic

Crystals seem to take delight in variation, and never more so than when they take shape in the form of flor de sal do Algarve. The occasional hefty pyramid of salt presides over smaller crystals: grains the size of pinpricks, lethal-looking microscopic spines, shards of tattered parchment, and plain old fleur de sel clusters. The diverse crystal composition of the Algarve's flor de sal celebrates the extraordinary merits of fleur de sel as a class of salt: a prodigal crystalline inventiveness. Flor de sal do Algarve is crafted by skilled artisans such as João Novalho, who earned an advanced degree in aqua culture before making salt his metier. There is no lack of skill in its production.

However, the flavor of the salt does not live up to the example set by the crystals. Alongside the Brittany salts, it comes off as astringent and metallic, sometimes intensely so. Eaten with food, these faults take on a moral tone: a warm smile greeting you at the door followed by recrimination and bitterness.

The flavor could be an indication of the salt's *meroir*, some twist of fate that turns the sea's Janus face from mirth to doubt, perhaps brought about by the unusual style of harvest practiced by many salt makers in the region. Fleur de sel is typically harvested in the afternoon right after the crystals have a chance to form, or in the case of a night-blooming fleur de sel, first thing in the morning when they've formed under the cooling air of night. However, it is possible in Algarve to wait. The fleur de sel that forms in the afternoon is allowed to grow, to thicken, and to continue to crystallize from the afternoon through the night and into the next morning. This permits the formation of a much thicker layer of fleur de sel—one with its own characteristic mineral profile and flavor.

When your meal is devoutly Portuguese—*pastéis de nata*, the classic Portuguese egg custard tarts; or the crazy-sweet angel hair pasta dessert *aletria doce*; or any of the super-saucy grilled or sautéed fish, oyster, octopus, or eel dishes, where bitter herbs, bold spices, and lots of wine and butter are all brought into play in a wonderful steaming sugar-steamy-herby salt-rush—then please, do use flor de sal do Algarve. Any salt with a death grip on the moment should not be forsaken, lest the dream escape.

Flor de Sal do Aveiro, Eduardo Oliveira

■ **ALTERNATE NAME(S):** none ■ **MAKER(S):** Eduardo Oliveira ■ **TYPE:** fleur de sel ■ **CRYSTAL:** fine; highly irregular ■ **COLOR:** gemstone of silvery oxide and milk ■ **FLAVOR:** balanced mineral; briny ■ **MOISTURE:** moderate ■ **ORIGIN:** Portugal ■ **SUBSTITUTE(S):** Flos Salis; fleur de sel de Guérande ■ **BEST WITH:** grilled and fried fish; fruit; the only salt worth flying to Europe for if you are making fire-grilled octopus; life-changing on a salad of edible flowers

This salt compares to the finest fleur de sel: luscious, lean, eternally youthful. Yet through diamond-like crystals that shine and shift, a road drifts into the distance of time, rippling in the summer heat. Aveiro's fleur de sel is the only example of its kind, and, oddly, it is not a relic of times past, but a figment of its own possible future. Talk of Aveiro's fleur de sel requires fortification. First, a light, slightly fruity white wine to accompany all dishes. I'd  start with something Brazilian-inspired, like grilled baby octopus with papaya, lime, and just a few grains of fleur de sel; then a white fish such as cod crowned with sautéed banana, lemon juice, and fleur de sel. Follow it with a green salad with strawberries and fresh goat cheese topped with fleur de sel, and finish off with a cool cup of port-infused Portuguese flan, a pinch of fleur de sel served on the side to spark a little extra flavor from the last few bites.

Yet ask the salt about itself and it chooses not to answer. Instead, it bristles with light and invites you into its crystals. Trapped there you might be blinded by their brilliance, but sprinkle them on food and you taste the salt maker's subtle appreciation for the salt's origins and a suggestion of its purpose.

Eduardo Oliveira has a strange way of looking at salt. More poet than artisan, more naturalist than businessman, his every word suggests his bafflement by the process he practices every day—yet he brings twenty-eight years of experience as a chemical engineer in the French cosmetics industry to his fleur de sel. He is the only man in memory to have made fleur de sel in Aveiro.

Oliveira is generous with his knowledge, but hesitant to support any conclusions you might draw. For example, it's his observation that a convergence of two freshwater streams is necessary for the formation of great salt. Is this because this water brings new minerals to the salt water? "Who knows?" he answers, then just says, "No." His is an observation, not a theory. Why, he is not sure. For those who would explain the creation of salt in terms of chemical processes, or in terms of artisanal processes, or in terms of any other processes for that matter, Oliveira offers not scorn, but a gentle glimmer of humor in the warm darkness of his eyes. Salt is a mystery, he says, and like nature in general, the important thing is to respect and appreciate it. Deep below the visual extravagance of his salt lurks an open-ended discussion with the experience of salt: how it plays with other flavors and then dissolves into an unknown connection with whatever comes next.

SALTED

Flos Salis

■ **ALTERNATE NAME(S):** none ■ **MAKER(S):** Marisol ■ **TYPE:** fleur de sel ■ **CRYSTAL:** superfine frizz of grains and microflakes ■ **COLOR:** lush white ■ **FLAVOR:** bright front; warm body; faintly metallic finish ■ **MOISTURE:** moderate ■ **ORIGIN:** Portugal ■ **SUBSTITUTE(S):** fleur de sel de Guérande; fleur de sel de Camargue ■ **BEST WITH:** foie gras; salt crust-baked bass; new potatoes

Sitting in the back seat of the car, about ten years old, my palms and neck are sweaty. My mind races in anticipation. After years of ogling, followed by begging and pleading—years peddling across town on a squeaky bike on reconnaissance; of lusting—I was getting a model train set. The joy! A miniature locomotive—smell the diesel, feel the devastating power of steel grinding on steel—soon would be mine, its meticulously crafted form and surprising heft clutched in my chubby hand.

So out of proportion to everything around us, such infinitesimal objects provoke the imagination to explore the cosmos of their secret charms. When I look at Flos Salis, the ten-year-old's anticipation—the jittery sensation of raw compulsion and unchanneled imagination—comes rushing back: crystals so faint, so frail, like mountain flowers seen through a telescope from outer space.

Each crystal has a flattened scalene structure, like cubes sliced diagonally, with a color clearer than any other fleur de sel (perhaps Camargue is a rival). While this clarity is not normally something I would favor—suggesting a density and uniformity to the crystal lattice making up the salt grain—in the case of Flos Salis, it creates an eye-catching jewel-encrusted effect. Its mouthfeel on food is like adding jimmies to ice cream: neat-o, and far more satisfying than some grown-ups would like to admit out loud.

Flos Salis is tart, bright, and slightly pungent, but in an agreeable way that is thirst-provoking without being parching. As usual, the mineral content of the salt tells us a little about the quiet alchemy that drives its flavors: 0.45 percent magnesium, 0.23 percent calcium, 0.17 percent potassium, and so on.

Marisol is among the largest producers of high-quality fleur de sel anywhere, harvesting thirty tons in 2009. Flos Salis, which is handled with special care to preserve its exceptionally delicate crystals, is the brainchild of impassioned Marisol founder Nico Böer, a renaissance man who, in addition to salt making, speaks forcefully on aquatic life, real estate, sailing, agriculture, and the environment.

Ilocano Asin

- **ALTERNATE NAME(S):** Pangasinan Star; Philippine fleur de sel
- **MAKER(S):** n/a
- **TYPE:** fleur de sel hybrid
- **CRYSTAL:** small crumpled boxes; highly irregular
- **COLOR:** dry oyster-shell
- **FLAVOR:** sun-warmed brambles; timothy grass
- **MOISTURE:** moderate
- **ORIGIN:** Philippines
- **SUBSTITUTE(S):** Sugpo Asin; fleur de sel de Guérande
- **BEST WITH:** rare, simply prepared meats: lamb carpaccio with lemon; aged porterhouse with cracked black pepper

Ilocano Asin is an exaggerated version of the classic French fleur de sel. Its lush, almost billowy crystals provide a sensuous crunch that separates it from the smaller crystals of the French fleurs de sel. Its place in the spectrum of fleurs de sel is defined by the fact that, well . . . it isn't exactly a fleur de sel at all. It looks like a fleur de sel and acts like a fleur de sel, but it's really a hybrid of fleur de sel and sel gris, containing both the fleur de sel crystals blossoming on the surface of the water and the nascent baby crystals of sel gris germinating below.

The crazy combination of nearly microscopic fleur de sel crystals and the larger, yet supple sel gris crystals in Ilocano Asin position it as one of the grand salts capable of crossing over from wonderfully dramatic play on the most delicate of foods to wonderfully subtle play on the most hearty foods. On a fried egg with wild mushrooms, its crystals will pop and sparkle warmly, lending richer flavor and a more pleasant crunch texture. On a braised leg of lamb with onions, chile peppers, thyme, and mango, it will resonate unobtrusively, allowing your palate to explore in peace the combination of fruity acidity, heady herbaceousness, and meaty opulence.

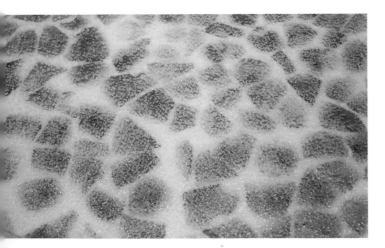

Containing just 85.6 percent sodium chloride, each crunch delivers a flavor that is rich, warm, and mildly sweet with a balance of 0.51 percent magnesium, 0.29 percent calcium, and 0.13 percent potassium. This sweetness is carried by a voluptuous body that makes the sensation last and last without becoming harsh or overbearing, guiding its perfectly balanced behavior on food.

While Ilocano Asin might be more technically placed among the sels gris, to do so would diminish its preeminence among the greatest and brightest of salts, sort of like calling the superstar of rock and roll Freddie Mercury an Asian rock star. Maybe I will start referring to Ilocano Asin as a sel gris when everyone else starts referring to Mercury by his birth name, Farrokh Bulsara.

Sal de Hielo de San Fernando

- **ALTERNATE NAME(S):** flor de sal de Cádiz ▪ **MAKER(S):** Salina San Vincente ▪ **TYPE:** fleur de sel
- **CRYSTAL:** microfine and very fine; constellations ▪ **COLOR:** wet snow seen through a windshield
- **FLAVOR:** reserved, calm; glittering sweetness over a faint buzz of pollen flavors ▪ **MOISTURE:** moderate
- **ORIGIN:** Spain ▪ **SUBSTITUTE(S):** fleur de sel de Guérande; Aguni Koshin Odo ▪ **BEST WITH:** raw vegetables; pastries; scattered willy-nilly on piles of fries, grilled steaks, and sausages

Each crystal of Sal de Hielo presents the mouth with a seemingly endless series of elaborations—crystals emulating plant life. The flavor lingers for minutes, first trying to find expression, then tiring of the effort and taking root in the darkness. There, eventually, it sprouts forth and you detect it: a series of tingling sensations. But then it fades away and nothing is left. And that is all.

Tasted on its own, without the fertile soil of a good food to give it purpose, the salt moves toward a sullen flatness that stops just short of bitterness. The flatness is not a shortcoming, but a reflection of the salt's rejection of silly ideas like tasting salt on its own. Chemically, Sal de Hielo is rich, containing a wide range of minerals—0.65 percent magnesium, 0.13 percent calcium, 0.41 percent iron, 0.17 percent potassium—and dozens of others in trace amounts: the salt really doesn't need to impress further.

One of the most masterful fleurs de sel you are ever likely to encounter, Sal de Hielo comes from an unlikely little salt farm, the Salina San Vincente, near Cádiz, an area not well known for its fleur de sel. If you visit the Salina San Vincente, you will find Don Manuel Ruiz Coto there, supervising younger members of his family at the fishing nets, grappling with a heavy pipe in the yard, or working in the salt fields. Coto, who is at once amused by other people's fascination with his work and proud to talk about it, says that no more than half a dozen saltworks in the region continue to employ traditional Roman salt-making techniques. Coto's salt is thought to be made in Roman era salt pans.

Sugpo Asin

- **ALTERNATE NAME(S):** n/a ▪ **MAKER(S):** n/a ▪ **TYPE:** fleur de sel hybrid ▪ **CRYSTAL:** large, crumpled boxes and wonky granules ▪ **COLOR:** flamingo dander ▪ **FLAVOR:** concentrated; sweet mineral water ▪ **MOISTURE:** moderate ▪ **ORIGIN:** Philippines ▪ **SUBSTITUTE(S):** Ilocano Asin; fleur de sel de Guérande ▪ **BEST WITH:** fresh tomatoes, onions, bananas, mangos, or papayas; fire-roasted clams; a haunch of venison blackened in embers

As in any land where nature thrives in close proximity to humanity, sensations here can seem so vibrant that it's sometimes hard to fully appreciate their subtleties, until you realize that it is all subtlety, that everything can be apprehended through the play of light on the white coral sands at the bottom of a deserted bay. Sugpo Asin, which emits the palest reflection of color (from carotene in the water from the shells of sugpo prawns), is the embodiment of this paradox. The subtlest of salts, it also radiates stark beauty.

The salt, produced by a small, family-operated business where everyone lends a hand, is exceptionally difficult to make. In addition to cleaning and maintaining the tile-lined crystallizing pans to allow for a high-quality salt, the salt makers take the utmost care with the ecology of the large holding ponds where seawater is conditioned prior to feeding the crystalizers. Most salt farms don't bother raising sugpo prawns because of the extreme difficulty of maintaining the proper pond ecology and shepherding the shrimps' development. The payoff is a salt with a tantalizing pale pink color, and a unique intense-sweet flavor.

The color of Sugpo Asin can range from batch to batch, from the palest pink to a warm ivory. The crystals have a wonderful lushness to them, with a beautiful, irregular structure. Poured into a moist pile on your upturned palm, the crystals fall loosely and pile up with profound loftiness.

Sugpo Asin is delicious in any dish that calls for fleur de sel. Its complex intensity makes it suitable for rich or bold foods, and for dishes where the pronounced (yet still nuanced) presence of salt is desired. Any seafood comes spectacularly alive with Sugpo Asin. It works great with lean cuts of venison, lamb, and beef (for fattier cuts, I prefer French fleur de sel for its clean minerality). For skirt steak, sliced paper-thin and fired a few seconds over hot coals, Sugpo Asin is the best salt in the world.

SEL GRIS

Grigio di Cervia

- **ALTERNATE NAME(S):** Riserva Camillone sea salt ■ **MAKER(S):** n/a ■ **TYPE:** sel gris ■ **CRYSTAL:** crumbled shortbread ■ **COLOR:** dissipating Swarovski jonquil ■ **FLAVOR:** firm yet lush roundness with a vibration of nectarine ■ **MOISTURE:** moderate ■ **ORIGIN:** Italy ■ **SUBSTITUTE(S):** The Meadow Sel Gris ■ **BEST WITH:** Parmesan-breaded veal scaloppini; chanterelle omelet; tannic dark chocolate; fresh ricotta; pasta

This salt's color hints at the warmth to come. Amber light flickers through the crystals of grigio di Cervia as if forever illuminated by the flames of a cozy hearth fire. But the salt's flavors come through with another sort of warmth altogether—more of a midsummer rain felt through a linen shirt than a cup of hot cocoa between chilled palms. Italians call salt from the region of Cervia *sale dolce*, or sweet salt. The salt makers credit this unique fruity-sweet flavor to lower than normal magnesium and potassium levels—even though sweetness is often a distinctive characteristic of some of the über-magnesium-rich salts of Japan,

THE SALT THAT PROSCIUTTO FORGOT

In medieval times, the legendary salt-cured hams of the Italian peninsula—such as the sweetly bold Prosciutto di Parma in Emilia-Romagna and the milder and faintly floral Prosciutto di San Daniele from Friuli—rose to become icons of regional prestige. While the terrain and climate, pig breeds and feeding, and myriad local techniques all contributed to the unique character of each ham, salt was no less a factor.

The essential ingredients for prosciutto are pork and salt. The great prosciuttos were as much testaments to their regions' salts as to curing expertise and animal husbandry. It was salt—the moisture in it, the way it was ground, the trace minerals and microscopic organic matter it harbored—that made a subtle but crucial difference in the texture and flavor of the finished ham.

The tidal wetlands of Cervia provided a mineral-sweet salt to the butchers of Parma, and the salt fields of Venice, among others, served Friuli. Prosciutto is now mostly made with salt transported by truck and railway from Trapani, far to the south. The lush flavor of the traditional salt has been swapped for a clear but faintly hot salt with no cultural or culinary connection to the original recipes. But you can still taste the near-maddening sweetness of a good Cervia salt-cured prosciutto in the regional charcuterie shops of central and northern Italy. ■

and magnesium, potassium, iodine, zinc, copper, manganese, and iron are all present in the salt. Chalk it up to nature's boundless appetite for mystery.

Grigio di Cervia is coarse, with moderate moisture lending suppleness to its crunch. Apart from its faintly amber color, its astonishing sweetness, its bubbly Champagnelike body, and crisp, honeysuckle-sweet flavor, it's tempting to compare it in stature to the French sels gris. Even though it is not gray, not French, not briny, and made from the Adriatic rather than the Atlantic, it's a true classic among sels gris.

It is hand-harvested daily in very limited quantities—which is fine, because this salt should only be used judiciously as a finishing salt. Yet the jar of grigio di Cervia in my kitchen looks battered and grubby from near-constant handling. How do I use it? Gently worked into the Parmesan breading of a veal cutlet or sprinkled on wild mushroom bruschetta, its sweetness satisfying the latent desires for earthy flavors with a spark of contrast.

Purchasing note: Grigio di Cervia should not be confused with the more widely available Riserva Camillone salt by Salina di Cervia that is sold in a cloth bag, which, while good, has a markedly different flavor and crystal structure.

The Meadow Sel Gris

- **ALTERNATE NAME(S):** Korean sel gris ▪ **MAKER(S):** n/a
- **TYPE:** sel gris ▪ **CRYSTAL:** museum-quality collapsible jewel boxes ▪ **COLOR:** clouds gone pale after rain
- **FLAVOR:** firm; round; vibration of nectarine ▪ **MOISTURE:** moderate ▪ **ORIGIN:** Korea ▪ **SUBSTITUTE(S):** sel gris de l'Ile de Ré; grigio di Cervia ▪ **BEST WITH:** all cooking uses; finishing on pork loin, roast chicken, steamed vegetables and butter, caramel

The crystal of this salt confronts you, asserting its identity like a cubic poem on the boundless iterations of geometry in nature. Then you put it in your mouth and it abruptly surrenders to your bite, eager to do your hunger's bidding.

The resemblance between good French sel gris and the The Meadow sel gris is akin to that of two adopted brothers: they share values and a common purpose in life, yet their attitudes, appearances, and proclivities are their own. The Meadow sel gris is luminescent opal color rather than grey. Its crystals are coarser and not granular, but a combination of tiny hollow pyramids, small boxes, and chaotic bits of stuck-together smaller pyramids and boxes.

The crunch is delicate, almost dainty—surprising for crystals of such heft. The flavor of the salt is so clean it might be called minty fresh, but there's no trace of herbal pungency. It has not the slightest trace of bitterness, nor the faintest of mineral flavors, but rather something suggesting the sweetness of tropical fruits tamed down. It's as if, after presenting itself to your senses with an entreating smile, it averts its eyes and walks away. Sprinkling Korean sel gris on food feels like a fleeting privilege, and every time you use it the sensation of your good fortune refreshes itself. It is at once sophisticated and a crowd-pleaser, and it's certainly one of my personal favorites as an all-around salt for daily use, for cooking, and for finishing any food substantial enough to benefit from a slightly larger but still supple crystal—from steamed summer squash to braised winter roots, from grilled fish to roast beef.

The salt comes from Korea's best salt fields located to the south on the constellation of islands off the mainland where the waters are renowned for their purity and their thriving marine life. The islands are remote, with only a few of the larger ones accessible by ferry.

The salt makers in the region also credit the pristine mud flats of the area for contributing additional mineral wealth to the salt. The region experiences large tidal variations that irrigate the mud flats and contribute to the nutrient-rich environment that supports the aquatic and bird life. There are also distinct dry and rainy seasons, so after each dry season at the close of the year's salt making, winter rains rinse the mountains, streams, salt fields, and surrounding waters.

Sal Marinho Tradicional de Aveiro

▪ **ALTERNATE NAME(S):** sal de Aveiro ▪ **MAKER(S):** independent ▪ **TYPE:** sel gris, or traditional salt and sel gris hybrid ▪ **CRYSTAL:** medium coarse; crunched blocks ▪ **COLOR:** lifting fog ▪ **FLAVOR:** sublimated mineral; faintly sweet; the smell of a Popsicle ▪ **MOISTURE:** high ▪ **ORIGIN:** Portugal ▪ **SUBSTITUTE(S):** any Portuguese sel gris ▪ **BEST WITH:** thick beef steaks; saucy fish dishes; heavy stews; roasted beets; fruit salad; goat cheese

Angular, more irregularly sized and shaped crystals, and a translucent whiteness distinguish Aveiro's sel gris from those of northern France. In fact, the salt

is barely gray at all, and the Portuguese refer to it by the no-nonsense name of *sal grosso*, coarse salt.

Sprinkled over fried bream with finely chopped herbs, the luscious crystals of this salt add crunchy mineral and herbaceous flavors to the moist, flaking flesh of the fish. Sal grosso de Aveiro is a great salt for all-around cooking, and also for finishing any dish where a strong, bold expression is desired. If you ever take an interest in curing, there is no better salt for salt-cured cod (*bacalhau*) or beef.

Two major environmental differences between Portugal and France relevant to salt making are the level of heat and the makeup of the soil. The regional salts reflect both of these differences, though in ways you might not expect. As in many southern European countries, heat shapes the work day in Portugal. The intense heat makes salt crystals form fast and furiously throughout the day and into the night. As a result, by the time the salt workers set out in the morning with their *rapãos do sal* (salt rakes) in hand, the salt crystals are considerably larger than those one would find up north in Brittany. The salt crystals of sal grosso de Aveiro tend to be large and ungainly, yet each is supple, yielding between your teeth with a satisfying crunch.

The weather and soil composition also influence the flavors of the salt crystals. Aveiro salt tends toward slightly more bitter flavors than those found in French salts. This is a characteristic of many Portuguese salts—likely the result of the rapid rate at which salt crystals form under a hot sun. If the salt is of good quality, this bitterness is not too pronounced and can actually provide penetrating complexity on heartier foods.

The salt made in Aveiro can range from an unappealing, dirty coarse salt to a lusciously whitish-gray crystal, depending on the producer. Aveiro's salt fields are formed in marshes thick with black sediments. Raking off the salt from the bottom of the pans too aggressively or too frequently stirs up the mud, which then contaminates the salt. While this has little effect on the healthiness of the salt, the excessive amount of insolubles can give it a gritty texture. More conscientious salt makers, by contrast, allow the salt to form a protective barrier on the bottom of the pan and then rake off only the top crystals.

Sal Rosa de Maras

■ **ALTERNATE NAME(S):** Peruvian pink; Peruvian warm spring, Inca salt ■ **MAKER(S):** n/a ■ **TYPE:** sel gris ■ **CRYSTAL:** clunky, irregular chunks and medium-fine cubes ■ **COLOR:** paper-thin tourmaline; cream ■ **FLAVOR:** tart boldness; mild sweetness; light funk of clay ■ **MOISTURE:** moderate ■ **ORIGIN:** Peru ■ **SUBSTITUTE(S):** Sugpo Asin or other coarse fleur de sel ■ **BEST WITH:** Burgundy-marinated grilled venison; ceviche tostadas; pan-fried trout

Below the ancient sacred city of Machu Picchu, deep in the Peruvian Andes, lies the town of Maras, founded on salt centuries before the arrival of the Incas. From a hot spring issuing from the western flank of Qaqawiñay Mountain, a tributary to the Urubamba River flows water with far higher salinity than the sea. The water is diverted into hundreds of rivulets spreading like capillaries from the main artery, feeding thousands of small ponds where the water is evaporated and the salt is skimmed with woven baskets. This salt is not a sea salt evaporated from ocean waters, but a mineral salt taken from warm saline springs.

Sal rosa de Maras is pretty, its pearl-pink crystals radiating the beauty of a child's quick laugh rippling from a hut on the banks of the Urubamba. The salt provides a zing of semisweetness and earthiness, though its chunky crystals lack the sumptuousness of the finest quality salts. This can be a good thing: think of using sal rosa de Maras atop the paper-thin, ice-hard glaze of a crème brulée. More culturally attuned ideas for the salt might trace history: sprinkled on pre-Inca dishes of tamales, potatoes, *huanaco*; river perch fired in a slipper of banana leaf; or an astringent ceviche. From there it finds a place in latter Criollo recipes such as *lomo saltado* and *papas a la huancaina*, based on the beef, chicken, and rabbit introduced with the influx of Spaniards, Italians, French, Germans, Chinese, and Japanese.

The salt fields at Maras lie in the Sacred Valley of the Incas at an altitude of about 10,000 feet. Water from rainfall and snowmelt higher up in the mountains makes its way through subterranean streams to a deposit of salt dating back tens of millions of years. The Salineras de Maras, comprised of about three thousand small pools, each measuring about fifty square feet, have been producing salt for anywhere from six hundred years to nearly two millennia, depending on whom you ask. The Inca, whose empire was cut short by the astonishingly bloodthirsty Francisco Pizarro, are credited with developing the elaborate system of salt pans terraced into the precipitous Andean slopes.

Sel Gris de Guérande

- **ALTERNATE NAME(S):** gray salt; Celtic Sea salt ▪ **MAKER(S):** cooperative; independent ▪ **TYPE:** sel gris ▪ **CRYSTAL:** highly irregular chunky boxes ▪ **COLOR:** semitranslucent blue-gray ▪ **FLAVOR:** muscular mineral body given shape by clean brine ▪ **MOISTURE:** moderate ▪ **ORIGIN:** France ▪ **SUBSTITUTE(S):** sel gris de l'Ile de Noirmoutier; sel gris de l'Ile de Ré ▪ **BEST WITH:** medium-rare 1¹/₂-inch-thick grass-fed rib-eye steak

Guérande's name suggests the essential link between the land, the sea, and the superb salts for which the region is famed. Guérande is from *gwen ran* ("white land") in Breton, the Celtic language of Brittany. It is a land ideally situated for the production of salt. Guérande's natural estuaries, bright days, and reliable breezes have been creating brilliant white lakes of salt for thousands of years, even before being discovered by civilized man. Surprisingly, things haven't gone too far downhill since then.

The lands surrounding Guérande have been preserved in part due to France's resurgent artisan saltmaking industry, but also because, frankly, much of the land there is a swamp. In Guérande during low tides, the sea can nearly disappear from view altogether before rushing back in to fill the estuaries, bays, harbors, and salt fields. The combination of high tides and flat coastline has protected the salt marshes for millennia, fostering the development of elaborate, meticulously engineered solar salt evaporation schemes that have proven capable of weathering a thousand years of fierce Atlantic storms.

Sel gris de Guérande's flavor and uses are commensurate with its history and geography. Complex mineral flavors with unapologetic briny notes contrast with and lend form to a huge variety of foods, from lean fish to fatty meats, from sweet caramels to astringent vegetables. Sel gris de Guérande (or its sisters from Ile de Ré and Ile de Noirmoutier) is also the natural choice for an all-around cooking salt. Finely ground and used in baking, it brings a barely detectable richness to other flavors—or, at the very least, that even deeper feeling of being rich yourself that great ingredients bring to the table. Thrown coarse into boiling water for blanching vegetables, rubbed whole over meats, or packed around lemons or fish for preserving, sel gris de Guérande has probably seasoned more of the most essential foods in the French culinary tradition than any other salt; it will do equal justice to your cooking at home.

Sel Gris de l'Ile de Noirmoutier

- **ALTERNATE NAME(S):** none ▪ **MAKER(S):** cooperative; independent ▪ **TYPE:** sel gris ▪ **CRYSTAL:** chunky jumbles of agglomerated nuggets ▪ **COLOR:** silvery gray to gray-silver ▪ **FLAVOR:** bold mineral; moderate brine; reminiscent of Mai Tai ▪ **MOISTURE:** very high ▪ **ORIGIN:** France
- **SUBSTITUTE(S):** sel gris de Guérande; other sels gris
- **BEST WITH:** roasted and grilled game of the winged and hoofed varieties

Noirmoutier's sel gris tastes different depending on what music you are listening to—it's racy and voluptuous under a live recording of Led Zeppelin; playful but a bit vacuous with the Steve Miller band; slightly bored by Jimmy Buffet. I won't even tell you what it tastes like when you listen to John Denver. The salt recoils at the often perky instrumentalism of Frédéric Chopin. Give it hip-hop and it behaves like a superstar in a nightclub: at ease, hip, radiant.

Two millennia of history undergird the porcelain clay salt pans where Noirmoutier sel gris crystallizes. It is harvested from warm brine by paludiers who work barefoot, sensing the formation of the crystals in the pans from the warmth of the dry clay at the sides. History, tradition, and artisanship lend the salt a profound sense of culinary identity, allowing it to posture without affectation and to contribute to the spirit of the moment with a diplomatic spark of genius. Sel gris de l'Ile de Noirmoutier tastes like what it is: a salt keenly connected to its ecology, intimately attuned to its circumstances, and yet sure of itself—a salt for the ages.

TRADITIONAL SALT

Alaea Hawaiian (Coarse)

■ **ALTERNATE NAME(S):** alaea volcanic, alaea salt, Hawaiian red salt (see sidebar, opposite) ■ **MAKER(S):** various ■ **TYPE:** traditional and/or industrial ■ **CRYSTAL:** coarse; masonry cut imperfectly by crickets ■ **COLOR:** brick to coral ■ **FLAVOR:** ocean with note of wet pavement ■ **MOISTURE:** very low to none ■ **ORIGIN:** United States ■ **SUBSTITUTE(S):** Alaea traditional ■ **BEST WITH:** fish; pork; hearty Mexican dishes like tamales; it is the soulmate of fresh fruits

Flex your jaw and feel the crystals punch into the flesh of ripe cantaloupe, sweetness blossoming steadily until a sudden hard crunch of salt bursts through. There are dozens of alaea Hawaiian salts on the market, each with crystals of varying size and hardness. The uncertainty of when (or, God forbid, if) the hardest of these salts succumbs to the effort of your mastication lends a degree of terror to eating. As with a rock salt such as Himalayan pink or Bolivian Rose, pitting your teeth against a minute slab of alaea Hawaiian is an impressively unpleasant experience—except when it isn't. Then it's really quite nice. The trick is to be mindful of the challenge of marrying hard granules to yielding foods. If the food is sumptuous enough, with enough substance to occupy the mouth fully (think chiles rellenos), then the salt actually provides a point of textural reference for your palate, like spotting a dot of dry land on the horizon of a vast sea.

Alaea is a red, iron-rich volcanic clay native to the Hawaiian Islands. It is held to be sacred, and is used both on its own and combined with salt for various religious and healing practices. Alaea Hawaiian salts are traditionally made from pa'akai, the crude white salt made on the islands. Some pa'akai made in traditional pans dug in the deep ochre-red, iron rich clay take on a pale salmon color from particulate stirred up in the harvest—much as French sel gris takes its pale gray color from the silver porcelain clay bottoms of the salt pans there. Many alaea salts today are made by mixing pa'akai or industrially-produced California sea salt with premium alaea clay sourced elsewhere—mainly from secret locations along river banks on Kaua'i.

SIFTING THROUGH THE ALAEAS

There are many kinds of alaea salts. Most come from just a few sources, though they are often rebranded with names that vary slightly from place to place. For example, alaea, alaea volcanic, alaea Hawaiian, Hawaiian Red, and so on can all refer to just one salt. But despite the interchangeability of

their names, not all are created equal. Colors of alaea range from pale salmon to rich brick, depending on the grade and quantity of alaea volcanic clay that is combined with the salt. Darker salts are not perforce of higher quality than lighter salts, though they do generally use a higher grade or greater quantity of sacred alaea clay. Regardless of their color, most of the alaea salts sold commonly (and legally) today are actually made using an industrially produced sea salt from California–and the chances are even the stores selling the salt will be unaware of the fact. A handful of traditional saltmakers continue to make alaea using traditional methods. If you don't have a knowledgeable saltmonger in your neck of the woods, premium brands of alaea such as Haleakala red or other brands bearing the name of the saltmaker on the label are the safest bet. The finest alaea salt from a base salt perspective available now is Haleakala red, evaporated in a greenhouse in open pans. The fullest expression of authentic alaea is found only in the many gray market alaea salts available on the Hawaiian Islands, or more commonly just offered as a gift. ■

ALAEA QUICK REFERENCE

Without resorting to proprietary names from reputable companies that explicitly state where their salt comes from and where it is made, it is difficult to know the origin of a specific salt.

PRIMARY NAME	SALT	COLOR	DESCRIPTION	ALTERNATE NAME(S)
alaea hawaiian	industrial and/or traditional	brick red	most commonly available alaea on U.S. mainland	Alaea Volcanic, alaea salt, Hawaiian red
alaea traditional	industrial and/or traditional	pale to dark salmon	varieties most commonly sold and consumed in Hawaii	Hawaiian sea salt, Bright Alaea, Hawaiian Pink salt
Haleakala Red	traditional	brick red	proprietary name	Haleakala Ruby
Molokai Red	traditional industrial salt blend	brick red	proprietary name	n/a

Traditional Hawaiian dishes that call for alaea salt include Kalua pork and *poke* ("cut pieces" in Hawaiian), a salad of raw or partially cured fish mixed with chiles, onions, tomatoes, and sometimes soy sauce. A favorite alaea salt recipe in our household is fish tacos with mango salsa sprinkled with alaea salt (see page 281).

Several major brands and varieties of alaea salt are available. The one described here is profiled because it is so commonly available. Despite the name, the salt itself is an industrial sea salt from California blended with premium Hawaiian alaea. Many, perhaps most, of the paler, traditional alaea salts sold in Hawaii are likewise actually California salt, in this instance blended with a paler but also pretty alaea. Virtually all Hawaiian salt makers are now forbidden to sell their salt, and legally can only give it away. As a result, traditional salt making, once a pillar of Hawaiian artisanship, has withdrawn to the fringes of Hawaiian culture.

Alaea Hawaiian (Fine)

■ **ALTERNATE NAME(S):** Alaea Volcanic (fine), alaea Hawaiian (fine), Hawaiian red (fine) ■ **MAKER(S):** various ■ **TYPE:** traditional and/or industrial ■ **CRYSTAL:** sand brushed off tops of feet ■ **COLOR:** terra cotta ■ **FLAVOR:** seawater drying off iron anchor ■ **MOISTURE:** none ■ **ORIGIN:** United States ■ **SUBSTITUTE(S):** alaea volcanic coarse or other alaea salt in a grinder ■ **BEST WITH:** Bloody Mary rims; blended with black-colored salts on mozzarella

---

Saturated with tangy rust, this salt becomes increasingly oceanic, then stalls before taking on water and sinking slowly into the black depths of the sea. Alaea in its finely ground incarnation is not a great salt, but using it at the right time and in the right place can yield great results. Its thin, cubic, somewhat irregular crystals and luminous pink color make it definitive on the rim of a cocktail glass—although one could achieve a subtly different result by rimming a glass with alaea volcanic coarse salt that's been run through a good salt grinder.

There are a number of fine-grind alaea volcanic salts, and some are better than others. The moister varieties have better flavor, but they are harder to sprinkle, and clumps of salt on food (even beautiful red salt) are rarely ideal. Still, moist or dry, better or worse, I keep coming back to this salt. When you bite into large crystals of coarse alaea volcanic you are hit with a pungent acidic quality, reminiscent of lime juice, but this quality fades when the salt is preground.

Alcochete Sal Grosso

- **ALTERNATE NAME(S):** sal de Alcochete; sal marinho tradicional de Alcochete ▪ **MAKER(S):** various
- **TYPE:** sel gris; traditional salt ▪ **CRYSTAL:** coarse; clumped, highly irregular shards ▪ **COLOR:** oxidized steel ▪ **FLAVOR:** sublimated mineral; faintly sweet, like the smell of a Popsicle ▪ **MOISTURE:** high
- **ORIGIN:** Portugal ▪ **SUBSTITUTE(S):** Brittany sel gris; Algarve sel gris; or traditional ▪ **BEST WITH:** butter; roasted marrowbones; mild cheeses; fish in rich wine sauces; ideal for salt crusts

The salt is coarse and often has pronounced inflections of gray color from the rich alluvial soils of the Tagus River. The flavor is mild, slightly warm, and without the subtle bitterness found in many Portuguese salts. Whether this is a testament to the centuries of masterful technique behind its production or to the temperate weather or to some quirk of the local geography is anybody's guess.

Salt has been in more or less continuous production in the area for nearly a thousand years. It was once a pillar of the Portuguese economy and a strategic resource for the fishing and shipping trade of Lisbon. For centuries, Alcochete's salt was among the most prized salts in the world for preserving cod, and was even exported to the New World for use in preserving meat and

tanning hides from the burgeoning cattle industry. But when the domestic and export markets turned to cheap industrial salts, the local salt fields were almost entirely abandoned.

My favorite experience with this salt was in the town of Alcochete itself, in a family-owned restaurant. By luck, the waiter, whose mother was the chef, was earning his degree as an English language translator. We spoke about how during the fourteenth and fifteenth centuries the nobility of Lisbon had crossed the Tagus River to live in Alcochete to escape the black plague, which was ravaging the capital. A bowl of the local sel gris appeared unannounced at the table. Sprinkling the large, slightly pungent crystals over crusty whole grain bread slathered with sweet cream butter, we ooh-ed and ahh-ed until the waiter couldn't restrain himself and accepted a piece of his own bread, butter, and salt from us to taste for himself.

Alcochete sal grosso could be worth eating just for the pleasure of seeking it out. I could only find two ways to buy the local salt: either from the salt museum, where it cost five euros for a few ounces of the stuff, or by stumbling across a storage shed inhabited by old men puttering on machinery and smoking hand-rolled cigarettes. I paid ten euros for an eighty-eight pound sack of salt that we lugged around for the rest of the trip, giving it away to whomever showed interest, and cooking as many meals in salt crusts as possible along the way to lighten the load before our return flight home.

Ittica d'Or (Fine)

- **ALTERNATE NAME(S):** none ▪ **MAKER(S):** Meliora s.r.l. ▪ **TYPE:** traditional ▪ **CRYSTAL:** fine; moderately irregular ▪ **COLOR:** silver oxide ▪ **FLAVOR:** clean fresh air from a still life painting ▪ **MOISTURE:** light, but adequate ▪ **ORIGIN:** Italy ▪ **SUBSTITUTE(S):** Ravida ▪ **BEST WITH:** raw sheep's milk cheeses; sheep's milk cheese in olive oil; olive oil

Crumpled, delicate, firm crystals offer an exceptionally fresh oceanic sensation to the mouth, like licking the shoulder of a mermaid. The salt also bears within it faintly acrid notes, which simultaneously diminish its perfection and add to it a certain humanity—like discovering that the mermaid wears sunblock. The provenance of the salt, however, is entirely respectable. Along the western Sicilian coast from Marsala up to Trapani lie famous salt pans located in natural reserves. The salt is extracted by the natural evaporation of seawater. Passing through a series of huge basins formed on the natural basalt of the bay, the seawater evaporates and leaves only the salt behind. The salt is harvested by hand with rakes and shovels, then dried under the Sicilian sun. This finishing salt is billed as a natural complement to fresh raw vegetables, salads, and fish, but I think its fine crystal structure and very full flavor make it better suited to gently sautéed vegetables, pasta tossed simply with olive oil and garlic, and the tender roasted flesh of small game birds.

Japanese Nazuna

- **ALTERNATE NAME:** nazuna ▪ **MAKER(S):** n/a ▪ **TYPE:** traditional ▪ **CRYSTAL:** adhesion of protopyramids, cubes, polyhedrons, plates ▪ **COLOR:** shocked ice ▪ **FLAVOR:** balanced; clear ▪ **MOISTURE:** high
- **ORIGIN:** Japan ▪ **SUBSTITUTE(S):** Halen Môn; grigio di Cervia ▪ **BEST WITH:** raw beef; salmon; butter

An almost sweet mildness ripples gently outward across the tongue, not gathering steam but not diminishing either. Then, finding the odd places at the edges of your mouth, the salt takes on a resonance—it gains a brassy note, ringing out with the random tones of a self-taught trumpet player in a subway tunnel. The crystal structure seems to be composed of salt crystals of every imaginable variety that are stuck together to form the beginnings of flakes. An abundance of moisture gives even the most fragile of these crystals the resilience to bring their faint individual voices to the flavors of a dish. The combined effect is powerful, yet restrained.

Nazuna is from Kyushu, the third-largest island of Japan. The salt is made by evaporating seawater sheltered from the rain in pyramid-shaped greenhouses. Crystallization takes place in pans made of Japanese cypress (*hinoki*).

Jewel of the Ocean

■ **ALTERNATE NAME:** Uni no Houseki ■ **MAKER(S):** n/a ■ **TYPE:** traditional ■ **CRYSTAL:** origami cardboard boxes ■ **COLOR:** partially melted paraffin ■ **FLAVOR:** balanced; clear ■ **MOISTURE:** medium-low ■ **ORIGIN:** Japan ■ **SUBSTITUTE(S):** Vietnamese pearl ■ **BEST WITH:** would make beautiful rock candy necklaces

Absurdly huge crystals the shape and size of engine bolts are reason enough for any sane person to avoid eating this salt. It would be fun to use as construction materials for a scale model of Athenian walls and other fortifications around your food, in defense against attack by hordes of blood-thirsty Spartans. But it is not for eating. Yes, it is very nicely balanced, with the classic rich-yet-clear profile of good Japanese salts. Yes, it has luscious color that makes me think of candlelit dancers behind rice paper screens. And, yes, it even has the requisite moisture to lend each unearthly crystal a yielding quality that makes you think about it for many minutes after its shimmering Scovillian zing has trailed off to nothingness.

Tension abounds in this salt. It is in its structure, and in the very mineral sources it comes from. The salt is made by combining deep seawater with more seawater from the surface of the ocean, joining the subtle magnesium-rich depths with the planktonic vitality of the shallower waters. Ocean currents convect minerals surprisingly little, so as far as salt harvesting is concerned, each

oceanic layer can be considered its own sea; it is the waters of these two seas that make up this salt. The brine is solar evaporated first, and then moved into handmade ceramic vessels inside solar greenhouses for crystallization.

To grind Jewel of the Ocean with a mortar and pestle (it is too coarse for any salt mill) is to throw away its entire raison d'etre. There is no way to combine this stuff with food without sacrificing its chief allures: bigness, and an ingenious structure evocative of architecture used millennia before history was written and possibly originating from outer space.

On the other hand, the impossibility of this salt may be reason enough to seek it out. The crystals do not occur as a solid block like a rock salt. Rather, a loose piece of salt is constructed as a thick-walled but hollow box, with spans of fibrous-seeming salt crystals stretched from one edge to the other, as if forming a taut, woven drum. Then, very fine crystals of geometric shapes are flung into this drum, where they stick. The interior walls of this salt box are thus filled with struts and smaller crystals of every imaginable shape, producing a kaleidoscopic effect in salt-silver monochrome. Under the spell of this play of light and lighter, the adventurous eater might feel obligated to seek out some showy use for the salt's natural glamour, much as a beachcomber tries to find just the right spot on the crowded mantel for a glowing bauble washed up by last night's storm.

Maine Sea Salt

- **ALTERNATE NAME(S):** Maine Coast - **MAKER(S):** Maine Sea Salt Company - **TYPE:** traditional
- **CRYSTAL:** medium to superfine crunched bits - **COLOR:** grated radish - **FLAVOR:** mineral bite; bracing; massive - **MOISTURE:** moderate - **ORIGIN:** United States - **SUBSTITUTE(S):** French sel gris; sal marinho tradicional de Alcochete - **BEST WITH:** lobster salad; grilled swordfish; bluefish with lemon and fennel; atop or in clam chowder; the best salt in the world for crabcakes

Salt making used to be a major independent enterprise in the United States, practiced by hundreds of small saltworks along the east and south coasts and at inland salt springs across the country. Maine, a logistical hub for the fishing industry, was no exception. But with short summers, dark winters, and generally cold, damp weather, making salt there has never been easy. Saltworks to the south and west and overseas put an end to most salt making in Maine two centuries ago.

This is a pity, because the sea in the Gulf of Maine has some interesting stories to tell. The Gulf Stream, a massive warm current from the equatorial Atlantic Ocean, sweeps up the Atlantic seaboard, spinning off the hip of North Carolina and heading out to sea. Icy waters from the Arctic fill the gap, chilling the Gulf of Maine 20° to 40°F cooler than waters just a few hundred miles to the south and east. In addition, the ocean's temperature decreases with depth, and drops abruptly across a layer called the thermocline. The thermocline in the Gulf of Maine is very shallow, often less than 150 feet deep. Circulated by powerful tides and currents, cold water from the thermocline introduces enormous organic fertility and mineral richness to the Gulf of Maine's pure Arctic waters.

Stephen Cook, who runs the Maine Sea Salt Company with his wife, Sharon, makes a bold, vigorous traditional salt. Water from the Gulf of Maine is drawn into greenhouses (salt houses), where sun and wind evaporate the seawater to the point of crystallization. The salt is harvested with no other processing.

Maine salt's bracing, intense crystals strike beautiful, flinty sparks of flavor on creamy crab and other seafood bisques. Cook's favorite use for his salt is gravlax, which he makes for special occasions—an operetta of Maine's nautical ties sung in sugar, salmon, and salt.

More on Maine: Another Maine saltworks, Quoddy Mist, wrestles with reverse osmosis and vacuum evaporators to make a wild and unruly tasting sea salt that introduces gale winds and the lash of frayed rigging to your mouth.

Moroccan Atlantic

■ **ALTERNATE NAME(S):** Moroccan sea salt ■ **MAKER(S):** n/a ■ **TYPE:** traditional ■ **CRYSTAL:** rubble of microfine bits to huge chunks ■ **COLOR:** cloudy; a faint blush ■ **FLAVOR:** hot; sharp ■ **MOISTURE:** low ■ **ORIGIN:** Morocco ■ **SUBSTITUTE(S):** coarse traditional salt ■ **BEST WITH:** spicy lamb stew; braised shortribs with *harissa* and yogurt; grilled seabass with cumin, caraway, and cilantro

Some salt is made with love; some is born of economic necessity. Once in a while, a salt comes along that has been made without thought for so long that its reasons for being are difficult to divine. Moroccans have been making salt for thousands of years. Why no longer matters. It just is. Hot, bold, untamed, and terminally uncouth, Moroccan Atlantic has all the charm of a cobra attached to the hollow of your ankle.

Most of the salt made along Morocco's 1,500 miles of arid coastline are ground into fine grains before they reach the consumer, but the raw, wild crystals that come from the traditional salt fields are the most interesting, if only because they leave you with the honor of hammering them into usable form yourself. Even pummelled a few times in your mortar and pestle, the salt will barely be able to restrain itself. It slants its viper eyes and says, "touch me," then leaves it to you to decide whether or not it's worth the risk.

Exercise a healthy viciousness yourself when cooking anything you intend to subject to this salt; or at least hold nothing back. My favorite is the inspired dish known unimaginatively in Morocco as "eggs," where about a gallon of olive oil is heated in a pan and eggs are tossed in to virtually deep-fry before being topped with a touch of cumin and maybe a chiffonade of fresh basil. Serve it up, salt it, and eat with thick crusts of fresh bread.

Muối biển (ruộng muối salt field)

- **ALTERNATE NAME(S):** Muối thổ (raw salt); Vietnamese sel gris; Vietnamese traditional = **MAKER(S):** n/a = **TYPE:** traditional = **CRYSTAL:** medium clusters of cubes and baby pyramids = **COLOR:** old lace
- **FLAVOR:** potato chip roundness slaked with flower nectar = **MOISTURE:** high = **ORIGIN:** Vietnam
- **SUBSTITUTE(S):** coarse traditional salt = **BEST WITH:** omelets; stir-fried anything; spicy beef soup; a defining force for slices of beef pan-seared with chile peppers, aromatic greens, and lemon

Huge jagged crystals yield between the teeth with a dreamy, softly crackling crunch. Then the flavor expands and evolves, like a whisper in reverse, and the soft sounds of sweetness find balance, growing in volume until you hear the murmured encouragement of the boldest flavors overtaking your mouth. Coarse, variegated, moist, tasty, and balanced, with the natural visible impurities of an authentic unrefined traditional gros sel: empires could be built on this salt. They were.

Vietnam has a long artisanal tradition of making salt from the sea, and the salt is generally wonderful. The country's traditional salts are solar evaporated and hand harvested, then drained and transported by hand in woven baskets to be consolidated into large mounds that are covered with thatch to protect them from rain. Muối biển (pronounced moo-ee bee-en), translated literally as "sea salt," is used to distinguish the natural, unrefined salt still very popular in Vietnam from Muối biển, the more generic term for edible salt reserved for refined salt. Unfortunately, very little Vietnamese salt is exported, despite the enormous potential for salt production along the country's 2,025 miles of coastline. It's the world's loss.

Papohaku White

- **ALTERNATE NAME(S):** Papohaku opal ■ **RELATED SALTS:** Haleakala red; Kilauea black ■ **MAKER(S):** n/a ■ **TYPE:** traditional ■ **CRYSTAL:** crumbled toffee ■ **COLOR:** moon white ■ **FLAVOR:** buttery fruit ■ **MOISTURE:** moderate ■ **ORIGIN:** Hawaii ■ **SUBSTITUTE(S):** Kona deep sea salt ■ **BEST WITH:** sautéed shrimp with chiles and ginger; sashimi; ground up fine on popcorn

Meditation is an important practice. It allows us to explore the contours of our mind, and then learn how these contours influence our perceptions of the world. It is especially important to meditate regularly, which is why I do it at least once every few years. Popohaku white offers a tasty alternative, or, better yet, at least a supplement, to any meditative regimen. Rich and buttery with a rounded, balanced body, the salt unexpectedly opens up within itself to reveal a labyrinthine mineral sweetness you could spend a lifetime exploring. The main difference between food finished with Papohaku white and a lifetime of profound mountaintop meditation is that it approaches the discipline as a full-contact sport.

Sprinkled on grilled fish and pineapple, it crashes over you with the force of a tidal wave. Part of the salt's impact is due to the crystal shape—a mishmash of ground-up shards and chunks with more class than a rock salt but none of the elegance of a fleur de sel or sel gris. This lack of crystalline sophistication would be a serious disadvantage in a lesser salt, but Papohaku white's truly magnificent mineral richness turns it into a virtue, like a bronzed warrior who recites poetry as he dispatches his opponents.

Papohaku white is made in the town of Kaunakakai, on the Hawaiian island of Molokai. Seawater is filtered, then condensed to six times its original salinity in a high-tech condenser; this concentrated brine is then pumped into small, freestanding solar evaporators resembling solar water heaters where, after weeks of further evaporation, the salt crystallizes. The resulting clusters of coin-sized crystals are harvested and ground to a desired consistency.

Papohaku white is the base for two other excellent Hawaiian salts. Kilauea black is made by combining Papohaku white with activated charcoal, resulting in an impossibly lush black salt reminiscent of the jungle at midnight, replete with all the sounds and smells of a savage yet ultimately harmonious place. Haleakala red is made by combining Papohaku white with a premium-grade variety of sacred alaea volcanic clay. With its bright, deep, meaty red color, Haleakala Red is the most scrupulously made and probably the finest quality Hawaiian alaea-style salt available.

But the proof is, as they say, in the pudding. Use Haleakala red on virtually any seafood or pork dish, and to spectacular effect on fruit salsas and ceviches. Kilauea black is great on fish, but also brings great visual impact and full flavor to mild, pale-colored foods from roast potatoes with sour cream and chives to steamed cauliflower to pasta. It's good on bread and butter, too. Use Papohaku white not just on grilled red meats and hearty fish dishes and soups, but also on . . . pudding. Butterscotch pudding, in particular, finds a new place in the pantheon of old-fashioned dishes gone wild, with Papohaku white spangling through its normally unrelenting richness.

Trapani

- **ALTERNATE NAME(S):** sale marino di Trapani; Trapani e Marsala salt; Sicilian salt ▪ **MAKER(S):** various ▪ **TYPE:** traditional ▪ **CRYSTAL:** micro to chunky shards ▪ **COLOR:** dehydrated white ▪ **FLAVOR:** neutral—the Switzerland of salt
- **MOISTURE:** none ▪ **ORIGIN:** Italy ▪ **SUBSTITUTE(S):** any finely ground traditional salt (fine); any sel gris (coarse)
- **BEST WITH:** olive oil and garlic pasta; sea snail bruschetta; fried sardines; delicate sauces; pasta water; pickling olives and mushrooms

"Master," said Sancho Panza. "Everything that gleams is not a giant." Don Quixote, roared, "Coward!" and spurred his Rocinante. Together they charged the windmill at a steady stroll. The wind picked up, Rocinante broke into a liesurely trot, and the windmill's blade struck Don Quixote a blow to the head, knocking him from his steed.

While the windmills of Trapani cannot count the valiant Don Quixote among their conquests, the salt they grind touches any food it seasons with a similar inanimate wallop. Trapani salt unapologetically dominates the compact piece of terrain it occupies in the flavor landscape. It is bright and blunt—the essence of salinity. That is the sum total of its virtues. The color of Trapani salts ranges from an opaque, indeterminate white to a more translucent, glittery indeterminate white. The fine grind—more or less a bunch of shattered specks—is basically a small version of the large, hard, rockier crystals from which it was ground. If none of this sounds particularly beautiful, it is because beauty is not what Trapani salts are about. They're mashed up, smashed up, dry, brittle crystals that hit hard and fast and then take their leave without further ado. They should count themselves fortunate to have the full majesty of Italian cuisine as their sidekick. Most of the natural salt consumed in Italy is now from Trapani.

There can be no better match for Trapani salt than a simple meal of grilled lamb rubbed with garlic, olive oil, and salt and drizzled with lemon juice—if only to lighten Sicily's load of sheep. (There are about 1.5 million sheep and 5 million people on the island, yet, especially in the countryside, it seems the opposite is true.) Sheep provide milk for most of Sicily's famed cheeses, which underscore the island's close relationship with salt. There are the heady pecorinos (*pecora* means "sheep") and ricotta salata, an aged sheep's milk cheese with a heavily salted rind and an unctuous, mild interior. Vastedda cheese starts its life as a delicate sheep's milk *tuma*, eaten right out of the mold, then evolves into primo sale after it is lightly salted, and finally becomes vastedda when fully matured.

Trapani salt is harvested twice a year, allowing sufficient crystallization time for magnesium and other salts to contribute a 2 percent trace-mineral content to the finished product. Salt has been made in the lagoons between Trapani and Marsala (from *Mars el'Allah*, Arabic for "Port of God") since Phoenician times. Neutral, dry, and easy to dose with the fingers, Trapani salts are good all-around cooking salts for those who insist on the familiar feel of an industrial sea salt but want the fuller flavor and more appealing aura of a hand-harvested salt.

Vietnamese Pearl

- **ALTERNATE NAME:** Vietnamese traditional ■ **MAKER(S):** n/a
- **TYPE:** traditional ■ **CRYSTAL:** immense, sheer-faced fortifications ■ **COLOR:** sunlight seen from inside a glacier
- **FLAVOR:** steel; pepper skins; baby chickens ■ **MOISTURE:** high ■ **ORIGIN:** Vietnam ■ **SUBSTITUTE(S):** Jewel of the Ocean ■ **BEST WITH:** sweet vegetables like pumpkin, butternut squash, creamed corn; infernally spicy foods; charred freshwater fish

Danger is the chief attraction of Vietnamese Pearl, like a cliff that beckons to your every suicidal tendency. Touch, bite, savor the sharp spicy flavor, and maybe you will survive. Vietnamese Pearl has two sides: on a good day, it's soft and bouncy, pliant as bubble gum, imploding into chewy, tropical-ice sunshine as you go merrily on your way. And on a bad day, things get scary. Suddenly the steering wheel comes off in your hands and you're hurtling toward the guardrail as a burst of sharp, rock-hard safety glass erupts like a car wreck in your mouth. Either way, it's fun.

Few salts can compete with Vietnamese Pearl for the sheer magnitude of its crystals, which can easily exceed a half-inch, and sometimes get much larger. For years, its structure found endless diversion in the geometries of the triangle. More recent batches seem inclined to pursue iterations of the triangle. The closest salt to Vietnamese Pearl, Jewel of the Ocean, occupies itself exclusively with the square. Either one will make any sane person quail. The saving grace for both salts is their very substantial residual moisture, which makes them crunchable, instead of hard and sharp, though Vietnamese Pearl is generally more malleable.

The trick to using Vietnamese Pearl effectively is to learn how it reacts in different conditions. Experienced users describe (in Vietnamese) heating it in a wok to the point where it explodes on contact with your mouth. This makes no sense to me. A quick hit with a mortar and pestle, however, tames reduces the pathological bulk of the crystals without diminishing its fractured intensity. Meals brainstormed up from extreme ingredients are the natural stomping grounds for this salt: chiles (Hanoi, hahong ku chu), pungent spices (fenugreek, coriander), cloying herbs (basil, tarragon), and singed bits of meats and vegetables fused into perfection by the natrium stridency smoldering within.

FLAKE SALT

Bali Kechil Pyramid

■ **ALTERNATE NAME(S):** coarse Kechil Balinese salt ■ **MAKER(S):** Big Tree Farms ■ **TYPE:** flake ■ **CRYSTAL:** heavy-bottomed shot glasses for mice ■ **COLOR:** rippled water ■ **FLAVOR:** bright; tidy; but with bitter aftertaste ■ **MOISTURE:** moderate ■ **ORIGIN:** Bali, Indonesia ■ **SUBSTITUTE(S):** Halen Môn silver ■ **BEST WITH:** shrimp and snapper satay; Balinese smoked duck; green papaya soup; tarte Tatin; the ultimate salt for home-made pretzels, bagels, and rolls

Kechil means "young," or "small." When I look at the salt, "cute" is the first word that comes to mind—in all the cuddly, gushing, annoying senses of the term. In some cute little atelier somewhere, little beings—beings smaller, even more ingenious, and far cuter than elves—must have made this salt.

From a distance, the crystals of Bali Kechil are more or less cubic, and don't ressemble a flake salt at all. Closer inspection reveals that they are in fact hollow boxes. Not neat boxes. The crystals are chunky and jumbled, with thick cubic bases and wobbly, ridged sides—childlike boxes. Getting past their adorableness is the chief challenge to using Bali Kechil. You have to put down the urge to snuggle, take a breath, stand up tall, and smack it around. Once you can do that, you are ready to enjoy the salt truly and openly.

Ten thousand feet below the base of Bali's sacred Gunung Agung volcano, Bali Kechil is made from water hauled by hand from the sea and poured carefully into basins carved in the black beach sand. After the water has evaporated, a thin layer of salt-crusted sand is skimmed from the basin and painstakingly rinsed in clean salt water to form a saturated brine. The brine is then reduced in bamboo basins until crystals form that can be harvested.

Scattered on food, Bali Kechil is a train wreck of crazy popping as the tiny crystals implode between your teeth. There is nothing cute about it—dazzling is more like it. Few salts offer a more vital experience of salt's physical presence with so light a flavor. Bali Kechil's little box crystals communicate in crystalline verbosity the pure essence of traditional Balinese flavors, like kaffir lime leaves, blue ginger, coconut, and bird's-eye chiles. In fact, eating the salt brings new sensations to the deeper regions of the mind (ones you may not even know you possess), like the puffy-crunchy texture of krupuk melinjo crackers made with gnetum gnemon fruit, or the earthy-sour flavors of tamarind pulp and pandan leaf. Bringing these sensations back home to your daily life, Bali Kechil is the best salt available for salted bagels, pizza crusts, pretzels, and focaccia.

Bali Rama Pyramid

- **ALTERNATE NAME(S):** coarse Balinese salt - **MAKER(S):**
Big Tree Farms - **TYPE:** flake - **CRYSTAL:** architecturally
implausible Aztec pyramids - **COLOR:** rippled water
- **FLAVOR:** electrified frost; potato chip of minerals; faint
bitter aftertaste - **MOISTURE:** low to moderate - **ORIGIN:**
Bali, Indonesia - **SUBSTITUTE(S):** Halen Môn; Cyprus flake
- **BEST WITH:** roasted cherry tomato salad; all roasted and
pan-fried seafood; oatmeal cookies

At the birth of a first child, there is no sudden parental transformation from self-centered dope to enlightened sage. You are just as self-centered; it's just that your self has now been expanded to include the wriggling critter in your arms. You are still a dope, too, and your materialistic obsession with glowing baubles and whizzing machinery persists, or may even be amplified. After days and weeks and months of sleepless nights spent obsessively staring at a new baby, you keep thinking, "Wow, this thing is German-engineered and superbly built." Bali Rama Pyramid provides the same materialistic rush of admiration coupled with unmerited pride.

Each grain of salt is a structure of starched crystalline sheets tautly strung against a sharply inclined pyramidal armature. As clearly as the salt sings of island flavors like galangal, coriander, salam leaves, and lemongrass, you need not limit its use to tropical seafood, pork, and fruit. The visual and textural luxury of Bali Rama Pyramid should be enjoyed like any baubel: often, but without betraying just how much you adore it.

Cornish Sea Salt

■ **ALTERNATE NAME(S):** n/a ■ **MAKER(S):** Cornish Sea Salt Company ■ **TYPE:** flake (barely) ■ **CRYSTAL:** medium-coarse adhesion of cubes and micropyramids ■ **COLOR:** pond ice ■ **FLAVOR:** sharp, metallic, and clear, but not entirely unbalanced ■ **MOISTURE:** medium-low ■ **ORIGIN:** England ■ **SUBSTITUTE(S):** Halen Môn; Japanese nazuna ■ **BEST WITH:** herbaceous pie of leeks, butter, and lardoons; steak and kidney pie; fried liver and onions; cottage potatoes and scallions

Each salt crystal is made up of a number of small, firm grains stuck together by tantalizingly close to nothing—static electricity, perhaps. Whatever the mechanism, the salt has an agreeable bulk, a weightiness that makes it pleasant to hold in the hand, something unsupervised children might be compelled to scatter like birdseed. The combination of crystalline heft and delicacy lends the impression that the very existence of this salt is fleeting.

With enough moisture to provide body on food, Cornish sea salt does everything in its power to seduce. But the flavor of the salt is less wondrous: flat, faintly bitter, and metallic: a shrill voice issuing unexpectedly from a pretty face. Yet for all that, when harmonized with other assertive ingredients, the salt communicates a certain sense of place.

Cornish food tends toward the substantial, and this salt fits right in. Good hiking and farming foods, like smoked oysters with duck egg, potted shrimp, "tates and mate" pasties, and clotted cream and jam on a scone: the crunch of Cornish salt on any of these dishes is warmly welcomed. I'll never forget sitting in a restaurant with a friend when they brought out stargazy pie, which was basically a fish pie of leeks, suet (possibly), and six fresh pilchards with their heads popping through the crust, gazing into my starry eyes. All it needed was a pinch of Cornish sea salt.

Cornish sea salt is made in Cornwall by Tony Fraser, founder of the Cornish Sea Salt Company, located at the extreme southwest of England, on the heel of the small boot of land that projects into the northern fringe of the North Atlantic at the mouth of the English Channel. Salt was made in this area, called The Lizard, possibly as far back as 3,000 years ago, in the Iron Age, using the traditional briquetage method, with seawater evaporated in clay pots over a fire of gorse and other shrubs. Today, seawater is drawn from Cornwall's desolate coast, then filtered and heated to condense the brine until salt crystallizes. The resulting salt is then hand-harvested from the evaporation pans, rinsed, and dried.

Cyprus Black Flake

- **ALTERNATE NAME(S):** Cyprus Black Lava; Turkish Black Pyramid ▪ **MAKER(S):** n/a ▪ **TYPE:** flake ▪ **CRYSTAL:** heavily built hollow pyramids ▪ **COLOR:** flinty gray to charcoal black (see sidebar, page 146) ▪ **FLAVOR:** earth- and tannin-enrobed electricity ▪ **MOISTURE:** none ▪ **ORIGIN:** Cyprus ▪ **SUBSTITUTE(S):** Cyprus flake; Molokai Black Lava ▪ **BEST WITH:** fresh chèvre; grilled asparagus

Cyprus black is intensely earthy, tannic, and bold, and is best used judiciously. It is also the opposite, and is best used freely. Or it is both.

Perhaps that needs some explanation.

Different people taste Cyprus black on different foods in different ways, on different days. Some call it subtle one year and intense the next. For others, it depends on what food the salt accompanies. As in quantum mechanics, the experience of Cyprus black changes the experience of Cyprus black. This is a difficult notion to wrap the mind around, but it doesn't matter. Regardless of our understanding, the salt is good—if unpredictable.

The color of the crystals ranges from flinty black to rain cloud gray, depending on manufacturing variations from batch to batch. The salt can also be classified as a modified salt, as it takes its characteristic color from activated charcoal added after crystallization. An especially saturated, obsidian black version of this salt is available under the name Black Diamond flake sea salt. The translucency of the tremendous pyramidal crystals lets lighter, brighter colors pass through. The flavor is relatively consistent when tasted alone, but highly responsive to other ingredients, or different people's tongues.

Cyprus black delivers a satisfying snappy crunch, and resists dissolving even on very moist foods. Massive pyramids of Cyprus black on a rich pumpkin soup topped with guacamole, cilantro, and toasted pumpkins seeds invite you to delve into the divine pleasures of Mayan cuisine. The salt's subtle tannic notes lend wonderful balance and structure to grilled asparagus and Brussels sprouts. On pasta, it mimics the pungent snap of fried garlic; on baked potatoes, or Cobb salad, it adds the crunchy contrast of bacon bits. My favorite is potato latkes topped with smoked salmon and tarragon crème fraîche, and a neat pinch of Cyprus black on top, a sort of poor man's caviar.

WHAT MAKES BLACK SALT BLACK?

Some salts are traditionally evaporated from waters that have filtered through or evaporated over volcanic sands, which suggests the term "volcanic" or "lava" salt. But the presence or absence of volcanic soils in the salt-making process has no bearing on the color of a salt. All these salts emerge from the salt pans in varying shades of brilliant white. During or after drying, they are combined with activated charcoal (also called active charcoal), which is highly porous (a single gram can have 1,640 square yards of surface area), making it incredibly absorptive and quick to adhere to salt crystals. Activated charcoal offers the added advantage of being a detoxifying agent; it is used in some instances to treat poisoning. From a gourmet standpoint, it lends black salts their characteristic color, plus the faintly earthy, oxidized flavor of charcoal. ■

Cyprus Flake

- **ALTERNATE NAME(S):** Cyprus Silver ▪ **MAKER(S):** n/a
- **TYPE:** flake ▪ **CRYSTAL:** heavily built hollow pyramids
- **COLOR:** shaved egg white ▪ **FLAVOR:** evaporated thunderbolt ▪ **MOISTURE:** none ▪ **ORIGIN:** Cyprus ▪ **SUBSTITUTE(S):** Hana flake; Maldon ▪ **BEST WITH:** canapés

Etiquette is not Cyprus flake's strong suit. Think of it as a three-hundred-pound middle linebacker. You have food (the quarterback), you have flavor (the ball), and you have a hulking impediment that is not only ready, but able to do anything necessary to make contact. Cyprus flake is one of the few salts capable of standing up to a sports analogy.

Visually, Cyprus flake is distinctive and rather alarming, like the hourglass of a black widow or the stripes of a scorpion fish—nature's way of alerting your mind and body to the forces of nature that are yet to unfold. The flake crystals of the salt, which measure between 1/8 to 1 inch, are among the largest, most architecturally rugged, and most regularly contoured—which is to say, perfectly pyramidal—of any flake salt. It takes work to crunch one. In your mouth, it remains defiantly voluminous, daring your teeth to bite. And when you do, its structure explodes in a mini supernova of crystalline slivers. The taste is pungent and bright; a little hot.

Cyprus flake's strange natural architecture lends visual drama to a dish—sort of like a nuclear alternative to the trusty sprinkle of parsley—and similarly asserts the physicality of salt as a force of nature in a recipe. Perch a flake on a pearl of salmon roe sushi. Challenge your molecular gastronomy skills by suspending silver pyramids of salt in a cube of aspic. Scatter some on a home-spun tuna melt, or over a thick potato-leek soup, or fissuring the skin of a crème caramel. Above all, Cyprus flake brings something refreshingly un-foodlike to blanched veggies and garden salads—a small, immaculate piece of titanium geometry unearthed in a verdant tropical chaos.

Halen Môn

■ **ALTERNATE NAME(S):** Halen Môn Silver ■ **MAKER(S):** The Anglesey Sea Salt Company Ltd. ■ **TYPE:** flake ■ **CRYSTAL:** laminated sheets crushed into trapezoids ■ **COLOR:** silvered ice ■ **FLAVOR:** mineral freshness with a touch of sun; clarified butter ■ **MOISTURE:** moderate ■ **ORIGIN:** Wales ■ **SUBSTITUTE(S):** Cayman sea salt; Cornish sea salt ■ **BEST WITH:** butternut squash soup; grilled fish; garden vegetable sandwich

Shards of fractured, flat geometric crystals layer one atop the other, reflecting and refracting light into infinite gradations of translucency the color of scattered memories. These stacked strata of salt crystals yield a dazzling crunch. A pleasant residual moisture lends a mellowing effect, releasing sea and sun flavors that disband casually throughout any food it seasons. Halen Môn offers a textural dimension beyond that of most other flake salts, its crunch-upon-crunch layers vanishing before calling undue attention to themselves, leaving behind a clearly defined structure and pleasant minerality, ponderings for the mouth that are as ungraspable as string theory.

Halen môn gwyn a glan o gymru means "pure white sea salt" in Welsh. If the translation does not do justice to the salt, the lyrical beauty of the original Welsh mirrors at least some of the salt's mysteries. For example, Halen Môn floats. Flicked across the surface of a lobster bisque or fresh corn chowder speckled with shaved truffles, Halen Môn (or Halen Môn oak smoked) stays buoyant, creating striations of mineral freshness that glide down your throat as the salt dissolves under the pressure of your tongue. My friend Christy, a Celtic raider of the produce aisle, finishes her signature butternut squash–and–every-vegetable-in-Oregon soup with Halen Môn, sparking intense bursts of flavors whenever a stray flake of undissolved salt crunches in the mouth.

Halen Môn is one of the few great culinary salts produced by the same vacuum boiler evaporation technique practiced by industrial giants. Pure seawater from the Menai Straits of the Welsh coast passes through two natural filters—a mussel bed and a sandbank—before being charcoal-filtered. The thrice-filtered seawater is heated in a vacuum, which encourages it to simmer at a low temperature, then the cool concentrated seawater passes into shallow crystallization tanks where, overnight, delicate crystals form on the surface and sink to the bottom. In the morning, the precipitated salt is harvested by raking up the sheets of flakes, which are rinsed with brine and dried.

Showier varieties of fleur de sel can't compete for modesty, more delicate sel gris can't compare for penetration, and high-contrast parchment-thin flake salts long for Halen Môn's deeper mineral clarity. The salt has a confident oddball identity that resists enlisting with any established camp, preferring to deliver its own style to meats and vegetables of every sort. This makes Halen Môn that rare bankable star with unshakable instincts about the roles it plays—the Johnny Depp of sea salt, but paler . . . Nicole Kidman.

Hana Flake

- **ALTERNATE NAME(S):** Hana no shio - **MAKER(S):** n/a
- **TYPE:** flake - **CRYSTAL:** sharp, flat pyramids - **COLOR:** sheet ice on a sail - **FLAVOR:** condensation on clean glass; Arctic Ocean air - **MOISTURE:** moderate - **ORIGIN:** Japan
- **SUBSTITUTE(S):** Halen Môn; Bali Rama Pyramid - **BEST WITH:** snow peas; foie gras; poached halibut

The best dishes in the world are true works of art, inscrutable, impossible to improve upon. Until they meet the right salt. At the restaurant Le Bernardin, I once had a dish of *mi-cuit,* goose foie gras on a tender trampoline of crisp-crusted halibut, capped with white grape and Sauternes coulis. I almost started attacking people in the restaurant, grabbing their lapels and shaking them. The torrent of pleasure and passion and adrenaline coursing through me didn't abate until hours later, after we had run down the sidewalks in the snow like unleashed poodles, yapping at the streetlights, youthful, imbecilic laughter trailing behind us. If Chef Ripert had just added a pinch of Hana flake, we might never have stopped.

Each crystal of Hana flake is defiantly clear and improbably sliced, like a diamond necklace run through a food processor, reassembled, and frozen in liquid nitrogen before being hit by a hammer. The taste isn't so different—a sharp blade of ice-water clarity. Hana flake is all about the tug of texture on flavor— all about the tensile strength of something designed to explode. Perfection is a place in time. Topping a dish with Hana flake offers something eternal.

Maldon

- **ALTERNATE NAME(S):** none - **MAKER(S):** Maldon Crystal Salt Company Limited - **TYPE:** flake - **CRYSTAL:** clutter of fine shards and small pyramids - **COLOR:** sheet ice
- **FLAVOR:** sea breeze with glitter in it - **MOISTURE:** low
- **ORIGIN:** England - **SUBSTITUTE(S):** Cyprus flake; Hana flake; Bali Rama Pyramid - **BEST WITH:** butter leaf lettuce salad

We all have good days. Days when the rhythms of life inexplicably synchronize—our socks match, all the traffic lights go our way, everything we say is witty, and the eyes of those around us glitter with a mix of friendly adoration and carnal lust. You can just feel it. You've got the groove. You *are* the groove. The next day, inevitably, you inexplicably get a bloody nose while brushing your teeth, you drop your keys through a sewer grate, you get caught in a lie, and the plumber figures out you're an idiot. But what if every day could be a good day, an eternally brisk and refreshing excursion, structured with the right balance of what we need to feel amazed at ourselves and our lives?

That isn't going to happen.

But Maldon doesn't have off days. The crystals are proportioned just so, an effortless balance of scintillating flakes and snappy pyramids. The flavor is silvery, fresh, and good-natured, igniting fresh contrast in the color, texture, and flavor of roasted meats and vegetables. Complementary as the salt may be to cooked foods, it is all but indispensable for finishing fresh green salads or any raw vegetable. It's also good almost anywhere else, lending a spark of contrast that demurely calls attention to itself.

Marlborough flakey is more delicate in crystal and refined in flavor, and Cyprus flake is heftier and bolder in all regards. What they leave untended is a sizable middle ground—which Maldon occupies with insouciance. Crushing Maldon between the finger and thumb, and letting the flakes fall to the surface of your favorite food is almost as satiating as eating it.

Maldon sea salt is made from seawater collected from England's Blackwater River estuary during fortnightly high tides, when the salinity is highest. After a brief stint in holding tanks to let ocean matter settle out, the seawater is filtered and passed into stainless steel salt pans. The brine is evaporated over fires mounted on an elaborate network of brick flues (natural gas has replaced coal as the fuel) that give the specific heating pattern required for the formation of Maldon's characteristic flake crystals. Crystals form on the surface of the water and sink to the bottom. After the water cools, the salt crystals are raked, drained, and dried. Salt has been produced at or near the site of the modern saltworks since the Iron Age. Entire hills of red clay in Essex are actually formed from red clay briquetage used in prehistoric production of salt. A 1086 survey noted forty-five salt pans in the Maldon area.

Marlborough Flakey

- **ALTERNATE NAME(S):** none ■ **MAKER(S):** Dominion Salt Works
- **TYPE:** flake ■ **CRYSTAL:** tufts of owl feather ■ **COLOR:** high-voltage sparks ■ **FLAVOR:** raindrop ■ **MOISTURE:** none
- **ORIGIN:** New Zealand ■ **SUBSTITUTE(S):** Murray River flake
- **BEST WITH:** snow peas; pasta primavera; mixed baby greens salad; chocolate cake

On the beach, sand twinkling on your toes, you feel the sun's last warm exhalation before it sinks below the horizon. The sea flashes into darkness, the sky plunges into color, and the heavens' passage through time is narrowed to a slit as the vastness of the universe condenses to a flicker. Marlborough flakey, with its blinding white, undulating, frothy crystals—unlike any other—regales you with promises of intensity that never materializes and of luminosity in shadow. The crystals torque into twisted shapes fringed with a lacework radiating ever outward with the ceaseless variation of a fractal. This is among the great salts for fresh vegetables and other foods whose flavors crave a salted contrast, but whose grandeur can only be experienced in glimpses.

The name "Marlborough flakey" provides some insight into the behavior of the salt itself, provided you are capable of burring your Rs. The salt doesn't so much crunch as *yield* in a quick succession of crackles, like the brittle softness of dried flower petals. The flavor is equally elegant. Much as when you capture a snowflake on your tongue and sense only fleeting moistness, so food finished with Marlborough flakey tastes not so much seasoned as graced. It carries with it distinct mineral notes that could be trace amounts of calcium and magnesium, and it finishes with the classic double-whammy of a great salt: faint bitterness overlaid by sweetness.

Marlborough flakey harmonizes with food. While the salt maker likes to talk about crushing it between your fingers for cooking, I think he is understating the pleasure to be had from letting your tongue, hard palate, gums, and cheeks take their turns collapsing and rolling the crystals, each part of the mouth receiving slightly different information depending on where the salt is in its rapid path toward dissolution. Cast it across a salad of fresh garden greens, where it contrasts with and softens the astringency of vinaigrette and accentuates the bitter and mineral flavors of the veggies. If nothing else, try it on pasta puttanesca, or mozzarella, or poultry.

Marlborough Flakey is evaporated by the sun and wind from the clear South Pacific current that sweeps up the east coast of New Zealand to mingle with the Tasmanian Sea. It is produced by Dominion Salt Works, which manufactures a variety of industrial, pharmaceutical, and animal salts in addition to a few premium culinary salts. The company also makes an iodized flake salt, which is unusual.

Murray River Flake

- **ALTERNATE NAME(S):** Murray Darling ▪ **MAKER(S):** n/a
- **TYPE:** flake ▪ **CRYSTAL:** scales from a mechanical fish
- **COLOR:** startled flamingo ▪ **FLAVOR:** distinct sunshine sweetness; tingle of warm minerals ▪ **MOISTURE:** low
- **ORIGIN:** Australia ▪ **SUBSTITUTE(S):** none ▪ **BEST WITH:** slices of grilled lamb topped with a salad of grapefruit, mint, fennel, and shaved Parmesan; caprese salad; grated cheddar and popcorn; tostadas; seafood frittata

Murray River flake is the cotton candy–pink Lamborghini of Slow Food. Everything about it cries speed, excess, pleasure. Eat this salt blindfolded and you will know exactly what it looks like—just a glint of chrome, a blur of color, an ineffable lightness, and it's gone.

This is among the most delicately formed flake salts, so fine and crisp and subtle that you can't help but throw it around recklessly. The crystals are foil-thin scraps of fragmented pyramids, evaporated naturally from a saline aquifer. They take their color from the carotene produced by microorganisms living in the underground brine. This color and the fluffy feel of it between the fingers suggest using Murray River flake more as a topping than as a salt. It nonetheless brings a muscular and purposeful fullness to moist foods, such as a salad of explosively ripe backyard garden tomatoes, sweet basil, and springy-yet-yielding buffalo mozzarella. Unless used on a relatively dry surface, such as goat cheese or scantily dressed greens, Murray River should only be applied at the table just before eating.

Fed by snowmelt, the Murray River descends from the Australian Alps where it joins the Darling River in a 414,000-square-mile basin (more than twice the size of California or Germany), where frequent drought has created naturally high concentrations of salt in the groundwater. In the dry season of 1829, the explorer Charles Sturt noted that the water was too saline to drink. Due to overfarming and other environmental damage to the area, salinity has only increased. Murray River salt is made from water drawn from this aquifer—one of the few salts made as part of a broader desalinization effort to rehabilitate land.

South African Flake

- **ALTERNATE NAME(S):** South African sea salt flakes - **MAKER(S):** n/a - **TYPE:** flake - **CRYSTAL:** platelets of agglomerated cubes - **COLOR:** fractured windshield - **FLAVOR:** hot; full; faintly aluminum - **MOISTURE:** high - **ORIGIN:** South Africa - **SUBSTITUTE(S):** Halen Môn - **BEST WITH:** dense soups; chili; braised meats

South African flake is intense to the taste, with a hotness that lacks the richer pungency of many other flake salts. Its classic translucent quartz color is pretty but a touch flimsy, and not among its chief charms. However, the salt brings a texture to the table that washes aside such shortcomings. Sheaves as jumbled and fractured as any ice floe challenge you to find a rightful place for them in the kitchen.

The salt is made from water collected at the edge of the sea—not from the ocean itself, but from an underground salt lake nearby (see South African pearl, page 171). After evaporating in a series of solar salt pans, the crystals are formed by allowing the delicate bloom of fleur de sel to continue to expand until it becomes a thin, brittle crust across the surface. When harvested, the crust crumples, resulting in shards. The outcome is flakes of salt made from several to several hundred miniscule cubic crystals—and none of them seems to want to touch, giving the impression that they could scatter at the least provocation, like minnows nibbling at the surface of a pond. Halen Môn appears similar from a distance, but seems born of the opposite inspiration: built up of flakes that are eager to snuggle and, in their eagerness, get piled up on top of each other in unexpected ways.

South African flake is an ideal finishing salt for dishes that would benefit from the obtrusive presence of a salt, such as lightly seasoned grilled meats. Alternately, it contributes both texture and a strident spiciness to vegetable dishes, such as a salad made of roasted peppers, avocados, cucumber, and a few tufts of leafy green.

蝦 SHIO

Aguni Koshin Odo

■ **ALTERNATE NAME(S):** Koshin Odo Aguni; Aguni no shio; Aguni salt ■ **MAKER(S):** Koshin Odo ■ **TYPE:** shio ■ **CRYSTAL:** very fine, fullerenelike composites; highly irregular ■ **COLOR:** winter-moon white ■ **FLAVOR:** sweet; elusive; cucumber ■ **MOISTURE:** moderate ■ **ORIGIN:** Japan ■ **SUBSTITUTE(S):** Shinkai deep sea ■ **BEST WITH:** rare beef filet; sashimi; barely cooked vegetables like peas; long-cooked vegetables like ratatouille; pinched into a cup of coffee

---

Allow the lattice-shell structures of ever-diminishing geodesic shapes tumble from your fingers, glinting with razor definition too small to discern, minerals mimicking in silvered origami the preprotozoan sex life of cells. Close your eyes. There is texture, certainly. But your fingers can't find it. They say the blind have more sensitive skin. Perhaps this salt is visible only to the sightless.

Tasting Aguni is similar to looking at it. Deprived of knowledge of the world, you might think the ocean tastes this way, but it doesn't. Nothing of the wildness remains, none of the sinus-shaving turbulence. And yet the feeling is not calm either. Sprinkle it on steamed vegetables, liberally or sparingly, and you taste: vegetables, and steam, and the fork. Sprinkled on the tongue, you taste, of all things, your tongue! The flavor is a series of "nots," a process of elimination. But not that either; it is The Process of Elimination.

Aguni Island is far enough away from the larger islands of Okinawa that the seawater from which Aguni Koshin Odo is made is free of pollutants. Water is pumped from the ocean up to the top of a thirty-three-foot-tall tower and allowed to trickle down the thousands of fine bamboo branches that hang from its ceiling. The water that reaches the reservoir at the bottom of the tower is pumped back to the top and allowed to trickle down the bamboo again. The tower's perimeter is built of blocks with large perforations, which allow the sea breeze to blow through and start evaporating the seawater as it picks up subtle flavors from the bamboo. After about a week, the water sitting in the reservoir is a concentrate (*kansui*), about six times as saline as normal seawater. The kansui is then divided into two batches so that two different methods of evaporating the remaining water can be employed.

In the first method, which yields the majority of Aguni Koshin Odo produced, workers take round-the-clock shifts stirring the kansui with a long-handled wooden paddle in a wide, shallow pan (*hiragama*) over a low fire of driftwood and scrap wood. Wood is used instead of gas because, while it is more difficult to maintain a constant temperature with wood, wood generates a wavelength of radiation similar to that generated by the sun. The constant stirring and the shallowness of the hiragama allow for quick, even crystallization. After two days of this, when the crystals are well formed, the slushy solution is transferred to a dehydration tank, where the last of the water is slowly removed over four to five days. The longer the salt spends in this tank, the more nigari (bittern) will crystallize into the salt. Finally, the salt is pressed through sieves for two days to mature.

The second method takes longer but produces a more sought-after salt. The kansui sits in a shallow tank inside a greenhouse for solar evaporation. It takes anywhere from three weeks (in the summer) to two months (in the winter) for the salt to crystallize out. The salt made using this method is preferred by many Aguni salt fans for its larger crystals and subtle taste, but is not easily found outside of Japan.

ODO'S EXPERIMENT

We think of seawater as salt water, but when we think of salt, we think of just one thing: sodium chloride. In truth, the sea contains many salts—and many other things. Sodium chloride represents only about 78 percent of the mineral content of seawater, yet refined salt is very nearly 100 percent sodium chloride. In other words, the mineral content of refined salt is wildly disparate from that of seawater, in which life thrives.

The salt maker Koshin Odo once performed an experiment to explore the value of natural salt to living organisms. He picked up a bunch of crabs off the beach. He put some of them in salt water made from a refined salt manufactured through ion exchange and vacuum evaporation. The crabs died almost right away. Some of the crabs he put in salt water made by combining fresh water and unrefined rock salt. The crabs died within two days. Then he made salt water using some of his own Aguni salt. The crabs lived. Furthermore, the aquarium holding the crabs began to produce more life, presumably from microscopic organisms already living on the crabs. Koshin Odo believes that the same subtle chemistry essential for the very survival of marine animals offers benefits to humans as well. ■

Amabito no Moshio

■ **ALTERNATE NAME(S):** moshio; ancient sea salt ■ **MAKER(S):** Kamagari Bussan Company ■ **TYPE:** shio ■ **CRYSTAL:** brown sugar ■ **COLOR:** cappuccino sea foam ■ **FLAVOR:** chicken-fried ocean ■ **MOISTURE:** low ■ **ORIGIN:** Japan ■ **SUBSTITUTE(S):** none ■ **BEST WITH:** cucumber sandwich; scallop sashimi; popcorn

Cliff-diving off some North Pacific archipelago just before a summer tempest provides the same sudden surge of warmth braced by brine and wind that amabito no moshio does—except amabito no moshio is like cliff-diving while eating a really good tuna fish sandwich. Amabito no Moshio brings to unassertive foods the definition that you would expect from any good salt, but it does so with a prejudice toward the savory. The salt's unique umami character—deriving from an infusion of seaweed—lends astringent foods richness and rich foods freshness. It is dry, but with a shio's typical fine, complexly articulated crystals and a luxurious beige patina like the interior of a Ferrari.

Amabito no Moshio is an adaptation of a 2,500-year-old salt-making method. In ancient times, salt would be hauled to shore and allowed to dry, sprayed with saltwater, and dried again, until the salt-encrusted seaweed could be rinsed into a concentrated brine and boiled over a wood fire for a salt that is high in seaweed ash. In 1984, archeological digging revealed a salt-making pot from the third or fourth century CE; that pot inspired the resurrection of this ancient salt-making tradition.

On Kami-Kamagari Island, seawater is collected and allowed to partially evaporate. Hon'dawara seaweed is then added to the brine to impart flavor and minerals. After the seaweed is removed, the brine is heated in an iron kettle and evaporated into a slurry. The slurry is spun in a centrifuge to remove most of the nigari (bittern), and then stirred over an open fire to evaporate off the remaining water and crystallize the remaining magnesium salts. The resulting salt is as supple as brown sugar and as savory as bonito-flavored potato chips.

It's easy to imagine making amabito no moshio your default salt for all savory dishes. Trout, pike, carp, hen, veal, pork, rice, pasta, potatoes, sunchoke, broccoli rabe, cheeses, yogurt—finding foods that would benefit from its umami minerality basically involves drawing up a shopping list. Sweets benefit from moshio as well— try it on 70 percent dark chocolate, or dusted on a chocolate soufflé.

Okinawa Shima Masu

■ **ALTERNATE NAME(S):** n/a ■ **MAKER(S):** various ■ **TYPE:** shio ■ **CRYSTAL:** fine; granular; slightly irregular ■ **COLOR:** wet paper white ■ **FLAVOR:** bitter; pickle; dull ■ **MOISTURE:** moderate ■ **ORIGIN:** Japan ■ **SUBSTITUTE(S):** Taiwan Yes Salt, cheap traditional sea salt ■ **BEST WITH:** soups; stews; braised meats and vegetables

Intense, slightly bitter, with clunky crystals that neither diminish nor heighten perception, this is a salt with no hope for glory. But then . . .

Oyakodon and Katsudon, two Titans of Japanese cuisine, wade through the early morning mist that mingles with the smoking wreckage of the city. The police commissioner, weary and smudged with grime, struggles to maintain an air of calm, lest the city sink into despair. How to tame these two rampaging monsters as they battle with indifferent ferocity across the broken land? As the commissioner strains to hear another dire report crackling from his walkie-talkie, little Chihiro emerges from the chaos of the crowded shelter, takes the commissioner's hand, and pours into it a fine, moist substance, radiant white against his unwashed skin. Could this be the answer? A flash of joy crosses the commissioner's face; he barks orders, starts to rush off, but suddenly remembers the young girl, little Chihiro. Kneeling down, he touches her chin, nods gravely to her: "Young one, you have saved us all."

CHIHIRO'S GIFT

Oyakodon and katsudon, two of Japan's most popular foods, are among a diverse family of foods called *donburi*—basically a protein piled on top of a bowl of rice, served with a few strips of nori seaweed. They are fast food in every sense of the term: batches of premade stew and rice, shoveled unceremoniously into the mouth. What salt do we dare dispense with such blithely consumed food? Now you know the answer. ■

Okunoto Endenmura

- **ALTERNATE NAMES:** not disclosed ▪ **MAKER:** not disclosed ▪ **TYPE:** shio ▪ **CRYSTAL:** fragments of dynamited abacus ▪ **COLOR:** x-rays of chrome ▪ **FLAVOR:** giant breaking waves over rocks, storm breeze, kelp, abandoned ship ▪ **MOISTURE:** moderate ▪ **ORIGIN:** Japan ▪ **SUBSTITUTES:** Shinkai deep sea salt, Aguni No Shio ▪ **BEST WITH:** shellfish, raw fish, beef carpaccio, rice and noodle dishes, eggs

Showering before dawn, lights flipped off, water cascading invisibly as you unconsciously lather and rinse your body, the rush of thoughts that courses through your mind can resemble the REM sleep you emerged from just minutes earlier. Okunoto Endenmura has the intensity of a dream's nocturnal rampage, but turns the mind toward action: cooking breakfast, diving into work, making love, rotating your tires. The salt is so brawny and reckless and at the same time so solicitous and cadenced that food reveals to it the unconscious purpose of its existence with simple clarity and perspective.

Okunoto Endenmura is a bear to make, and the fact that it exists at all is a testament to the intensity of Japan's cultural ties to salt. The *shio hama* or "salt beaches" of the Noto peninsula are the unassuming artifacts of the earliest salt making traditions, the only place where you can see in action Japan's once-dominant *Agehama-shiki* method. Seawater is repeatedly sprayed over sand-covered salt fields (*enden*), causing the crystallization of salt over the sand. More seawater is poured onto the salt-crusted beach to create a concentrated brine (*kansui*) that is then evaporated over a wood fire in a large pot (*kama*).

Practiced nowhere else in Japan today, *Agehama-shiki* was a major industry by 1627 when salt was monopolized by the Kaga clan. The method continued until 1905 when techniques such as *Ryuka-shiki*, employing the wind to evaporate sea water, were increasingly substituted. In 1959 salt production laws passed signaling the demise of the *Agehama* methods. But the death blow didn't come until 1971, when the Japanese government abolished all artisan methods and mandated ion-exchange membrane electro-dialysis salt production nationally.

In 2008, a simmering popular interest in posterity (and the tourism that could be spurred by it) led the government to give the Kakuhana household in Suzu special permission to make salt using the region's traditional methods. Production is as limited.

Sara-shio

- **ALTERNATE NAME(S):** none ■ **MAKER(S):** n/a ■ **TYPE:** shio ■ **CRYSTAL:** powdered milk ■ **COLOR:** fried egg whites ■ **FLAVOR:** fruit; aspartame; candy wrapper ■ **MOISTURE:** very low ■ **ORIGIN:** Japan
- **SUBSTITUTE(S):** Uminosei Yakishio Syokutakubin ■ **BEST WITH:** rice; noodles; rice candy

Sara-shio is crystallized over fire in open pans from seawater collected off of Oshima Island. Its fine crystals stop just short of the texture of talc, and with no moisture to alter the course of things, they vanish instantly on contact with food or tongue. As with the great Japanese sea salts, like Shinkai deep sea salt, sara-shio offers near-microscopic fronts of crystalline mystery to ply your senses. The flavor it brings is elegant and multifaceted, yet provocatively incomplete. Tasting it on a rice ball or sprinkled directly on your tongue, you sense fervent, reaching desire, and half expect something more to come. It may bother you, but there is nothing to be done about it: something is flirting with you, just out of reach. The opulent pleasure that might be yours touches your wrist and beckons you onward—but to where? There is a residue of loneliness.

JAPANESE DEPTH PERCEPTION

The Japanese, surrounded by oceans on all sides, study the seas much as farmers observe the plains. They are seekers of its most elusive mysteries and connoisseurs of its most refined pleasures. What might pass as a nuanced idea in the West is a self-evident fact in Japan. The ocean's currents are a case in point. The Japanese (and their island neighbors the Taiwanese as well) have observed that water drawn from different ocean locations and depths imparts different flavors and nutritional values to the salts produced from it. Deep sea currents are driven by different sources than the better known, shallower currents above 650 feet. Shallow currents are often propelled by atmospheric conditions, causing them to move quickly. Deep sea currents are driven by differences in density in different regions of the ocean (these are caused by differences in temperature and—surprise, surprise—salinity), and move much more slowly than surface currents. It is estimated that it takes two thousand years for deep sea currents to complete a cycle, meaning that much of the water at significant depths is believed to be free of industrial contaminants (some of the water in these deep sea currents has likely been below a depth of 650 feet since before the advent of human industry). It is also believed by some that these currents' slow travel along extremely cold landmasses aids in the accumulation of an ideal mineral solution. ■

Shinkai Deep Sea

- **ALTERNATE NAME(S):** none ■ **MAKER(S):** n/a ■ **TYPE:** shio
- **CRYSTAL:** fibroradiated fronds of glauconitic minerals . . . impenetrable ■ **COLOR:** bottomless polar white, like partially melted paraffin ■ **FLAVOR:** luminescent scoop of Arctic snow brought into a warm kitchen; clear with ineffable sweetness ■ **MOISTURE:** moderate ■ **ORIGIN:** Japan
- **SUBSTITUTE(S):** none, but Aguni Koshin Odo in a pinch
- **BEST WITH:** raw or rare Kobe beef; oysters on the half-shell

A white flash, a trembling afterglow, a whisper dissipating, then . . . nothing. A small pinch of Shinkai deep sea salt strikes the tongue with all the subtlety of a lightning bolt, tripping across the taste buds like some giant circuit breaker that sends the brain's voltage into the ether. A tumultuous ocean brininess (see sidebar, page 160) looms threateningly, then slides into a cleansing breeze that slowly ebbs and finally, just before it dies away altogether, asserts itself with a faint brambly-fruity note, like berries ripening in a thicket somewhere on the other side of a sand dune. It is impossible to describe Shinkai without drawing references from just beyond the horizon. Shinkai tastes like salt distilled from our deepest human essence: pure, powerful, innocent, and existentially happy.

As with many finishing salts, it is Shinkai's delicate crystals combined with abundant residual moisture that lend the salt its wild-yet-measured behavior. The fine flakes seek to dissolve in a rush of passion, succumbing to the moisture of the mouth, but the moisture trapped in the flakes slows things down ever so slightly. The effect is flawless shapes revealed in extraordinarily clean lines, secrets in contour.

Shinkai produces such a lush palette of flavors that condiments and fancy cooking techniques—indeed any elaboration—become unnecessary. Serve it on sashimi or carpaccio, and additional seasonings are a distraction, or even counter-productive. Generally speaking, the salt's mineral combination is best on fatty foods such as dark-fleshed fish, well-marbled meats, and fried vegetables. It also lends depth to chocolate and dairy dishes. While the beauty and delicacy of Shinkai suggest that it is best used as a finishing salt, it brings unsurpassed elegance when dissolved into delicate broths such as miso. Shinkai should not be used on astringent vegetables, such as asparagus, or acidic fruits, such as citrus. It can turn bitter in combination with such tastes.

THE MAKING OF A MASTERPIECE: THE THREE MUSES OF THE SALT WORLD

An appreciation for the care that goes into making Shinkai deep sea salt may help prepare you for the mad rush of tasting it (and the equally mad feeling that may strike when you first encounter its price tag). The process for making Shinkai was developed by a man named Shoji Koyachi; it originated in a small research project aimed at bring a salt-making business back to what had been a historic salt-producing region. While salt has been produced in Noto since the sixteenth century, industrial salt manufacturing brought an end to artisan production by the beginning of the twentieth century. After three years of research and development, he founded the Shinkai Shio Sangyo Company in 1998 to initiate production based on forgotten techniques.

Shinkai comes from the Noto Peninsula, where the waters are among the cleanest in Japan. 20,000 gallons of ultraclean seawater is harvested four times a month from more than two thousand feet beneath the surface of the ocean at a location where warm and cold currents of the Pacific Ocean collide and salinity is especially desirable. Waters at this depth part of the high salinity halocline, especially rich in ions like magnesium. For a week to ten days, this salt water is sprayed over bamboo mats suspended from the ceiling and reaching to the floor of specially constructed greenhouses, evaporating its moisture, until it reaches 10 to 11 percent salinity. The brine is then placed in a large stainless steel cauldron and boiled vigorously over a wood fire, to a concentration of 20 percent salinity. Next, the concentrated brine is tended constantly as it is slowly simmered over a low wood fire for twenty-five hours. A mound of salt slowly emerges from the steaming cauldron. This is raked off by hand and carefully dried.

The result is a single four-hundred-pound batch of salt that is exceptionally rich in minerals, with 16.2 percent of its content comprised of trace elements and moisture. The primary elements, magnesium (0.80 percent), calcium (0.19 percent), and potassium (0.40 percent), with dozens more in lesser quantities, give shape to a cleansing freshness on the palate, a subdued sweetness that commingles easily with the gentle turmoil of ocean bitterness. The crystals are formed in exceptionally fine, almost invisible flakes. Three women do virtually all the work: Junko Tsunetoshi, Tadako Shimo, and Eiko Miyashita. Dazzling and at the same time delicate, wild and yet measured, Shinkai is the distilled taste of nature's majesty coupled with human craftsmanship. ■

ROCK SALT

Bolivian Rose (Coarse)

- **ALTERNATE NAME(S):** Andes Mountain Rose ▪ **MAKER(S):** various ▪ **TYPE:** rock ▪ **CRYSTAL:** gravel
- **COLOR:** liquid cotton candy ▪ **FLAVOR:** salt spring with a lollipop dissolving at the bottom
- **MOISTURE:** none ▪ **ORIGIN:** Bolivia ▪ **SUBSTITUTE(S):** Himalayan pink ▪ **BEST WITH:** chiles rellenos; fried plantains; river trout fried in butter

---

If you believe that satisfying passions is an unnecessary indulgence, this salt is not for you. If you had a million dollars and you spent it all on Bolivian Rose, you might come away with more than you need, but you would still need all of it. When it walks into the room, you might have a hard time not staring at it in an inappropriate manner.

Bolivian Rose is not to be confused with the evaporative salt from the Salar de Uyuni, the vast remains of a prehistoric salt lake that once covered most of southwestern Bolivia. But Salar de Uyuni offers a glimpse at the origins of Bolivian Rose. A chalk-colored crust of a salt pan formed from an ocean evaporated eons ago was buried under ten thousand feet of shifting continental plates, only to emerge three million years later as a stone that can be ground up and eaten with butter-fried river trout like so many cranberry and tangerine capsules of time.

Large crystals of Bolivian Rose resist the mouth's first overtures; they put up a fuss, then shyly relinquish their subtle flavors. Bolivian Rose is surprisingly mild for a quarried salt, well-balanced and slightly sweet, with a clean finish. Tasted on its own, it has a consistent silky sweetness that goes on and on and on, fading imperceptibly until you suddenly recognize it isn't there at all—sort of like Girl Scouts knocking politely at the door to sell you their cookies, leaving you something nice to show for your time, then disappearing without a fuss.

In combination with food, Bolivian Rose provides a bold rush typical of rock salts, but the rush is one of mirth rather than of fury. The secret lies in the salt's mineral makeup: it's naturally rich in calcium and potassium with about 0.7 percent of each by content, and contains lots of magnesium as well, with trace amounts of iron and other minerals. Compare Bolivian Rose to Himalayan pink, and you will experience as clearly as possible the amazing differences that can arise from the subtle mineral combinations harbored in a salt crystal. Himalayan pink is as intense and spicy as Bolivian Rose is clean and sweet. Try Bolivian Rose on seafood, ceviche, and salads of cucumber, lime, and chiles.

Bolivian Rose can be bought as a fine or coarse grind. Buying it coarse gives you the opportunity to pound it in a mortar and pestle or grind it in an adjustable mill to the desired grain size. Once ground up, the salt's exceptional physical beauty is lost, shattered into a dull pink powder. Such is the ephemeral beauty of even the most eternal of salts.

Himalayan Pink

- **ALTERNATE NAME(S):** Himalayan rock salt, sendha namak (India), Pakistani namak (India) ▪ **MAKER(S):** various
- **TYPE:** rock ▪ **CRYSTAL:** pebbles ▪ **COLOR:** transparent to blood red ▪ **FLAVOR:** pungent, with lasting spicy heat over a lean mineral body ▪ **MOISTURE:** none ▪ **ORIGIN:** Pakistan
- **SUBSTITUTE(S):** Bolivian Rose; Jurassic salt ▪ **BEST WITH:** negroni cocktail rim; roasted game birds; venison or buffalo steaks; salt brittle; shaved over green apple or sashimi white fish or shellfish

Life is not all about wholesomeness. There is an edge to our existence, and explorers of that edge come to appreciate its flavor. It tastes like fun, fear, bubbling laughter. The irony of Himalayan pink salt is that it is widely marketed as a wholesome health food, a miracle mind-and-body relaxant, a purifying tonic. While neither affirming or disputing these claims and perceptions, it is worth mentioning that they are beside the point. Himalayan salt is crazy. It is fun. It is ancient, even in cosmological terms; comes from a savage wilderness; glows with brooding intensity; lends itself to as many creative uses as any salt on the planet; and lets loose its unique spicy-hot pungency with all the subtlety of a medieval army—and with twice the ingenuity.

Himalayan pink salt is mined from the south-facing scarp of the Potwar Plateau in the Punjab region of northern Pakistan, between the Indus and Jhelum Rivers. Buried amid an unruly jumble of sedimentary rocks spanning much of the Paleozoic era—from the Cambrian period (543 to 490 million years ago) to the Upper Carboniferous period (320 to 290 million years ago)—folded up among deposits of dolomite and beds of oil-shale, vast strata of salt up to eight hundred feet thick penetrate deep into the earth, swirled into bands of marl and gypsum.

For at least two millennia, men have dug these mountains for salt, cutting and hauling it by hand for transport to the cities below. The salt that comes from these mines is beautiful, and remarkably pure, ranging from 99 to 97 percent sodium chloride. The hills surrounding Pakistan's Khewra salt mine harbor some 6.7 billion tons of rock salt reserves, an estimated 220 million of which are deemed commercially accessible within the current extent of the mine. There are several mines in the area, making Pakistan's salt resources effectively unlimited.

Jurassic Salt

■ **ALTERNATE NAME(S):** Real Salt ■ **MAKER(S):** Redmond ■ **TYPE:** rock ■ **CRYSTAL:** aquarium gravel ■ **COLOR:** calico ■ **FLAVOR:** hot; flat; big ■ **MOISTURE:** none ■ **ORIGIN:** United States ■ **SUBSTITUTE(S):** Himalayan pink ■ **BEST WITH:** stews and soups; pasta water; pickling vegetables

The Cyclops ate fat rams by the handful for snacks, gobbled up men whole and screaming, armor and all. He was purported to have thrown boulders the size of chariots hundreds of yards out to sea in blind fury against nobody. I know what salt Cyclops preferred.

Moistureless, rock-hard, symmetrical as camphor pellets, Jurassic salt crystals lean into your mouth like a bear scratching its haunches on a tree—and with the same disconcerting tendency for unwanted friendliness, the flavor taking on a mildness on the back of the tongue and refusing to leave. Though balanced, with only a hint of bitterness, its amiability cannot escape a generally flat, heavy affect on the palate.

Jurassic salt is an unrefined mined salt, and as such has all the trace minerals that occur naturally in salt deposits. This deposit has sat for millions of years deep under the earth, where it has been heated and compressed into crystals of solid rock, and is utterly free of external contamination—at least until it is blasted from the mountain and hauled away in heavy trucks. To make rock this hard edible, it must be ground with industrial stone grinders. Regardless

CLASH OF THE TITANS: THE BEST KITCHEN SALT

Searching for a single salt that will do everything? A nice flake salt or fleur de sel will serve just about every imaginable application, from finishing to baking, but it will cost three to ten times more than equally wholesome and tasty alternatives that are simply less suited to finishing. Below, four major salts are considered in light of general kitchen usage. ■

	JURASSIC SALT	HIMALAYAN PINK	TRAPANI SALT	SEL GRIS
WHOLESOMENESS	~97 percent sodium chloride; virtually no contamination from industry or pollution	~97 percent sodium chloride; virtually no contamination from industry or pollution	~97.5 percent sodium chloride; very little contamination from industry or pollution	~85 percent sodium chloride; very little contamination from industry or pollution
ARTISANSHIP	Mined with industrial-scale heavy equipment; hand sorted; mechanically ground	Quarried by hand from the earth; hand sorted; mechanically ground	Harvested by hand from the sea; hand or mechanically ground	Harvested by hand from the sea
FINISHING SALT	Hard, rocky, dry crystals make this less than ideal, though radically better than, free-flowing iodized salt	Hard, rocky, dry crystals make this less than ideal, though radically better than, free-flowing iodized salt	Fine, dry, powdery crystals; easy to sprinkle but very quick to dissolve and gets lost in moister foods; overly hot and bright for many finishing uses	Supple, moist, crunchy crystals make this a great finishing salt on steaks, lamb, hearty vegetable dishes, and desserts; must be ground for other uses
COOKING SALT	Good for any use that will dissolve the salt completely, such as pasta water or sauces. Can be ground fine for baking	Good for any use that will dissolve the salt completely, such as pasta water or sauces. Can be ground fine for baking	Dissolves rapidly in food, is easy to dose. Bright, clean flavor makes it useful for delicate sauces, pickling. Dry crystals suitable for curing	Good for pasta water and sauces, it is also an excellent all-around cooking salt. Rub on roast meats and vegetables, or grind lightly for added sparkle when baking
APPEARANCE	Crystals lack the gemstonelike appeal of some quarried salts, but have a rustic charm	Luminescent pink crystals make this one of the most beautiful salts	Flat, deathly white crystals of no discernible shape	Depends. Dull gray crystals are rough, hearty, and may be unappealing to fussy sensibilities or for elegantly styled presentations. Opalescent sel gris can be beautiful
HOW LOCAL? (Assuming you're in North America.)	Produced in Southern Utah, 876 miles from Rugby, ND, the center of North America	Produced in Pakistan, 7,001 miles from Rugby, ND	Produced in Sicily, 5,183 miles from Rugby, ND, but just 1,194 miles from Rugby, England	Produced in Western France, 4,202 miles from Rugby, ND, and 352 miles from Rugby, England
ECONOMIC SYMPATHIES	An industrial company, no matter how well-disposed toward its workers, perhaps needs your support less than others	The folks in Pakistan are faced with dire economic and political challenges, and their emails and phone calls suggest a near-desperate need for our business	The Sicilians have overrun much of Italy and the rest of the world with their salt. That said, they're still artisans working in a traditional manner	When you buy sel gris, you are supporting policies for sound agricultural, cultural, and environmental stewardship the rest of the world can follow

of how finely it is ground (grinds range from aquarium-gravel coarse to beach-sand fine), the rockiness remains, so Jurassic salt crystals are primarily good for cooking when dissolving salt into food is intended.

Jurassic salt is a rock salt that enjoys considerable popularity, particularly among the health-conscious who seek the advantages of an unrefined salt over industrially harvested and refined sea salt. But Jurassic salt is not exactly "artisan salt." For a large order of road salt from a major customer, like the state of Colorado, sixty rail cars of road salt will rumble out from the salt mine, each car carrying a hundred tons of salt. Nonetheless, the salt may be a good fit for some people: relatively devoid of industrial contamination, it is unrefined, has a flavor that is decent enough, and is dang interesting to look at.

Kala Namak

- **ALTERNATE NAME(S):** black salt; Indian black salt; sanchal ▪ **MAKER(S):** various ▪ **TYPE:** rock
- **CRYSTAL:** fine powder to large rocks ▪ **COLOR:** oxblood ▪ **FLAVOR:** volcano; egg; dragon breath
- **MOISTURE:** none ▪ **ORIGINS:** India; Pakistan ▪ **SUBSTITUTE(S):** Korean bamboo salt ▪ **BEST WITH:** chaats; popcorn; fruit salad

O Ganesha, Lord of Beginnings, Remover of Obstacles, deva of the intellect and of wisdom. We beseech you: what food is also a medicine, curing ills even as it brings umami to the aqueous cucumber, imparts mouthwatering heartiness to popcorn, requites the vegans' hankering for oöspheric savoriness on their tofu, and makes fruit salads levitate? What whitens our teeth as it freshens our breath? And, o Ganesha, what is black and white and red all over?

In rock form, kala namak is dark purple bordering on black. Ground up fine and seen up close, it is pink bordering on white. But it is pink leaning toward red when sprinkled on food.

Kala namak is ancient, sung of in ancient Vedic hymns, and identified by Maharishi Charak, the 300 BCE father of ayurvedic medicine. Ayurvedic healers claim that kala namak possesses several therapeutic qualities, and they use it to pacify the bowels. As a digestive remedy, a fresh piece of ginger is soaked in lime juice spiced with kala namak, which is purported to induce salivation and digestive enzyme production. Kala namak is also claimed to aid in both appetite loss and obesity. The salt is used in medicinal formulas for combating hysteria. In combination with a number of herbs, it can be crushed into a powder believed to be good for dental hygiene. A common dentifrice includes kala namak mixed with alum or white oak bark powder, black pepper powder, turmeric and a dash of camphor or clove oil.

Although relatively uncommon in the West, kala namak is widely used in Indian cuisine, particularly in the north. The salt is standard in chaats (nibbles and tidbits of various forms sold from carts on practically any street corner in urban India) and in the summer drink jal jeera. But kala namak easily transcends cultural boundaries. It is exquisite and addictive on popcorn, naan, focaccia, or bagels.

Kala namak is made from pink rock salt (*sendha namak*) from Pakistan; it is imported into India in bulk by Indian companies, though they are loath to disclose their sources. The sendha namak is converted into kala namak using a centuries-old process. Heated in the presence of spices until it melts, the resultant compound is cooled, stored, and aged. When finished, the salt is rich in iron, sulfur, and many other elements and compounds. So ask yourself, are you worth your kala namak? You know the answer.

Mongolian Blue Steppes

■ **ALTERNATE NAME(S):** jamts davs ■ **MAKER(S):** various ■ **TYPE:** rock ■ **CRYSTAL:** coarse gravel; chunks of rock; sculpted pie wedges ■ **COLOR:** blood orange; dawn reflected off wet pavement ■ **FLAVOR:** sweet; starchy; complex minerals ■ **MOISTURE:** none ■ **ORIGIN:** Mongolia ■ **SUBSTITUTE(S):** Andes mountain rose ■ **BEST WITH:** seafood pasta, pasta with truffles; lemon and salt-crusted chicken thighs stuffed with cheese and herbs; guacamole and chips; duck confit crostinis; venison carpaccio

If you had only one seasoning for your kitchen, what would it be? The Mongolians, over millennia of hardship and privation, chose salt. Or rather, it chose them. The Mongolian steppes, a vast expanse of highland savannas, offer relatively little in the way of herbs and spices. Saline lakes provide one source of salt, but the most characteristic salt of Mongolia has to be rock salt, which serves not just human needs but those of the livestock tended by these nomadic herders as well.

In addition to an intensely saline lake, the great northern basin of Uvs Nuur features deposits of rock salt of the most astonishing colors, ranging from tangerine to candied orange and from steely gray to predawn blue. Chunks of the salt are often left in their coarse, rocky form, and then shaved atop everything from a glass of mare's milk to spit-roasted meats. It can even be carved into beautiful, eminently giftable shapes that are easy to handle and easy to pack.

Some anthropologists theorize that early Neolithic people were drawn into the land that is now Mongolia by its salt resources. Grating a powdery mist of minerally, sweetly vegetal salt over the tongue gives us an idea of the primordial draw salt must have had on the first settlers of the Mongolian steppes. This is one of the most complex and unabashedly delicious salts on the planet.

Persian Blue

■ **ALTERNATE NAME(S):** none ■ **MAKER(S):** various ■ **TYPE:** rock ■ **CRYSTAL:** gravel ■ **COLOR:** sky-transparency studded with stars of tanzanite and sapphire ■ **FLAVOR:** mild; silken sweetness of Popsicle on edge of porcelain cup ■ **MOISTURE:** none ■ **ORIGIN:** Iran ■ **SUBSTITUTE(S):** Himalayan pink ■ **BEST WITH:** parsnip puree; poached perch; pears

There is no nightlife in Tehran. The metropolis shuts down at midnight; people go to bed. The snowcapped crest of Mount Damavand puffs sulfur clouds like an old man blowing smoke rings at the silver moon. But within this nocturnal austerity there lurks a salt, one with a private jet and a posse. Sprinkled over Champagne from an amulet strung around the neck of a Nubian supermodel in a swishy nightclub in Moscow, Persian blue salt is a culinary bauble: rare, beautiful, and gracefully useless.

Certain mines in Mongolia, Poland, and Iran produce salts across a spectrum of blues, from gunmetal blue to topaz to purplish tanzanite to deepest sapphire. While many bluish colors can appear in chunks and even whole veins of salt, the most ferocious peacock hues, like those of Persian blue, appear only in glints suggestive of mystery. Some minerals are idiochromatic, meaning their composition is what colors them. Salt, clear as eternity, is not idiochromatic. Salt can be either allochromatic, meaning it takes its colors from trace impurities in its composition or from defects in its structure; or it is pseudochromatic, meaning its colors are due to tricks played by light as it diffracts along internal flaws. Persian blue's colors are a bit of a mystery, possibly taking their tint either from an uncanny interaction between sylvite (potassium chloride), dispersed metallic sodium, and other minerals alloying the salt, or from the diffraction of light through the crystals, or both.

The enigma of the salt's colors is counterbalanced by its pedestrian, down-to-earth flavor. The grains are hard as any rock salt, with a faintly sharp but clean taste—milder than Himalayan salts, though with a similar unidimensionality. An overtly vampire-proof dish, like roasted garlic puree on a halibut steak, would be an acceptable volunteer from a flavor standpoint. Rim a cocktail glass with it; scatter it on fish carpaccio; or take it to bed to ogle under the beam of a flashlight, muttering softy in Russian.

Salzburg Rock Salt

- **ALTERNATE NAME(S):** Altaussee Stone; Austrian rock salt; Hallein rock salt; Hallstatt rock salt
- **MAKER(S):** various ▪ **TYPE:** rock ▪ **CRYSTAL:** gravel ▪ **COLOR:** russet breadcrumbs ▪ **FLAVOR:** warmed, newly cracked granite ▪ **MOISTURE:** none ▪ **ORIGIN:** Austria ▪ **SUBSTITUTE(S):** Jurassic salt ▪ **BEST WITH:** steamed potatoes; buttered dinner rolls; cheese and nutmeg spätzle

A Neolithic sadness glimmers in the crystals of Salzburg rock salt: the deep light of longing and forgetfulness. Time slides to a halt. Imagine Audrey Hepburn as the cosmically beautiful young princess in *Roman Holiday*, klieg lights glittering in her murky eyes, poetry lilting off her half-sleeping lips. Tasting the sizzling coolness of Salzburg rock salt, you are her urbane and handsome chaperone, wise in the world but caught off-guard by an apparition who makes the present vanish. Befuddled, mankind's prehistory looms like a  dark cloud over the brief spark of your own life. This all must take place in your imagination, however, as the culturally pregnant Salzburg rock salt offers only a muted spicy mineral flavor and a rock salt's indifferent hardness.

Salzburg rock salt and other more or less identical rock salts formerly or presently produced by the mines of Hallstatt, Hallein, and other towns in the Salzkammergut region can be named rather freely, but all the colorful, natural-looking rock salts you come across there are more or less identical. This is convenient, because finding any at all can be challenging. Solution mining has replaced rock-salt mining over time as the veins of 80 percent or purer salt were depleted, leaving only clay-dense veins of just 40 percent salt open for exploitation.

A stag horn pickax found in 1838 suggests that salt may have been mined in the region in 5000 BCE, and Celtic settlers appear to have mined salt since the fifteenth century BCE, hauling oxhide bags laden with rock salt from the depths of the earth on their backs or on pack animals. Salt was harvested for local use and trade abroad from the salt springs in the region by Celtic settlers at least since 700 BCE, and rock salt pulled from veins in the mountains brought a sustained population boom to the area well before the early Middle Ages. Salt also brought war, resulting in Bavaria and other states taking control of the mines' wealth; the poverty of the salt miners became proverbial. Altaussee is one of the few old mines still making rock salt, a relict of the Celts who first settled there and saw beauty in stones of salt.

Timbuktu Salt

■ **ALTERNATE NAME(S):** Sel de l'Azalaï; Mali salt, Sahara desert salt ■ **MAKER(S):** various ■ **TYPE:** rock ■ **CRYSTAL:** tailings of dune sand ■ **COLOR:** lightbulb ■ **FLAVOR:** clean; warm stones ■ **MOISTURE:** none ■ **ORIGIN:** Mali ■ **SUBSTITUTE(S):** Jurassic salt ■ **BEST WITH:** curries; lamb; couscous; fresh fruit; salt-preserving lemons

Nature writes its poetry in water and salt, the two elements that have brought so much human suffering and happiness. Like suffering and happiness, water and salt can also be lost to time. Two hundred and twenty million years ago, much of what makes up the Sahara Desert today was an ocean.

Beneath the desert sands in northern Mali, the sea's petrified remnants are cut from low-ceilinged excavations and expertly cleaved into large tablets. Tuareg nomads lead caravans of a hundred camels with hundred-pound slabs of salt strapped to each flank on the five-hundred-mile trek over sand dunes and hardscrabble from the Taoudenni mines in heart of the desert to Timbuktu—an ancient caravan called the Azalaï. There the salt is rinsed, pounded in ebony mortars, and packaged. Taoudenni produces several grades of salt: grayish salt for animals; pale for regional use; and mottle white for export.

For millennia the salt trade made Timbuktu a crossroads of Saharan Africa, eventually leading to the city's emergence as one of the world's leading centers of Arab scholarship and literary production. Today, the universities and temples of Timbuktu seem on the brink of being consumed forever by the brutal and increasingly vast desert.

UNCONVENTIONAL SALT

Icelandic Hot Spings

- **ALTERNATE NAME(S):** n/a ■ **MAKER:** Reykjanessalt Ltd. ■ **TYPE:** unconventional ■ **CRYSTAL:** dried fudge
- **COLOR:** rice paper cinders ■ **FLAVOR:** scissors, paper, rocks ■ **MOISTURE:** moderate ■ **ORIGIN:** Iceland
- **SUBSTITUTE(S):** potassium salt ■ **BEST WITH:** reindeer, penguin

The idea of a low-sodium salt has been circulating for some time. The problem, of course, is that the reason we like salt in the first place is that we are wired to crave sodium. In fact, the wiring itself is made of sodium, the positively charged ion that conducts the impulses of life. Our craving for the sodium in salt is inviolable. Some folks in Iceland decided to take the salts that normally play only minor roles in natural salt and make them major constituents in a culinary salt. From a 4,724-foot-deep borehole, 563°F geothermal brine is pumped into a wild-looking array of vacuum evaporators and crystallizers powered by geothermal energy. A salt of 71 percent $NaCl$, 11 percent $MgCl$, 6 percent $MgSO_4$, 3 percent $CaCl_2$, 3 percent other minerals (including silica and calcium), and 6 percent moisture results. It is a sensation to embrace, an alkaline-tasting oddity reminiscent of chocolate with all the flavor, mouth-feel, aroma, and color sucked out of it, leaving only an ashen memory in its place. People love it.

South African Pearl

- **ALTERNATE NAME(S):** n/a ■ **MAKER(S):** n/a ■ **TYPE:** unconventional ■ **CRYSTAL:** hammered BB pellets
- **COLOR:** candlelit cream ■ **FLAVOR:** intense; faint dry bark; hot finish ■ **MOISTURE:** low ■ **ORIGIN:** South Africa ■ **SUBSTITUTE(S):** none ■ **BEST WITH:** citrus and mint salad; steamed snow peas

Biting into South African Pearl will give you an idea of how a giant might feel biting into a geode that has been scrupulously boiled to soften it: the fascinating but slightly infuriating sensation of an innocuous little pellet that powderizes recklessly in a spangle of intensity.

South African Pearl is basically a snowball of powdered salt. As you bite, the salt's pearllike shape vanishes before you can identify its presence; only the finest film of salt remains, and this, too, dissolves instantly into whatever moisture is present, be it your food or your mouth. My best experience with this salt has been to use it as a finishing salt at the table on the barely moist flesh of steamed vegetables. On chunks of sautéed fish it provokes thoughts of fish roe, and maximizes its tactile and visual pleasures. Invite your guests to ogle and touch it, then roll the little spheres off the tops of their fingers to fall to their plates. The salt will either bounce off dry ingredients and roll around the plate, or stick to moist ingredients and quickly dissolve, depending on its chance encounters.

An alternate way to understand this salt requires a shift in thought. Advanced mathematics postulates that time-space is actually folded, so that planes of one four-dimensional sheet of reality are actually stretched and flexed to form different shapes, like a bow on a prettily wrapped package. In this same perfectly unintuitive and utterly ridiculous way, these little orbs can be flakes. Drop one on the glistening petal of your well-dressed green salad, take a bite, and pop! a snap of saltiness not unlike something you will experience with Maldon flake sea salt—albeit devoid of crispy texture. Think of it as a flake salt from another universe.

The salt is made by introducing a powder of fine moist sea salt into a drum and then rotating the drum, sending avalanches of salt down the sides so that bits of salt coalesce and roll, forming little white balls in much the same way you might roll up snow to make a snowman. The result is white pellets that make formidable projectiles. It would be unwise to leave this salt unattended in the presence of children familiar with the fine art of shooting spitballs.

MODIFIED SALT

Amethyst Bamboo Salt 9x

- **ALTERNATE NAME(S):** 9x bamboo salt; juk-yom; jook-yeom; ja-jook-yeom ■ **MAKER(S):** n/a ■ **TYPE:** sel gris; roasted
- **CRYSTAL:** shattered gemstone ■ **COLOR:** amethyst
- **FLAVOR:** soft-boiled quail egg ■ **MOISTURE:** none ■ **ORIGIN:** Korea ■ **SUBSTITUTE(S):** 9x bamboo salt; in a pinch, kala namak ■ **BEST WITH:** braised pork belly with green onions (*dwejigogi pyeonyook*); bread dipped in olive oil; spicy fried or grilled fish

Amethyst Bamboo Salt 9x smells like something dragons must use to season their victims before eating them. The salt belongs to the crowded and opinionated family of East Asian foods that are prized not just for their flavor, but also for their efficacy. In other words, they are expected to do something beyond just taste good. The salt is recognized for its antioxidant qualities and is highly prized in Taoist medicine: it is believed to inhibit the growth of cancer cells, cure fevers, relieve edema, disinfect, promote antibacterial activity (bamboo salt water washes are used as a cure for acne), and to detoxify by counteracting poisons, particularly heavy metals. Its anti-inflammatory effects have been studied scientifically. Amethyst Bamboo Salt 9x also stimulates qi, which translates as both mental and physical vigor. But what is most intriguing to a Western practitioner is that the salt tastes totally crazy.

Savory, sweet, smoky, seaweed, and a myriad of weird, hard-to-identify flavors are gobbled up by a ravenous, intensely sulfuric volcanic egginess. If your mouth has a hard time of it, that's nothing compared to what the salt has been through. Bamboo salt is made by putting gray sea salt in cylinders of three-year-old bamboo, capping them with special yellow clay, and roasting them in a furnace fired by pine firewood and resin at above 1000°F for eight hours. This process is repeated eight times. At a final ninth firing, the salt is heated to 1500°F, at which point it melts and pours forth like a breath of liquid fire, then cools into amber, red, black, blue, and (the most treasured) amethyst colored crystals.

The 9x salts are often consumed dissolved in water as a tonic, but can also be pulvarized and eaten on food or mixed with regular sea salt or a lesser bamboo salt to attenuate their intensity in daily culinary use. A little goes a long way. Spicy sauces, pickled and fermented foods, and dumplings are its natural compatriots. Try it on chicken breast, broccoli, and bamboo shoots stir-fried with some sesame oil.

Black Truffle

■ **ALTERNATE NAME(S):** truffle salt; sale al tartufo; sel aux truffes ■ **MAKER(S):** various ■ **TYPE:** traditional; infused/ blended ■ **CRYSTAL:** fine; slightly varied ■ **COLOR:** speckled beach ■ **FLAVOR:** truffle ■ **MOISTURE:** very low ■ **ORIGINS:** Italy; France ■ **SUBSTITUTE(S):** none ■ **BEST WITH:** eggs; mushrooms; steak; French fries; popcorn

Men and women wise in the ways of animals contend that pigs are highly intelligent. If the acuity of the nose is any indication of the perspicacity of the mind, pigs are surely geniuses. They are expert at scenting, unearthing, and wolfing down the finest things in life, from tubers and berries to eggs and birds, but the truffle is the pièce de résistance of the porcine probiscus. Truffles are found in Oregon and Washington, though the best—aromatic on a level unequalled by any other food—live in France and Italy.

Wild boar are not native to North America, no doubt because of the lack of great truffles. Humans love truffles, too. While the boar's earnest passion for truffles is evidenced by the continents upon which it deigns to live, we express our passion with our wallets. Great truffles sell for thousands of dollars a pound. In fact, few of us can afford to buy one. This is where truffle salt comes to the rescue. It is the most cost-effective way to keep truffles in your diet. A pinch of truffle salt made from French black truffles or Italian white truffles costs pennies but delivers a good measure of the aromatic impact of a freshly sliced truffle. While the human passion for truffles puts us among the smarter animals of the planet, our invention of truffle salt is as good an example as any of what sets us near the top.

Buying tip: Most of the white truffle salts I have tasted are cloying at best and horrid, acrid monstrosities at worst. An organic compound called 2,4-dithiapentane, which is added to olive oil to make virtually all truffle oil, is also used in many truffle salts. This can take an evil turn. Unless you can smell and taste before purchasing, avoid white truffle salt.

Danish Viking Smoked

- **ALTERNATE NAME(S):** Viking salt ▪ **MAKER(S):** n/a ▪ **TYPE:** traditional; smoked ▪ **CRYSTAL:** fine aquarium gravel ▪ **COLOR:** root beer ▪ **FLAVOR:** leather in a campfire; bouillon cubes; fish; marmite sucked through a black hole ▪ **MOISTURE:** very low ▪ **ORIGIN:** Denmark ▪ **SUBSTITUTE(S):** Maine mesquite- or hickory-smoked ▪ **BEST WITH:** meat dishes; mashed potatoes; transformative on hard cheeses

There are two aggressive forces in this salt: aroma and texture. The aroma is of an old, warm Nordic kitchen hearth used for decades to smoke and salt-cure reindeer and salmon. The texture is odd, and unpleasant: an electrical, nine-volt-battery feeling on the tongue layered with thirty feet of smoked animal flesh. The salt contains virtually no moisture, 0.04 percent calcium, 0.10 percent sulfate, and very little magnesium, if any at all. The paucity of minerals is matched by the unimpressiveness of the crystals. They are hard, dry, and entirely dull on their own—a rare example of nature failing to exercise creativity: hailstones instead of snowflakes.

Yet Danish Viking smoked salt has its place: with hearty foods—anything really, so long as its texture is heavy and devoid of nuance (think ten-year-old Cheddar without a cracker, or Sonny without Cher).

Fumée de Sel

- **ALTERNATE NAME(S):** barrique Chardonnay ▪ **MAKER(S):** n/a ▪ **TYPE:** fleur de sel; smoked
- **CRYSTAL:** crumbled graham cracker ▪ **COLOR:** weathered graham cracker ▪ **FLAVOR:** balsamic oak
- **MOISTURE:** low ▪ **ORIGIN:** France ▪ **SUBSTITUTE(S):** Halen Môn oak smoked; Kauai guava smoked
- **BEST WITH:** pasta with butter and crab

The French, connoisseurs of the ménage à trois, have brought together the winemaker, the cooper, and the salt maker and made music from their congress. Fumée de sel's toasty golden grains offer a well-rounded interpretation of salt, smoke, and wine, with notes of wine vinegar, caramelized sugar, and carpentry. The salt is made by cold smoking French fleur de sel with the French oak casks used to age Chardonnay. The structure of the fleur de sel suffers from the smoking process; it takes on an awkward, lumpy graininess.

If you have a moral qualm with a fleur de sel that lacks the intrinsic crystalline beauty of the species, then try to overlook the minor iconoclasms of this salt and relish it with full-bodied foods—roasted meats and seafood, pastas, potatoes, and omelets—that provide cover for its break from convention.

Halen Môn Oak Smoked

■ **ALTERNATE NAME(S):** Halen Môn gold ■ **MAKER(S):** The Anglesey Sea Salt Company Ltd. ■ **TYPE:** flake; smoked ■ **CRYSTAL:** laminated sheets crushed into trapezoids ■ **COLOR:** photographs of candlelight ■ **FLAVOR:** warm oak; wet bark; glucose; mineral astringency ■ **MOISTURE:** moderate ■ **ORIGIN:** Wales ■ **SUBSTITUTE(S):** Mediterranean smoked flake; Maldon smoked ■ **BEST WITH:** vanilla bean ice cream; sweetbreads; ravioli

Cupping a moist mound of this salt in your hand is like holding a treasure of crystals brilliant enough to mount on a gypsy queen's anklet and precise enough to be the mechanism of a train conductor's Swiss pocket watch. But there is really nothing orderly about Halen Môn oak smoked. Its crazy trapezoidal flakes give off the fiery amber glow of a Celtic oceanside bonfire, sublimating into sweetness.

Halen Môn's exciting texture in the mouth pairs with the moody smokiness of Welsh oak to create a salt that is exceptionally deft at coaxing nuance from virtually any dish it finds. This is the salt for winged creatures such as roasted pegasus, or, more practically, pigeon or guinea fowl, or sea creatures such as rockfish, abalone, and mussels. Chicken or salmon are good matches, too. The flakes also perform miracles on ice cream and crème brûlée, where they blink on and off across your mental radar screen, blips the color of salted caramel. Asked at the age of five what his favorite dessert was, my son, Austin, replied: "Flambéed bananas with chocolate syrup and smoked salt."

Iburi-Jio Cherry

- **ALTERNATE NAME(S):** none **MAKER(S):** Namahage no Shio Company **TYPE:** shio; smoked **CRYSTAL:** silken fabric granules and flecks **COLOR:** burnt caramel **FLAVOR:** cherry smoke; sweet hardwoods; bacon **MOISTURE:** moderate **ORIGIN:** Japan **SUBSTITUTE(S):** Kauai guava smoked **BEST WITH:** beef filet; raw salmon; ice cream sandwich; toast

Few things provoke blind carnal hunger like bacon. But imagine bacon on the big screen— bacon on IMAX, in 3-D, with digital THX Audio surround sound shaking the seats, and maybe a wind machine tossed in for good measure. Iburi-Jio Cherry has the supple, moist body and rich caramel color suggestive of something delicious, but it is nonetheless impossible to anticipate its sensory impact. The rush of Iburi-Jio Cherry is so big and true that you momentarily forget your hunger and lose yourself in the story. But then the curtain falls, the lights go on, you snap back, and dreams of the foods you want to eat come flooding forth.

The trick to this salt is that there are no tricks. It is the product of an unscrupulous pursuit of quality. It starts with the harvest of deep sea water from the Oga Peninsula in northern Japan. After naturally condensing, the brine is simmered over a wood fire for three days to crystallize the salt. The salt is then smoked with cherry wood, using a highly controlled cold-smoking technique that preserves the salt's essential, magnesium-rich moisture. The resulting amber crystals might be extracted from the piggy squeal of all that is good.

Meat dishes are the obvious destination for Iburi-Jio, where it elegantly lends a multitude of new flavor dimensions. But there really are few foods that do not fairly hum with happiness under its influence: apples, beer, cabbage, donuts, eggnog, fajitas, gravy, hoagies, iguana, jambalaya, kale, lobster, melon, nuts, oatmeal, plantains, quiche, romaine, souvlaki, turtle, umeboshi, vichyssoise, wontons, xigua, yams, and zucchini. Few things in life taste as good as grill-toasted ciabatta with butter and Iburi-Jio.

Kauai Guava Smoked

■ **ALTERNATE NAME(S):** Guava wood smoked Hawaiian sea salt ■ **MAKER(S):** Tiki Spice ■ **TYPE:** traditional; smoked ■ **CRYSTAL:** cracked gravel ■ **COLOR:** weathered teak ■ **FLAVOR:** caramel-vinegar woodsy smoke ■ **MOISTURE:** low to moderate ■ **ORIGIN:** United States ■ **SUBSTITUTE(S):** Iburi-Jio Cherry ■ **BEST WITH:** seafood omelet

The aura of a salt might come from the sea that originates it, the climate that shapes its birth, the culture of the people who rely on it, the individuals who make it, or any combination thereof. Kauai guava smoked radiates with an easy confidence and a cheerful spirit, born from the harmonic convergence of all elements of a beautiful place.

Kauai guava smoked salt is solar evaporated from twice-filtered seawater and smoked with guava wood harvested from the Kauai mountains. Full, sweet, faintly bacony, Kauai guava smoked can be used on anything that would benefit from the rich flavors of tropical woods, from hearty soups to toasted cheese sandwiches, from grilled fish with mango to a tangy ginger-infused flan.

WHAT SALT ARE YOU SMOKING?

If you are a home smoker, try smoking your own salt. While it can be difficult to rival the most masterfully smoked salts such as Iburi-Jio cherry, with a little experimentation you can successfully marry a good sea salt with any number of smoky flavors, from hardwoods to herbs. Cold to warm smoking is the general rule of thumb, with good results achieved in the 85° to 150°F range. Some salt smokers aim for 200° to 225°F.

Spread the salt one inch deep in a large baking pan. Set your smoker to low and smoke the salt for at least twelve hours; ideally, for twenty-four hours. Every three or four hours, stir it to allow the smoke to reach all of the crystals, or skim the surface of the pan to remove the smoke-infused top layer, and then recombine everything at the end. Store in a sealed glass container.

Just as important as the smoking technique is the choice of salt. A number of factors influence how effectively smoke penetrates a particular salt, as well as how full and complex the finished flavors will be. The salt should be coarse enough to give sufficient aeration between crystals, so the smoke can penetrate all the crystals of salt in the smoking pan. The salt crystals should be irregular enough that salt grains overlaying one another produce lots of nooks and crannies. The salt should be as moist as possible to encourage the uptake of smoke. In this vein, a moist traditional salt or sel gris provides an excellent choice for smoking. ■

Maboroshi Plum

■ **ALTERNATE NAME(S):** maboroshi no ume shio ■ **MAKER(S):**
n/a ■ **TYPE:** shio; infused ■ **CRYSTAL:** laser-printer toner
■ **COLOR:** scarlet magnolia ■ **FLAVOR:** lick from salt-dusted
persimmons and green apples ■ **MOISTURE:** low ■ **ORIGIN:**
Japan ■ **SUBSTITUTE(S):** none ■ **BEST WITH:** rice noodle
salad; soft boiled eggs

The Japanese obsession with the pickled plum borders on pathology. Fortunately, they are similarly keen on salt, soy, fish, rice, fresh vegetables, miso, sake, and other foods. Japanese eaters tend to balance their obsessions against one another, which gives their passions a semblance of modesty and well-roundedness. Maboroshi plum salt takes this common food a step beyond polite conventions, like a muddy-cleated *geta* on a bamboo mat.

A homemade tradition since the eighth-century Nara period, the pickled plum condiment, umeboshi, is made by packing plums in a jar with high-quality sea salt until 20 to 30 percent of the plum liquid has been extracted. This plum juice is referred to as plum vinegar. The plum and the plum vinegar are common condiments—the ketchup of Japan. Maboroshi plum salt is crystallized from the plum vinegar. It includes crystallized citric acid from the plum vinegar, sugars, complex flavor compounds, and a beautiful plum-pink color from the plum.

Use maboroshi plum salt with broiled white fish, sashimi, and sushi. Bakagai (orange clam) is great. I once just stir-fried baby bok choy, napa cabbage, snow peas, or broccoli and seasoned it with maboroshi. Young Hugo, an unrepentant antivegetarian, silently polished off first his own, then the rest of our plates.

Maine Apple Smoked

- **ALTERNATE NAME(S):** Apple Smoked Maine Sea Salt
- **MAKER(S):** Maine Sea Salt Company • **TYPE:** traditional; smoked • **CRYSTAL:** potatoes the size of aquarium gravel
- **COLOR:** coffee • **FLAVOR:** campfire on the Atlantic seaboard • **MOISTURE:** very low • **ORIGIN:** United States
- **SUBSTITUTE(S):** other Maine smoked salts; Danish Viking smoked salt • **BEST WITH:** grilled cheese sandwich

Salt crystals fresh and briny as an Atlantic oyster offer a contoured seascape of sharp smoky aromas, like a life raft on fire. Each grain of salt is hard, irregularly oval as a lizard egg, with colors ranging from coffee bean husk to the grinds scooped from an espresso maker—shades that betray distinctive personalities. A chief charm of Maine apple smoked is that it is painstakingly hand-smoked (often in the twenty-degree cold of winter, which is physically tough and presents a variety of technical challenges); and it is the imperfections, the variations in smokiness among grains, that gives this salt its distinction.

The vigorous, slightly harsh, medium-bodied smoky flavors of Maine apple smoked are perfect for hearty meats like goat, lamb, and thin slices of beef flank or skirt steak. Ground fine, dust it onto hard cheese or over a lavish garden salad of greens, sprouts, squash, nuts, and dried gogi berries.

Maine salts are also smoked with maple, hickory, mesquite, and alder. Each variety is smoked the same way, so they share the same campfire qualities and evince only subtle differences in aroma and flavor.

Roasted

- **ALTERNATE NAME(S):** parched salt • **MAKER(S):** various • **TYPE:** sel gris or traditional; roasted
- **CRYSTAL:** crumbled pumice sand • **COLOR:** whitish beige to grayish white • **FLAVOR:** freeze-dried ocean • **MOISTURE:** none • **ORIGIN:** Korea • **SUBSTITUTE(S):** none • **BEST WITH:** pan-fried fish; spicy-sauced short ribs; sautéed vegetables

If you ask a Korean grocer for a salt that will go with everything, she will blink at you uncomprehendingly and say nothing. If you ask her for her favorite salt, however, you will get a detached gesture toward shelves piled high with bags of several varieties of roasted salt. If you actually buy the salt, go home and use it to make dinner, and race back to the store and give your grocer a hug, she will smile and blush and twirl the toe of her shoe on the ground like a little girl. Then she'll share with you the recipes her grandmother used to make.

The odd fuzzy-crunchy texture of roasted salt is thrilling but safe, like decaf espresso. Its flavor is earthy, faintly tannic, and mild—think beach sand that dissolves on contact with your tongue. In Korean cooking, roasted salt is commonplace—a staple salt used in finishing and in cooking—but for the rest of us, roasted salt introduces a highly palatable exotic sojourn into our daily cooking.

Roasted salt is made by baking Korean sel gris in a furnace at temperatures ranging from 900° to 1400°F. Roasted salts are similar to bamboo salts, except they are generally baked in clay ovens rather than bamboo cylinders. Makers offer grinds ranging from fine sand to coarse gravel.

Saffron Salt

- **ALTERNATE NAME(S):** none ■ **MAKER(S):** various ■ **TYPE:** traditional; infused/blended ■ **CRYSTAL:** pulverized sand ■ **COLOR:** corn yellow ■ **FLAVOR:** eau de saffron ■ **MOISTURE:** none ■ **ORIGINS:** Italy; elsewhere ■ **SUBSTITUTE(S):** none ■ **BEST WITH:** Mediterranean sea bass baked in salt crust (or parchment) with fennel; Bloody Mary rims; chocolate ice cream

You're feasting in the candle glow of a cozy restaurant in Greenwich Village. There's a succulent chunk of branzino steaming at the end of your fork, and you inhale—saffron. You take a bite—more saffron. You are eating saffron. The valiant predator that gave up his sleek body for you has died in vain. Not even the gulp of crisp, fruit-splashing Riesling you swish around in your mouth can give integrity back to the beast. Now that you are attuned to it, saffron has inveigled its way into your senses and taken over. The vase of gardenias on the table smells of saffron; you smell saffron from the passing waitress; the movie star sitting in the adjacent booth has saffron on his breath. It's stuck in your head like an ABBA loop. This is a sad state of affairs, because you love saffron.

Saffron is potent. One overstep in the kitchen with whole threads of quality saffron and you are done for. Saffron salt is an invaluable tool because it allows saffron to be meted out with laser precision. Most good saffron salts are made with hand-harvested salt from Trapani, which provides a bright and neutral foundation for the saffron and at the same time honors your food with natural, unprocessed salt. Just loosen a few grains, evaluate, and add more. Saffron salt is effective in steamed recipes where ingredients are enclosed and the vapors contained, but often it does its best work when added at the end, just before or after the dish is served. Stir a few pinches into rice routinely before serving.

Sal de Gusano

- **ALTERNATE NAME(S):** worm salt - **MAKER(S):** various - **TYPE:** traditional; blended - **CRYSTAL:** ground crust with variously perceptible vegetal and insectile bits - **COLOR:** orange-ochre - **FLAVOR:** savory broth of fire, earth, and smoke - **MOISTURE:** none - **ORIGIN:** Mexico - **SUBSTITUTE(S):** grasshopper salt (dried grasshopper with legs removed added to chile and salt); scorpion salt (of which I have heard only rumors) - **BEST WITH:** ceviche; mescal; likely the best salt on earth for tropical fruit

The Azetec emperors craved few things more than a meal of roasted maguey grubs, the exceptionally nutritious and delicious caterpillar that feeds on maguey and agave plants. Also called the *gusano rojo* or *chinicuil,* this red-colored caterpillar is a delicacy to this day, sold live in markets or strung through and dried out in necklace fashion for those who prefer to wear their food. Gusanos are best known as the little worms found in the bottom of a mescal bottle, though most premium and all wood-conditioned mescals do not include the worm. The aversion to grubs among "civilized" eaters is unfortunate, as the delicate, meaty flavor of the gusano is as palatable as chicken, and its texture is no less satisfying than a French fry. If given the opportunity, definitely try gusano tacos or a plate of fried gusanos served with guacamole or salsa verde.

Sal de gusano is the least terrifying and most versatile way to enjoy gusanos. Oaxacan salt is ground up with mild chiles such as pasillas and sprinkled on food. Tuna ceviche, served in a sundae cup rimmed with sal de gusano, is a dish I remember fondly from long-ago travels. More recently, but more poorly recollected, were the nights out dancing in clubs and drinking mescal with a lick of sal de gusano from the sweaty wrist of a friend, followed by a bite from a slice of lime. Broadly speaking, sal de gusano is the steak-and-egg lover's ultimate all-purpose seasoned salt, blending the popular appeal of zesty deliciousness with the serious culinary street cred that only desiccated insects can bring.

Salish Alder Smoked

- **ALTERNATE NAME(S):** red alder smoked • **MAKER(S):** n/a
- **TYPE:** industrial; smoked • **CRYSTAL:** aquarium gravel (coarse grind); fragmented sand (fine grind) • **COLOR:** wet bark • **FLAVOR:** firepit • **MOISTURE:** very low • **ORIGIN:** United States • **SUBSTITUTE(S):** Maine hickory smoked
- **BEST WITH:** venison or elk steaks; ostrich burgers

One of the more aggressive smoked salts known to man, powerful and intense, and at times a bit shrill—a war cry. A pebble of the salt sizzles with intense smoke flavors gathered up from slow smoking over red alder in a tradition inspired by the Salish Indians, who inhabited a large swath of the country west of Washington's Cascade Mountains (Puget Sound was once called the Salish Sea). The trick is to use it sparingly. Sprinkling or grinding a few crystals over hearty dishes effortlessly evokes the traditional flavors of the Pacific Northwest.

While Salish alder smoked salt's more natural uses are with game and hearty roasted vegetables, it lends an amazingly pleasant fragrance to salads such as romaine with goat cheese and nuts, or rich desserts such as cheesecake drizzled with maple-blueberry coulis. Unlike subtler smoked salts, Salish seems to bring its own agenda to the table, suggesting that it might be preferable to celebrate the salt by making it a focus of the dish, or by using it in stealth—a sly tip of the raccoon pelt hat to culinary traditions now lost.

Takesumi Bamboo

■ **ALTERNATE NAME(S):** none ■ **MAKER(S):** n/a ■ **TYPE:** shio; roasted ■ **CRYSTAL:** basaltic rubble ■ **COLOR:** sun-bleached lava ■ **FLAVOR:** carbonated mangrove wilderness; crispy edge of tortilla ■ **MOISTURE:** none ■ **ORIGIN:** Japan ■ **SUBSTITUTE(S):** none ■ **BEST WITH:** cod; rice; raw oysters; tropical fruits; best salt ever on lean meats like venison, bufallo, ostrich

The crumbling texture in the mouth is like asphalt embedded in your hands after a fall, but this instantly dissolves into the sweetness of fizzled Poprocks, which just as quickly vanishes altogether. Was there more? Something profound and true was going to reveal itself to you in that first bite of Takesumi Bamboo salt, but the moment passes and you are left slightly dazzled, with a drifting sense of anticlimax. Then you relinquish the need to pinpoint the sensation and you are left with a revived and heightened satisfaction in the fleeting pleasure of requited eating.

My first meal with this salt was bourbon-glazed venison on a plate dotted casually around its rim with molten-hot jalapeño pepper and little volcanoes of takesumi bamboo salt piled at the side. Never have color, flavor, and texture been so implausibly and perfectly married. This salt would do well by any barbecued meat or grilled fish, or, at the other end of the food spectrum, sushi or stir-fried vegetables. I can even attest to the merits of takesumi bamboo pinched into a cup of coffee. It bridges extremes, from daunting meats to ingratiating fruits, though at the same time it can be too subtle for the hordes of foods in between.

This salt is made by packing salt into the hollows of bamboo and incinerating the stalks for three days and three nights in a charcoal kiln tended constantly by artisans. Then the stalks are split and the carbon-infused salt is scraped out.

Takesumi bamboo salt is believed to help rid the body and spirit of low energy *kegarechi*—from which only stultification and suffering can flow—and supply us with the high energy of *iyashirochi*—making us more prosperous and happier, and ensuring that our chickens lay more eggs. Better than a toaster, takesumi bamboo would be a great wedding gift, suggesting, as it does, the fleeting nature of our quest to understand and appreciate everything around us.

INDUSTRIAL SALTS

Kosher Salt

■ **ALTERNATE NAME(S):** koshering salt ■ **MAKER(S):** various ■ **TYPE:** industrial ■ **CRYSTAL:** dandruff; scales hammered from galvanized siding ■ **COLOR:** white plastic cup ■ **FLAVOR:** metal; hot extract of bleach-white paper towel; aerosol fumes ■ **MOISTURE:** none ■ **ORIGIN:** no specific origin ■ **SUBSTITUTE(S):** For cooking, any dry traditional salt such as Trapani, where dry salt is required; otherwise, any moist sel gris. For finishing, any flake salt or fleur de sel. ■ **BEST WITH:** marsupial roadkill

One fine day many years ago, an emperor who cared for nothing but his own appearance was duped into ordering a set of the most beautiful robes woven in the most beautiful colors with the most elaborate patterns, that gave the power of invisibility to anyone who was unfit for his post, or just plain stupid.

Kosher salt is used in many professional kitchens because it is easy to grasp with the fingers, easy to scatter into food, quick to dissolve, convenient to purchase, and very, very cheap. The modicum of texture it offers compared to free-flowing iodized salt leads some to believe that it's somehow more natural. The combination of professional endorsement and perceived naturalness has led to the widespread acceptance of kosher salt as "gourmet." But everyone saying it does not make it so.

Kosher salt is a processed food, with all mineral and moisture qualities intrinsic to real salt stripped away, and with a crystal structure fabricated by automated processes. The flavor is antiseptic, like the bright fluorescence of a laboratory on a spaceship drifting aimlessly away from earth. The texture crackles and bounces on your tongue like an undead pet, a battery-operated puppy with no hair, trying to comfort you with its soulless antics. When we cook with kosher salt we sanctify the artificial, we embrace emptiness, we become unfit for our posts—a nakedness far worse than embarrassment.

> *When everyone is against you, it means that you are absolutely wrong— or absolutely right.* —Albert Guinon

SHOULD YOUR SALT BE KOSHER?

Koshering salt originates in the laws of Torah, which forbid the ingestion of animal blood. This requirement means that observing Jews must prepare their meat with a salt that draws out available fluids. Coarser, drier salts with more porosity are more effective at this. Industrial kosher salts that are manufactured specifically with these absorptive properties in mind are called kosher salt, but koshering traditionally relied on natural evaporative or rock salts to do this job.

Each crystal of industrial kosher salt is composed of many cubes stuck together to create a very porous surface. The salt is generally 99.9 percent or higher refined sodium chloride, with all the natural minerals of the sea or underground deposit it came from processed out, though sodium ferrocyanide or other chemicals may then be added afterward. This makes it perform its koshering role quite well, though the blunt, artificially pungent flavor of the salt is biting and harsh on the palate and can lend an eerie sharpness to the flavors of foods.

Technically, such salts are called koshering salt, as all natural salt is inherently kosher, provided it conforms to the proper standards, such as having any brine shrimp (crustaceans) removed. Kosher certification attests to the salt's conformity to the laws written down in the Torah. It is unconcerned with the crystalline form of the salt, and, contrary to what many people believe, it has nothing to do with the naturalness or relative wholesomeness of the salt. Muslims also have their own dietary laws as part of Islamic law, or Sharia. Most rules relate to meat—the species of animal and the method of their slaughter. Food that is permissible as defined in the sacred text of the Qur'an is called halal. All natural salts are halal. Fortunately, a host of excellent salts are kosher certified. A more natural—and equally or more effective—salt for kosher salt users is Trapani or other hand-harvested and ground traditional sea salt. ■

Prague Powder #1

■ **ALTERNATE NAME(S):** pink curing salt; Insta Cure No. 1; sel rose; fast cure; speed cure; quick cure ■ **MAKER(S):** various ■ **TYPE:** industrial ■ **CRYSTAL:** gritty cubes ■ **COLOR:** sun-bleached coral ■ **FLAVOR:** n/a ■ **MOISTURE:** none ■ **ORIGIN:** various ■ **SUBSTITUTE(S):** none ■ **BEST WITH:** large variety of cured meats, except most dry cures

The somewhat plastic-fume chemical aroma of Prague powder #1 should warn you to stay away from the stuff in its raw state, even if its irrationally delicious-looking cotton candy–pink crystals do not second the warning. Prague powder #1 is tinted with a small amount of red dye specifically to alert us to the potential hazards of the salt. What a strange idea: sort of like putting excessive amounts of gladiatorial armor on children, giving them lots of pointy objects, and warning them to be careful.

Prague powder #1 is an extraordinarily valuable salt—the key ingredient for many wonderful cured meats. It contains 6.25 percent sodium nitrite and about 92 percent sodium chloride. Other ingredients vary from manufacturer to manufacturer, but it generally contains a very small amount of FD&C Red No. 3 and a fairly high proportion of anticaking chemical agents. Some brands contain no more than 1 percent sodium carbonate as an anticaking agent, while others use as much as 2 percent sodium silicoaluminate and propylene glycol. Note that there is no visible difference between Prague powder #1 and Prague powder #2 (see below), so be sure to read the label of your curing salt carefully. Half an ounce of Prague powder #1, with the additional amount of regular salt called for in the recipe, will cure fifteen pounds of meat.

Prague Powder #2

▪ ALTERNATE NAME(S): Insta Cure No. 2; Slow Cure ▪ MAKER(S): various ▪ TYPE: industrial ▪ CRYSTAL: gritty cubes ▪ COLOR: sun-bleached coral ▪ FLAVOR: n/a ▪ MOISTURE: very low ▪ ORIGIN: various ▪ SUBSTITUTE(S): sel rose ▪ BEST WITH: dry-cured meats

Throwing myself at the mercy of the salt gods, I once tasted this salt on its own (never do this, as even a slight overdose of its active ingredient, sodium nitrate, can prove fatal). A first burst of harsh sodium chloride tugged briefly at the base of my eyeballs before vanishing; it was followed by a sharp tang of steel ground in bearing grease, which was replaced quickly by a final long, sharp thrust of intense salinity. Risking death for such a tasting is a rather hollow gesture—in fact, it's completely pointless.

The sodium nitrate contained in Prague powder #2 is a time-release version of the sodium nitrite contained in Prague powder #1. It is essential for dry-cures because it works deep into a meat to kill botulism. But, as it cures, nitrate breaks down into nitrite. By the time the cured meat is eaten, the nitrate is gone; hypothetically, it is never actually consumed. So now that we have dispensed with the danger, let me add that the nitrates used to cure meats are one of the most miraculous poisons ever contrived by man, a chemical sleeper cell that slowly works its way into the very heart of enemy territory where it sets to work disabling harmful bacteria that could turn a translucent sliver of luscious prosciutto into a lethal weapon.

In the modern kitchen, Prague powder #2 replaces the antiquated use of saltpeter, which is pure potassium nitrate. Prague powder #2 contains 6.25 percent sodium nitrite, 4 percent sodium nitrate, and 89.75 percent of the salt is refined sodium chloride. Half an ounce of Prague powder #2, with the amount of regular salt called for in a recipe, will cure fifteen pounds of meat. (See page 215 for more information.) Use Prague powder #2 to make hard salamis, prosciutto hams, and dried farmers sausages that do not require cooking, smoking, or refrigeration. Note that there is no visible difference between Prague powder #1 and Prague powder #2, so be sure to read the label of your curing salt carefully.

PICKLING SALT

Additives in salt can react badly during prolonged interaction with foods. In particular, the iodine in iodized free-flowing salts will discolor and add bitterness to salt-preserved foods. In addition, anticaking agents can provoke a cascade of chemical reactions with unpredictable results. Pickling (preserving with salt and an acid such as vinegar) and salt preserving (where only salt is used) require salts with no additives. Some industrial manufacturers market salts specifically as "pickling salt," but the term really just refers to any salt without artificial additives. Sel gris or finely ground traditional salts such as Trapani are trusty standbys. ■

Saltpeter

■ **ALTERNATE NAME(S):** saltpetre ■ **MAKER(S):** various ■ **TYPE:** industrial ■ **CRYSTAL:** fine-grained globs ■ **COLOR:** innocuous white ■ **FLAVOR:** tannic steel ■ **MOISTURE:** none ■ **ORIGIN:** various ■ **SUBSTITUTE(S):** Prague powder #2 ■ **BEST WITH:** dry-cured meats

Saltpeter is one of the more versatile and impressive culinary chemicals. It is an ancient medicine, considered among other things to be an anaphrodisiac, reducing sex drive, which seems odd given the carnal urges it inspires in dishes like fresh figs baked in prosciutto. Mixed with sulfur and charcoal, it is the primary oxidizing agent in gunpowder. The first written instructions for making saltpeter are found in *The Book of Military Horsemanship and Ingenious War Devices,* written in the thirteenth century by the Syrian chemist and engineer Hasan al-Rammah. But the Chinese were making gunpowder at least four centuries before that, and they had been using saltpeter for medicinal and culinary purposes at least since the first century CE. A fifth-century Chinese document observes that it burns with a purple flame—a phenomenon I have not succeeded at replicating. I have, however, used it to cheat death, giving months of delicious life to two dried sausages.

Saltpeter is potassium nitrate, which goes by the chemical formula KNO_3. The name derives from the Medieval Latin *sal petrae,* or "stone salt," probably from the fact that it forms in plumelike "brushes" on the stone walls of caves and basements, especially in proximity to urine from bats or livestock.

Since saltpeter is pure potassium nitrate, most curing experts and probably every sensible person will tell you to use Prague powder #2 instead of saltpeter, to water down the potential toxicity. If you are fixated on using saltpeter's potassium nitrate rather than Prague powder #2's sodium nitrate, you can opt for sel rose rather than saltpeter. But if you are a curing expert, or just naturally predisposed to taking risks with your life and the lives of your dinner guests in pursuit of the ultimate salted meat snack, saltpeter combined with a good sea salt can be used in accordance with traditional charcuterie recipes.

Sea Salt

■ **ALTERNATE NAME(S):** California Sea Salt; sel de mer; industrial sea salt; chemical feedstock salt
■ **MAKER(S):** various ■ **TYPE:** industrial ■ **CRYSTAL:** coffee ground ■ **COLOR:** starch ■ **FLAVOR:** hot, oxidized metal ■ **MOISTURE:** none ■ **ORIGIN:** anywhere ■ **SUBSTITUTE(S):** Trapani salt; any fine traditional salt; sel gris ■ **BEST WITH:** chemical processing

Those leveling criticism at strip malls need some perspective. They need to look at so-called sea salt.

Two hundred years ago, there were dozens of salts for every region and culinary tradition—tens of thousands, perhaps hundreds of thousands of salts. Each artisan salt was the singular reflection of a specific geography, climate, technology, diet, culture, and even individual. Salt and people were intimately linked, so

we could explore entire worlds of flavor diversity through salt. Mechanically harvested industrial sea salt put an end to that.

Most artisan salts are sea salts, but most salts that call themselves sea salts are actually industrial salts made from seawater. The term "sea salt" has been co-opted by industrial salt manufacturers, who do nothing to disabuse us of the impression that theirs is a natural salt crafted for culinary purposes. Vast evaporators collect water from any available source regardless of the purity of the water. (For example, sea salt made in America comes from the industrial heart of San Francisco Bay.) Popular brands may contain additives such as magnesium oxide and/or sodium ferrocyanide. Ninety percent or more of the salt made in typical industrial sea salt evaporators goes toward deicing, the chlor-alkalai chemical process, and other industrial markets. A small amount of the remaining salt gets washed down and purified to make it safe for human consumption. Go shopping elsewhere.

Table Salt

■ **ALTERNATE NAME(S):** iodized free-flowing salt ■ **MAKER(S):** various ■ **TYPE:** industrial ■ **CRYSTAL:** homogeneous cubes ■ **COLOR:** abandoned factory windowpane ■ **FLAVOR:** phenolic paint followed by rusted barbed wire ■ **MOISTURE:** none ■ **ORIGIN:** various ■ **SUBSTITUTE(S):** anything ■ **BEST WITH:** shuffleboard lubricant

---

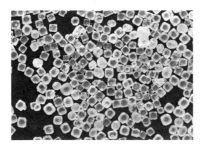
Digital audio systems are an amazing deal. For less money than it takes to buy a steak dinner, we can have an entire stereo system manufactured by robots. Automated factories in a country ten thousand miles away can stamp out products on an inhumanly vast scale with inhumanly perfect precision, all from thousands of inhumanly perfect parts provided by undifferentiated suppliers located anywhere.

Standardization → Optimization → Perfection: the calculus of industrial logic. We have a word for the sensuality of industrial logic when applied to food: processed. Make a perfectly standardized product on an inhumanly global scale from unnaturally pure chemicals and you get . . . I leave it to your imagination. Iodized salt is a processed chemical. And it tastes like it: harsh and bitter, with such perfect homogeneity that your tongue actually recoils from the encounter. Parching your flesh, the flavors evolve from bad to worse, gaining an intense acridness.

The free-flowing salt crystal is crystal identically cubic, dull, 99.5 percent or higher sodium chloride. The only reason it isn't purer is that it needs additives such as 0.04 percent dextrose (the sugar in corn syrup) and/or sodium thiosulfate, sodium carbonate, or sodium bicarbonate (baking soda) to keep the potassium iodide, potassium iodate, sodium iodide, or sodium iodate from breaking down into iodine and evaporating away.

To keep this refined chemical amalgam flowing smoothly—for instance, in a salt shaker—iodized salt needs anywhere from 0.5 percent to 2 percent anti-caking agents such as calcium silicate, sodium ferrocyanide (yellow prussiate of soda), or magnesium carbonate to absorb water from the atmosphere so the salt crystals do not glue themselves together. Aluminum calcium, ammonium citrate, ferric silicon dioxide, magnesium silicate, propylene glycol, silicate, sodium aluminosilicate (sodium silicoaluminate), and calcium phosphate are also anticaking agents. But that's not all. The anticaking agents may also need chemicals of their own because they too are prone to caking. Any number of humectants (anticaking compounds for anticaking chemicals) may be added to them to facilitate their use in the manufacturing processes. The salt shaker is a shining symbol of the chemical industry's triumph at the table.

One merit of iodized salt is its tactical use in the prevention of iodine deficiency, which may pose a risk to as many as two billion people in the world, mostly in poorer countries. However, those wishing to supplement their diet without resorting to iodized salt can take a natural kelp-based supplement such as Liqui-Kelp or Liqui-Duls, for about a penny a day. Not a bad price to pay for independence from the industrial maw.

SALTING

SALTING STRATEGICALLY

Everything is vague to a degree you do not realize till you have tried to make it precise. —Bertrand Russell

Salt is the most potent, versatile, and able-bodied ingredient in your kitchen, utterly unique in its collaborative powers. Salt binds moisture to protein in meat. Salt controls fermentation in baking, cheeses, and pickles. Salt is a preservative, warding off harmful organisms. Salt develops and protects the colors of everything from cured bacon to blanched string beans to baked bread crust. Salt develops textures, strengthening gluten in bread, firming cheeses, tenderizing meats, and hydrating a variety of foods. And, of course, salt improves flavor. The miracle is how the right amount of the right salt can heighten the flavor of food without changing its character, making ingredients communicate more truthfully and passionately. Whatever you are preparing, how you salt, when you salt, and what kind of salt you use all make a difference.

Salt is also a strategic ingredient; the way you use it sets the tone, or even the entire course, of your cooking. What do you want from your food? That's the question you should ask every time you salt. Use your memory, your imagination, your anticipation of what you are about to prepare to help you visualize what you're after. Where are you? Is the landscape exotic or familiar? Are you standing in your backyard garden, pitchfork in hand, taking in the fragrance of ripening vegetation; or are you crouched in the tall grass, clutching bow and arrow, nostrils flaring as you track the path of fugitive meat scampering through the underbrush?

Consider your ingredients and the techniques you will use to prepare them. All food is not created equal. The animal flavors of a long-braised brisket are not the same as those of a rare steak. Why salt them the same? Pasta ragued with the bold, musty flavors of foraged morels is nothing like blond curls of fettuccine tangled with chunks of raw ripe tomato and glistening with a sheen of fruity olive oil. Why not honor those differences with the considered application of distinctive salts?

Salting is an opportunity. What do you want salt to do for your dish? Set high expectations, then consider how salt can help you achieve those goals. Do you want the salt to spark and vanish or persist and penetrate? Do you want to build a crescendo or diminuendo of flavor? What textures do you want: a quick snap, a subtle crackle, a just-perceptible crunch? How prominent a role do you want to allot to salt: do you wish to hear only the voices of the other ingredients, or can salt chime in as a chorus, or even grab the microphone for a verse? Salting strategically deepens your connection to your ingredients, allowing you to cook them more considerately and creatively.

HOW MANY SALTS DO I NEED?

There are thousands of salts in the world, and there is no reason not to explore as many as inspire you. On the other hand, salting effectively can be achieved with the simplest of resources. Here are four common approaches to selecting salts for your kitchen:

THE SINGLE ESSENTIAL: One variety of sel gris or coarse traditional salt is all you need to cook well. Use it in most cooking applications, and for finishing hearty or very moist foods. Grind some up lightly in a mortar and pestle for finishing more delicate or drier foods and for baking.

THE THREE FOUNDATIONS: A fleur de sel for finishing fine foods, a flake salt for snappy contrast on fresh vegetables and other dishes, and a sel gris for everything else, as described above.

THE SIX STARTERS: one fleur de sel, one sel gris, and one flake salt for the foundation; one colorful flake, one colorful traditional, and one choice smoked salt for play.

THE TWELVE KINGS: two fleur de sels, distinguished by either flavor or crystal delicacy; two flake salts, distinguished by color and or heft of the crystal; one sel gris for the uses described above; one shio for raw proteins, prized broths, and for play; one rock salt to lend a gemstone look to food once in a while; two traditional salts that revel in the color, crystal, and mineral diversity of this broad class of salt; two smoked salts, one flake and one traditional or one bold and the other subtle; one flavored salt like truffle salt for a sneaky shortcut to decadence. ■

THE FIVE RULES OF STRATEGIC SALTING

1. Eat all the salt you want, as long as you are the one doing the salting.
2. Skew the use of salt toward the end of food preparation.
3. Use only natural, unrefined salts.
4. Make salting a deliberate act.
5. Use the right salt at the right time.

Strategic Salting Rule #1
Eat all the salt you want, as long as you are the one doing the salting.

Admittedly, this first rule may sound crazy. It might sound more reasonable to just say, "eat less salt." But that is the inevitable result of salting your food at will. Whole foods are naturally very low in salt, which is why we developed a taste and traditions for salting. When you are the one adding the salt, you are allowing your own sensibilities to find the balance of flavor that's appropriate to your taste.

We've spent so many thousands of years alert to the allure of salt that we're almost certainly predisposed to salting without even thinking about it, driven by an instinct that says, if salt is available, let's taste it. The industries built around our busy lives take full advantage of this instinct. Salting is an easy way to create a powerful flavor impact, which is why many restaurants tend to use a lot of salt, as do most packaged food manufacturers.

If we took out all the salt put into food by food chemists and chefs, our salt consumption would drop radically; 75 percent of the salt we eat comes from processed or prepared foods. Only 10 percent of our dietary salt comes naturally in the foods we eat (and far less if you are a vegetarian), and typically only 15 percent from salt we add ourselves. If you follow all of the tenets of strategic salting, your discretionary salting will likely drop even further. Following Rule #1 can reduce your salt consumption dramatically.

The two main benefits of salting your food yourself are better nutrition and better flavor. With your own hand adding the salt, you will instinctively rely on the natural calculations made by your mind and body about your nutritional needs, and you will get the most desirable taste sensations and impact from whichever salts you use.

Strategic Salting Rule #2
Skew the use of salt toward the end of food preparation.

This is not to say you shouldn't cook with salt. The culinary arts rely dearly on salt for both cooking and seasoning, but more often than not you need less than you might think. When you add salt near the end of cooking or right before eating, it is incorporated into the food less homogenously and provides more layered flavor; often more of the salt that enters your mouth is undissolved, giving your palate the stimulation of salt crystals frisking about.

Strategic Salting Rule #3
Use only natural, unrefined salts.

Unrefined salts, especially those produced by small manufacturers that are not governed by the economics of industrial-scale manufacturing, contain larger quantities of minerals and more carefully crafted crystal profiles. This gives you better flavor and greater nutritional value. And using natural salts in your kitchen sets the bar for all the foods you use: once you get hooked on the beauty of natural salts, it is nearly impossible to sacrifice that beauty on substandard ingredients.

SUPERMARKET SALT

Sodium content is a good measure of how much salt is in a food (almost all mass-produced foods are made with industrially processed salts, which are at least 99.5 percent sodium chloride), so shift your shopping habits toward foods that have more natural sodium levels. The amount of sodium in unprocessed meats and produce is very low. In natural low-fat milk, sodium content is 100 milligrams per serving. In raw beef, it's 140 milligrams per serving. An apple contains about 2 milligrams of sodium. A serving of green beans contains 7 milligrams.

By comparison, a single tablespoon of a popular brand of salsa *picante* contains 250 milligrams of sodium. Refined salt is about 40 percent sodium and 60 percent chloride, so that equals 635 milligrams of salt. If you eat salsa like I do, you are in for at least four such "servings" (I call them "bites") at a sitting, which is the equivalent of half a teaspoon of industrial table salt.

If the foods you are buying have either absurdly small serving sizes or very high sodium levels (over 200 milligrams per serving), there's a good chance a food chemist has done some serious salting on your behalf. You don't need other people salting your food for you. Leave those foods on the shelf. (To find sodium levels in most common foods, visit www.nutrition data.com.) ∎

Strategic Salting Rule #4
Make salting a deliberate act.

Challenge your salting habits. Think of salting as an opportunity rather than routine. You are enlisting the help of one of the most potent forces in cooking, and doing it thoughtfully establishes a new relationship between food and salt and enhances your skill and awareness as a cook. Never salt by rote. Aim to make whatever you are cooking better than the last time. Try something new once in a while.

Strategic Salting Rule #5
Use the right salt at the right time.

Salting is about two things: how salt chemically and physically modifies food, and how the interplay of salt and food affects the senses. The ionic properties of salt (see page 258) cause chemical changes to take place in food as it is prepared, whether you are roasting, curing, boiling, or baking. Finishing with salt is less about the chemical connections between salt and food and more about sensuous interplay between the salt and you. It allows the salt to project its crystalline character, which interacts with the textures and flavors of the food and the moisture and physiology of the mouth. The powers of salt in cooking and finishing are not discrete and exclusive. There is plenty of overlap: finishing with salt alters the surface of ingredients chemically; and salt added during cooking affects the flavor of food and stimulates taste buds.

FINISHING SALT

Three things are good in little measure and evil in large: yeast, salt, and hesitation. —The Talmud

All conversations on salting should start with this most ancient and effective, yet most radical and mistrusted, idea: you make the most of the natural character of food—and even improve it—when you finish it with salt. Finishing with salt is the linchpin of strategic salting: it's a versatile cooking technique and one of the most effective ways we have of playing sensually with what we eat.

The idea is simple: bring food, salt, and your palate into the most intimate possible contact, and the relationship of salt and food evolves with every bite. As you eat, food and salt combine—first a flash of salt . . . then the food . . . a flicker of salt . . . now fuller food flavors . . . then a faint spark of salt catching at the complex afterglow of the food.

The practice of finishing with salt is straightforward: choose an artisan salt, scatter it across the surface of your food, and eat. The goal is to enhance both the intensity and the subtlety of flavors, illuminating their full panorama. The rewards are increased intensity and complexity of flavor, surprising textures, unexpected aromas, and a heightened awareness of the process of tasting food.

Three characteristics of salt come into play when it's used to finish foods: crystal, mineral, and moisture.

Crystals are complicated beasts. The size of the crystal, its shape, and how it is composed have a variety of implications ranging from how it catches and

SERVING AND STORING SALT

Salt should be served fresh. Obviously, this sounds funny. Many of us were brought up with salt stationed permanently at the table. If we were lucky, pepper was ground fresh. Salt never received such consideration. But many salts are moist. If the moisture dries up, they become hard and brittle and lose their charm. For the best results, salt should be thought of as a perishable food. If you are preparing a dish that will be finished with a moist salt such as sel gris or fleur de sel, put your salt out on the table just as you would a condiment. After you are done, put away the salt in an airtight container.

Fleur de sel, sel gris, and other moist salts especially should be stored in an airtight container, preferably glass. The amount of moisture in the salt is typically a matter of much consideration by the salt maker, so keeping the salt hydrated to near the level it had when it was made is vital to preserving it in its original, intended form. Yet over time, moist salts can dry out even in the best of containers. If you find your salt has grown hard, brittle, or crumbly, you can add about 1 teaspoon of water for every 8 ounces of salt in a glass jar, stir a few times with a nonreactant object like a wooden chopstick, and reseal for six hours. Then stir the salt again and inspect it by pinching some between the forefinger and thumb and rubbing hard. If the salt breaks apart into a silky smooth sheen of finer crystals, it is properly rehydrated. If not, and the crystals are either hard or brittle, repeat the steps above until the proper texture is restored.

If dealing with a finer salt like a shio or delicate fleur de sel, care needs to be taken to avoid dissolving the delicate crystals. Fill a cup with 1 tablespoon of water and stir in a few pinches of the salt until the water is saturated with it and a small amount of salt remains undissolved on the bottom. Now spoon the saturated brine into the salt and stir or gently shake as described above. Because the added liquid is already saturated with salt, it will not dissolve the crystals of your finer salts. ■

refracts light to how it perches on top of or dissolves into a food to the texture it provides in your mouth. Granular crystals are firmer and more substantial than flake crystals. Solid crystals are harder than composite crystals. Larger crystals communicate more autonomy than smaller crystals. Flake crystals burst in an instant of irrepressible enthusiasm while granular crystals can be more urbane, taking their sweet time. Within an artisan salt of any given type, subtle or not so subtle variations from crystal to crystal can span an entire spectrum of texture and flavor combinations.

Mineral composition varies enormously from salt to salt. The minerals in some salts lend a sweetness, in others they have the effect of bitterness. The many types of fleur de sel on the shelves at The Meadow are arranged loosely from the super mineral-brine flavors of the North Atlantic, to the spicy notes of the mid-Atlantic, to the neutral complexity of the Mediterraneans, to the warm Indonesians, to the sweet Adriatics. The minerals in salt provide a variety of sensations, some of which progress while you taste them. A salt could start buttery and finish sweet. It could start out bitter and trickle off to a springwater freshness. Mineral composition often shapes the subtlest qualities of a salt.

Every salt also has a characteristic water content that influences its texture and how it interacts with food, from saturated sel gris at 13 percent residual moisture to desiccated Cambrian era rock salt at 0.01 percent residual moisture. Moisture provides two major things: mouthfeel and resiliency on food. The moister the salt, the less it will interact with the moisture in your food. Sprinkle supermoist sel gris on a juicy steak and the salt will just hang out, doing nothing, waiting for you to bite. A dry salt will instantly wick up the steak's moisture and dissipate, leaving behind a miniature puddle of brine. Moisture is also key in determining a salt's mouthfeel: the more moisture it contains, the less it draws from your mouth. Saturated salts will loll about and have a pool party in your mouth while the driest salts will raid the bar and drink everything in sight. The first is nice. The second, more often than not, is not.

There are other ways that salt enlists the mind and the senses. Aesthetics contribute as much to the quality of an experience as anything, and salt is often visually stunning. The glinting geometry of a choice salt perched on an enticing dish provides another facet of beauty to the food. And, of course, there is romance. Every salt partakes of culinary and cultural associations and is born of varied terrain and seas and climates. Handmade salts bring realms of places and people to your cooking, joining their geographies and cultures to yours.

Almost any food prepared with fire or spices or oils or acids or any combination of these will taste good on its own—and then radically more nuanced with a sprinkle of artisan finishing salt. Case in point: tomato, basil, olive oil: sliced, drizzled, and served. Top with flake salt (crackling sparkles). Now, shio (invisible umami or sweetness). Now, fleur de sel (briny mildness). Now, sel gris (mineral crunch).

Making the most of every opportunity to use finishing salt is a matter of understanding the behaviors of different types of salts and then picking a salt that you think will fulfill the mission you set for it. For example, finish with a fleur de sel when you want delicacy and balance hiding in every bite, or a flake salt when you want sparkle and contrast that says hello then leaves you alone. Finish with sel gris when you want a powerful intonation that endures well after the fork has left your mouth, or finish with a smoked salt when you want the natural aromas of cooking to greet you from the plate.

GETTING IN TOUCH WITH YOUR SALT

Never eat more than you can lift. —Miss Piggy

Many of the recipes in this book call for salt by the pinch. A two-finger pinch is the amount of salt that can be gently grasped between the thumb and forefinger. A three-finger pinch is the amount of salt that can be gently grasped between the thumb, forefinger, and middle finger. (The chart on page 204 provides conversions from pinches to grams and teaspoons for those who would prefer to measure salt by weight or volume even after reading the following paragraphs.)

Measuring salt using the fingers provides several advantages over relying on more fixed measures. Because of differences in weight, volume, and consistency, the amount of salt in a teaspoon varies enormously from salt to salt. And teaspoons themselves vary in shape: a shallow teaspoon will hold less of a coarse granular salt than a deep one will. Furthermore, so much of a salt's character stems from its crystal structure and moisture that it's difficult to understand fully what it will do on your food without touching it. Pinches will obviously vary from hand to hand, but once you begin handling salts, you'll find you quickly learn how the feel of various salts translates to their impact on foods. (My pinch-tester for this book was selected for her persnickety food sensibilities and her medium-size hands.)

QUICK GUIDE TO SALTING COMMON FOODS

INGREDIENT	TECHNIQUE	DESCRIPTION	TYPE OF SALT	WHEN TO SALT
Steaks: beef, lamb, or veal	GRILLING: direct high heat	1 to 2 inches thick, tender	Sel gris or coarse traditional salt to cook; sel gris to finish	Lightly, ten to thirty minutes before cooking. The more time the salt stays on raw meat, the thicker the crust on the steak after grilling, but the salt will lose its crunch.
Whole tenderloin or loin: beef, lamb, or veal	GRILLING OR ROASTING: high heat to brown, finish with medium-low heat	2 to 4 inches thick, extremely tender	Sel gris, coarse or lightly crushed	Very lightly, ten to fifteen minutes before cooking; meat is so tender the surface will break down quickly when salted.
Rib roast: beef, lamb, veal	ROASTING: high heat to brown, finish with medium heat	Wide eye, thick fat layer, bone-in	Sel gris, lightly crushed; use coarse for leg of lamb; fleur de sel to finish	Twenty to thirty minutes before cooking; season thicker cuts with a finishing salt after cooking.
Burgers: any meat	GRILLING OR PAN-FRYING	Ground meat patties	Sel gris, fleur de sel, or medium to coarse traditional salt	Mix in shortly before cooking; season with a little more after cooking.
Pork: fresh hams, chops, loins, tenderloins, or rib roasts	GRILLING, ROASTING, OR PAN-FRYING: medium heat	At least 1 inch thick	Fleur de sel, coarse traditional salt, coarse sel gris, or modified salt such as parched salt	No salt needed for cooking; use finishing salt. Option to brine.
Shoulder (chuck) or breast: beef, lamb, or veal	BRAISING: brown over medium-high heat; simmer slowly in liquid	Large, tough, fatty cuts	Any salt for cooking, but a waste to use flake salt. Flake salt, fleur de sel, or sel gris for finishing.	Minimal salting shortly before browning; salt to taste after cooking.
Game meats	ROASTING: brown in hot oiled skillet or high heat oven; cook at medium to high heat depending on size	Medium to large roasts	Sel gris to cook; fleur de sel, sel gris, flake salt, or modified salt such as parched salt to finish	Minimal salting shortly before roasting; salt to taste after cooking.
Poultry	ROASTING: medium to high heat	Whole birds	Sel gris to cook; fleur de sel, sel gris, or flake salt to finish	Minimal salting (mostly in cavity) shortly before roasting; salt to taste after cooking.

QUICK GUIDE TO SALTING COMMON FOODS

INGREDIENT	TECHNIQUE	DESCRIPTION	TYPE OF SALT	WHEN TO SALT
Poultry	FRYING: medium heat	Legs, breasts, thighs, etc.	Fleur de sel, sel gris, flake salt	No salt needed for cooking; use finishing salt.
Fish and shellfish	ANY QUICK-COOKING METHOD USING HIGH HEAT		Fleur de sel, flake salt, or shio on delicate flesh; sel gris or medium traditional salts for heartier or moister flesh.	No salt needed for cooking; use finishing salt.
Sauces	ANY	A liquid of concentrated flavors to enhance any food	White-colored salts such as Trapani, pale sel gris, or fleur de sel to season; option to finish with fleur de sel or sel gris	Add salt slowly, tasting with each addition; leave slightly under-salted if finishing salt desired.
Pasta, potatoes, or rice	BOILING/SIMMERING		Sel gris or any traditional salt for cooking; fleur de sel flake salt, or modified salt such as parched salt for finishing	Salt cooking water assertively; salt food to taste after cooking.
Tender vegetables or blanched tough vegetables	SAUTÉING OR FRYING: medium-high to high heat	Cut or torn into bite-size pieces	Fleur de sel, flake salt, or modified salt such as parched salt	No salt needed for cooking; use finishing salt.
Tough vegetables	BLANCHING: boil rapidly for a short time and shock in ice water to stop cooking	Cut or torn into bite-size pieces	Sel gris or any traditional salt for blanching; any finishing salt to finish	Salt blanching liquid assertively; finish with any finishing salt.
Cucumbers, eggplant, cabbage	MACERATING	Sliced, raw	Any finely ground traditional salt	Sprinkle with small amount of salt, rest over porous surface to drain, squeeze dry before serving or preparing further.
Fruits and vegetables	RAW	Cut or torn into bite-size pieces	Flake salt or fleur de sel	Salt just before eating.

For most of history, recipes didn't call for salt by the teaspoon or tablespoon, but used less precise language: a pinch, a dash (sometimes understood as two pinches), or a smidgeon (sometimes understood as half a pinch). The point of such measurements is their inexactness. How could you know how much salt to call for in a tomato sauce recipe if you don't know how big the tomatoes were, how sweet, or how flavorful? Every garden in the world produces different tomatoes, and the differences only increase among different terrains, climates, and tomato varieties. Culinary salts are as distinctive as any tomato. Seventy-five milligrams of intense, dry Tunisian traditional salt will have a radically different effect in a recipe than seventy-five milligrams of mild, moist Brittany fleur de sel.

The advent of industrially refined table and kosher salts gave cooks a standardized, characterless salt, and salt measurement has since been specified in terms of teaspoons or grams—though a substantial number of recipes still recommend salting to taste. The conceit of the modern recipe is that if you follow the directions exactly, you will get the correct result. Some recipe publishers are so good at testing and adjusting their recipes that it seems no matter who you are and what you do they come out great every time. Even so, there is a drawback to this approach. If instead of food that is predictable and uniform, you would rather taste the seasonal and regional qualities that make foods special, you will get much better results by paying close attention to the character of the ingredients and adjusting your recipe accordingly. If the tomato is plucked warm from the sunshine of your backyard garden and smells like it's about to burst with sweetness, you should not follow a recipe developed for people who have ice-hard supermarket tomatoes artificially reddened in a haze of ethylene gas. Show the true colors of your food by touching it, smelling it—knowing it. Assist it with any shortcomings and give it room to show its virtues. Pinching salt onto your food not only gives you a better connection with your salt, it encourages you to think about the individual character of each of your ingredients. The gram figures are the number of grams in each type of pinch, whereas the teaspoon measurements indicate the number of each type of pinch it takes to make up the measurement.

SALT PINCH EQUIVALENCIES

SALT TYPE	GRAMS CONVERSION		TEASPOON CONVERSION	
	Two-finger pinch (g)	Three-finger pinch (g)	Two-finger pinches (tsp)	Three-finger pinches (tsp)
Fine industrial sea salt	0.73	2.23	20	8
Table salt	0.49	1.33	15	6
Kosher salt	0.30	0.50	11	5
Fine traditional salt	0.60	1.77	13	5
Fine rock salt	0.49	1.07	11	8
Coarse rock or sea salt	0.70	1.59	9	4
Fleur de sel	0.80	2.29	5	3
Sel gris	0.96	1.98	5	3
Flake salt	0.50	0.92	4	3
Shio	1.20	1.84	11	5

Coarse traditional salt is not included because of enormous variation in crystal size among salts. Refer to sel gris for the closest approximation to coarse traditional salt.

HOW TO SALT A SOUP

The proper salting of a soup requires a genuine sensitivity to the nature of the soup. The traditional way is to add all the salt needed to fully season the dish into the liquid. The result is that the first bite and the last have identical flavors of salt. But stratified, clustered flake salts like Halen Môn and Cornish sea salts have the potential to change all that.

Make your soup, adding less than half the salt that you normally would. When you serve it, pass flake salt at the table. The right flake salt (or even sel gris) sprinkled on your soup will float on the surface for minutes before dissolving. So when the liquid with this crystalline flotilla slips off the spoon across your tongue, the crackling mineral architecture of the salt catches your attention. Your tongue then presses the salt up against the roof of your mouth, arresting its movement toward your throat, and the liquid around it glitters, an eddy of freshly salted intensity, until it is swirled away by the next sip. Finishing a soup with salt tunes our senses to the singular sensation of salt and frees the rest of the soup to tell a tale of its own quieter mood. ∎

UNCOOKED

Quails, ducks and smaller birds are salted and eaten uncooked;
all other kinds of birds, as well as fish, excepting those that are sacred
to the Egyptians, are eaten roasted or boiled. —Herodotus

Salt breaks down the cell structure of most fresh raw ingredients, which is why salt lingering on lettuce will turn it limp, and burying a fish in salt will cause it to experience the kinds of changes usually associated with cooking (firming flesh, loss of moisture, changes in color and opacity) without ever exposing it to heat. The changes become noticeable the second the salt starts to dissolve and progress steadily but slowly as long as the salt stays in contact with the ingredient. This is yet another reason why I suggest salting raw food just before eating it: to get the greatest sensual pleasure from the salt while impacting the physical nature of the food as little as possible. This is especially true when you are preparing fresh raw ingredients. There are times when you want to take advantage of the physical effects of salt on food (when curing salmon or pickling cucumbers, for example) by letting the elements commingle for minutes or days, but mostly the pleasures of salt on raw food are sudden and impactful, like a first kiss that gets you playfully slapped, turning someone you thought you knew into something much more.

Nothing could be simpler or more potent than sprinkling salt on a sliver of avocado or a just-shucked oyster. Part of the sensation comes from the texture of crunchy crystal against yielding ingredients. Part comes from the timeless minerality of the sea playing upon the fleeting flavors of the flesh. But the overwhelming power of salting uncooked food comes from salt's chemical and physical effect on the palate, the chain reaction of ionic violence that sends cells bursting and juices rushing.

UNSALTED BREAD WITH UNSALTED BUTTER AND SALT

MAKES ONE 1¹/₂-POUND LOAF; SERVES 12

Salt that is everywhere is nowhere. Burying food in layers of salted homogeneity gives you nothing so much as a lot of salt. Yes, salt can be used to subjugate other flavors, bending them to an evil imperial will, enslaving them to the offensive goal of not offending anyone. The dark lords of homogenous salting hold cocktail parties where they try to keep everybody in the usual safe conversational ruts—children, sprinkler systems, geopolitics—while you, a rebel with your feathered hairdo or cinnamon buns attached to the sides of your head, try to bring light, freedom, and individual expression to the sensory galaxy. Allow your ingredients to converse, each reflecting upon what it has to say before sharing with the others. Heavily salted breads and presalted butter have possibly done more than any other two foods to reduce the net amount of mirth and pleasure experienced on earth. Unsalt them, and then set them free with your salt. A small amount of salt can be added to round out the bread's toasty flavors without detracting from the salt's romp through fields of buttered grain.

2 cups bread flour, plus more for sprinkling

¹/₂ cup rye flour

¹/₂ cup whole wheat flour

¹/₂ teaspoon instant yeast

1 three-finger pinch of fine traditional salt (optional)

¹/₄ pound good, fresh unsalted butter, preferably Irish or locally made, slightly softened

Small pile of sel gris, preferably a mineral French sel gris such as sel gris de l'Ile de Noirmoutier

Combine the flours, yeast, and salt in a large bowl. Add 1⁵/₈ cups of water and stir until blended; the dough will be shaggy and sticky. Cover the bowl tightly with plastic wrap and let rest for 12 to 18 hours at room temperature. It is ready when its surface is dotted with bubbles.

Turn the dough out onto a lightly floured board, flour the top, and fold the dough over itself once or twice. Cover with plastic and let rest for 15 minutes.

Using just enough flour to keep the dough from sticking to your hands, quickly shape the dough into a ball. Place a flat-weave (not terry) kitchen towel on a sheet pan and coat the towel with flour. Put the dough, seam side down, on the towel. Sprinkle generously with more flour and cover with another towel. Let rise for 2 hours, until the dough does not readily spring back when poked with a finger.

At least 45 minutes before the dough is done rising, put a 6- to 8-quart covered Dutch oven (plain or enameled cast iron) in the oven and preheat the oven to 450°F.

When the dough has risen, remove the top towel. Slide your hand under the bottom towel and gently flip the dough into the hot Dutch oven, seam side up. Shake the Dutch oven to position the dough in the center. Cover and bake for 35 minutes. Uncover and bake for about 10 minutes more, until the top is very crusty. Let cool on a rack.

To serve, cut the bread into thick slices and serve with the butter and a small pile of sel gris.

STEAK TARTARE WITH HALEN MÔN

SERVES 2

With a feast of raw meat, the only things separating a gritty fifth-century encampment at the foothills of the Altai Mountains in Kazakhstan and a bistro in Paris, Buenos Aires, New York, or Tokyo are the trimmings. In the modern case, these might involve a glowing egg yolk cradled in a caldera of flesh, slivers of oily anchovy, the pickled plumpness of capers—an interplay of texture and flavor, of raw and cured, oils and acids, aromatics and salt. The spectral freshness and crackling crunch of Halen Môn penetrates through this wonderful exchange and substantiates it—footnotes in the secret life your mind leads during the most intense moments of pleasure at the table.

12 ounces well-trimmed lean beef tenderloin

1 1/2 teaspoons Worcestershire sauce

Freshly cracked black pepper to taste

1 tablespoon Dijon mustard, plus more for trimmings

2 egg yolks

4 anchovies

20 capers

1/2 teaspoon sherry wine vinegar

1 tablespoon extra-virgin olive oil or anchovy oil

2 tablespoons finely chopped red onion

1 tablespoon chopped chives

2 three-finger pinches of Halen Môn

4 slices of baguette, toasted, for serving

Slice the tenderloin thinly. Cut the slices into strips and the strips into small pieces. Chop until the meat is fine enough to mold, but is still in discernible pieces. Mix in the Worcestershire sauce, pepper, and mustard until well blended. Using your fingers, shape the meat into two small rounds, no more than 4 inches across, on two plates. Make a deep well in the center of each meat patty and put an egg yolk in each well.

In a small bowl, lightly mash the anchovies and capers with a fork. Mix in the vinegar and olive oil. Dollop half of this mixture on each plate at 12 o'clock. Mix the red onion and chives together and put a small mound on each plate at 6 o'clock. Put a three-finger pinch of salt on each plate at 3 o'clock and a spoonful of mustard at 9 o'clock.

To eat, mix the anchovy-caper mixture into the egg yolk with a fork. Work the egg mixture into the meat, incorporating the onion mixture, salt, and pepper to taste. Eat on or with toast.

RADISHES WITH BUTTER AND FLEUR DE SEL

SERVES 4

Imagine a garden. In it are Black Spanish, Burpee, Champion, Cherry Queen, China Rose, Early Scarlet Globe, Easter Egg, French Breakfast, Fuego, Icicle, Plum Purple, Snow Belle, Tama— all radishes. The best way to eat all of them, to savor their isothiocyanate heat, to luxuriate in their woody density, is with butter and salt. The silken texture of the butter plays off the radishes' crunch, and the two take a honeymoon together, visiting the sultry destinations of spiciness and cream. Fleur de sel is the key. Its moistness helps its crystals ride out the voyage long enough for the radish and butter to make their acquaintance in your mouth. It also lends mineral richness and texture to both. Fleur de sel, a pat of butter, and a radish— a poem penned by summer.

12 spring or summer radishes, washed and thoroughly dried
2 tablespoons unsalted butter, softened
French fleur de sel, such as fleur de sel de Guérande

If the greens on your radishes are pretty, leave them on; if not, trim off the greens. If your radishes aren't completely dry, the butter will not cling to them. Arrange the radishes on a plate. Put the butter on the plate or in a small crock and the fleur de sel in a small pile on the plate or in a small dish.

To eat, spread a thin film of butter on a radish, sprinkle with fleur de sel, and insert into your mouth.

SALTED BUTTER: THE OTHER PROCESSED FOOD

Possibly the best way to experience the pleasures of artisan salt is to use it on the simplest of foods. Make toast, butter your toast, sprinkle with a pinch of fleur de sel, and bite. A shimmer of salt, a wave of butter, a harvest of grain, and your mouth is alive. Which brings me to my point:

Never, ever, ever buy salted butter. Ever. Why sully your butter with the refined industrial salt invisibly blended into butter when instead you could bless each bite with a kiss of fleur de sel and ascend to paradise?

Of course, never, ever, ever is a long time. If you go to France and have a chance to buy *beurre salé*, a lovingly crafted butter typically using cream from grass-pastured cattle in Normandy combined with top-notch fleur de sel from south of Brittany, do so. Beurre salé is to mass-produced salted butter what fresh sushi is to frozen fishsticks. If you are like me, you will just grab a baguette, find a park bench, and sit there, watching the lovers stroll by and making sweet, sweet romance with your butter and bread. ■

SHINKAI AND OYSTERS ON THE HALF-SHELL

SERVES 2 TO 4

Whether in food or in adventure, our great life-affirming moments often come when nature and sentience find themselves suddenly on intimate terms. Gulping a fresh oyster from the half-shell can be as exhilarating as sailing headlong into white-capped seas with only the song of steel-cold air in the rigging to keep you company. This is why I never tire of the fall season's promise for new discoveries in oysters. I recently discovered the Totten Inlet Virginicas from the southern Puget Sound: minerally, fresh, and clean with a consistently firm meaty texture. Introducing Shinkai deep sea salt to the Totten was an opportunity for a culinary adventure I could not pass up. The mineral flavors of the oysters amplify the abundant steely flavors already apparent in the salt, and bring to light glints of sweetness and kelp that you might never find on your own. A drop of mignonette and a pinch of Shinkai deep sea salt; the sea god Neptune never had better.

2 tablespoons red wine vinegar

1/2 shallot, minced

1 dozen briny oysters, such as Totten Inlets, Kumamoto, or Olympia, shells scrubbed

1 teaspoon cracked black peppercorns

2 teaspoons finely chopped flat-leaf parsley

Shinkai deep sea salt

Combine the vinegar and shallot in a small bowl suitable for serving and set aside.

Put the oysters on a rimmed sheet pan and freeze for about 10 minutes to numb their adductor muscles; this will make them easier to open. To open, hold the oyster firmly, either in your hand or pressed down on a work surface, and work the point of an oyster knife between the tips of the shells to pop the shells apart. Run the knife along the inside of the top shell to cut the meat from the shell, and then remove the top shell. Run the knife under the oyster to detach it from the bottom shell, but leave the oyster nestled in the shell. The oyster's liquor should be clear; cloudiness indicates that the oyster is not completely fresh and should be discarded, or at least regarded with suspicion. Pick out any shards of shell that might have broken loose during shucking.

Add the pepper and parsley to the vinegar-shallot mixture. This is the mignonette.

Arrange the oysters over crushed ice on a platter large enough to hold them in a single layer. Make a pile of the salt to one side of the oysters or in a separate dish and serve the bowl of mignonette alongside with a small spoon.

To eat, spoon a drop or two of mignonette into an oyster shell and season with a pinch of salt. Immediately slide the oyster, salt, and sauce from the shell into your mouth.

NOTE: Instead of a regular platter of crushed ice, chill a large block of Himalayan salt in the freezer for 6 hours and use it as a beautiful, dramatic serving platter that also keeps the oysters cool. See page 267 for more about using Himalayan salt blocks.

CHÈVRE WITH CYPRUS BLACK FLAKE SEA SALT AND CACAO NIBS

SERVES 8 AS AN APPETIZER

Sometimes ingredients make strange bedfellows. Chocolate and cheese are not the most natural mates, but when the cheese is a heady, acidic, barnyard-fresh goat's milk cheese and the chocolate is bits of roasted cocoa bean, unsweetened and compact as an espresso bean, unexpected things happen. You get something more. But you can't quite tell what. The flavors square off, then shift, then subvert one another. Then they take a pause. The air is thick with tension, but nothing stirs. Suddenly, like a gunshot comes the massive crunch of Cyprus black flake sea salt and everything is movement. It all becomes clear in an instant: a dish that's as comforting as grandma's chicken potpie and yet uncivilly decadent. . . . A secret pleasure of serving this dish is watching even the most well-bred guest slyly supplement each bite with an added pinch of black salt crystals.

1 cup unsweetened cacao nibs
1 (8-ounce) log fresh goat cheese
2 three-finger pinches of Cyprus black flake sea salt
1 (8-ounce) baguette

Spread the cacao nibs in a single layer on a sheet of foil. Roll the log of goat cheese carefully in the nibs so that cheese doesn't stick to your fingers. Once the cheese is well coated, roll the log with a little more pressure to embed the nibs into the cheese. Place on a serving plate.

Sprinkle the cheese with salt, allowing the crystals to tumble across the plate.

Cut the baguette into thin slices and arrange them around the cheese log or place them in a basket to serve alongside.

To show guests how to serve themselves, cut a round of cheese from the log and place it on a slice of baguette; top with a few of the scattered chunks of black salt.

BUTTER LEAF SALAD, SHALLOT VINAIGRETTE, AND MALDON

SERVES 4

If there is any dish that could be served with every meal, every day, morning, noon, and night, it's butter leaf lettuce salad. Eggs Benedict with butter leaf lettuce salad; cheeseburgers with butter leaf lettuce salad; pasta alla carbonara with butter leaf lettuce salad. Or, for a snack, just butter leaf lettuce salad. Its acidic elegance balances out the heartiness of any meal. The trick is the dressing. Making your own vinaigrette is among the biggest single improvements you can do in the kitchen—it becomes a distillation of your aesthetic defined by acid, oil, sweetness, and salt. Jennifer's mastery of the vinaigrette has done more to promote the advancement of cuisine in our house than anything else: the shallots discover a plump, inner sweetness in the vinegar; the olive oil expresses its spicy-green spirit in response to the pepper; and the mustard emulsifies so that the dressing coats the lettuce in silkiness. Then the Maldon, strewn across the surface of the dressed salad—a glittering fencework of flakes perched along the crests and vales of lettuce—snaps like static electricity to stimulate the palate—a flash of pungency that illuminates everything so quickly and clearly that it is gone before you have time to fully comprehend what happened. This is Maldon's raison d'etre: to reveal and amplify, then vanish, leaving you with only the desire for another bite.

SHALLOT VINAIGRETTE
1 small shallot bulb, halved and thinly sliced
1/4 cup red wine vinegar
1 teaspoon Dijon mustard
3 tablespoons extra-virgin olive oil
1 two-finger pinch Maldon flake salt
3 grinds black pepper

2 small heads butter leaf, broken into leaves, washed, and dried
Maldon flake salt for the table

To make the vinaigrette, combine the sliced shallot and vinegar in a small cup. Set aside for at least 15 minutes or up to several hours. The longer the shallots soak in the vinegar, the more their natural sugars will dissolve in the liquid and the sweeter the vinaigrette will be.

When you are ready to dress the salad, mix the mustard into the vinegar and add the oil a little at a time, whisking until the vinaigrette is smooth and lightly thickened. Season with the salt and pepper.

As soon as the dressing is ready, put the lettuce leaves in a salad bowl. Add the dressing and toss to coat with wooden salad utensils or your hands. You are less likely to bruise the lettuce if you toss it with your hands.

Serve on individual salad plates and season each salad with an additional pinch of salt, or allow each person to salt their own.

VARIATIONS: If you have a shallow dish or plate of Himalayan pink salt (see page 163), add diced green apple, walnuts, and Roquefort to this salad and serve it on the salt plate to bring out an unexpected nutty sweetness. Substitute 1/2-inch chunks of cucumber, tomato, and avocado for the lettuce, and presto, you are eating a luscious summer salad of another stripe. Substitute Bibb or red leaf lettuce if you like.

CURING

Ham: 40 days in salt, 40 days hanging, in 40 days eaten. —Joseph Delteil

Sometimes salt's dehydrating effect is exactly what is needed. Before the advent of refrigeration and home freezers, retarding the growth of pathogenic bacteria by embedding perishable ingredients in salt (dry curing) or brine (wet curing) was the principal way that the shelf life of fresh ingredients was prolonged.

Salting changes the texture and moisture content of cured foods. All food cells are filled with water. Salt and water are both polar molecules, which means they are potentially attracted to one another. When they are mixed together, it is inevitable that some of the water is going to bind with some of the salt. In this way, salt draws water out of food, dehydrating it. Since microbes that cause spoilage need water to live, they are destroyed in the process. Likewise, the salt-cured food becomes a less hospitable spot for the growth of harmful (or toxic) bacteria. Cured foods may be stored without refrigeration for weeks or months. Salt curing also makes foods texturally denser and more concentrated in flavor. In meats, curing breaks down and tenderizes tough protein fibers, resulting in, for example, the compact yet tender texture of dry-cured prosciutto.

Cures for meat traditionally contained potassium nitrate (saltpeter) or sodium nitrate (Chile saltpeter or Peru saltpeter), which morphs into potassium or sodium nitrite during curing. This conversion from nitrate to nitrite is a time-release function, giving the cure time to slowly work its way deep into meats. For briefer cures when nitrate's time-release effect is not needed, sodium nitrite curing salts are used. In both instances, nitrite helps delay spoilage, especially from anaerobic bacteria, and it sets the red pigment in meats into the permanent rosy pink of cured ham, corned beef, and hot dogs. Nitrite and nitrate salts are both toxic: curing is the art of using this toxicity to kill bacteria without harming the eater.

The inclusion of nitrite in cures used to be ubiquitous because it was the only form of salt that inhibited the growth of dangerous bacteria such as *Clostridium botulinum*, which causes botulism. Because *C. botulinum* only produces toxins in anaerobic environments, it is not a hazard in cured meats other than very large dense hams and dry-aged meats in casings such as some sausages. Most cured meats (bacon, hot dogs, bologna) can be made nitrate-free without sacrificing safety, though they will lack the bright color and tang of traditionally cured meat. When nitrites interact with the amino acids in meats in our stomachs or in high-heat cooking, potentially carcinogenic nitrosamines are formed. However, during curing most of the nitrite breaks down to nitric oxide, a harmless chemical found naturally in the body.

Curing salts today are made primarily of sodium chloride, with a small percentage of nitrite and nitrate salts added. Prague powder #1 (also called Insta Cure No. 1 or simply pink curing salt), for example, contains 93.75 percent sodium chloride and 6.25 percent sodium nitrite, a ratio of about one ounce per pound. (A touch—0.004 percent—of FD&C Red #40 is added for color, and less than 1 percent sodium carbonate may be added as an anticaking agent.) Both #1 and #2 curing salts are tinted pink to ward off accidental consumption, which is why they are sometimes collectively called pink salt, *sel rose*, or, less romantically, tinted curing mixture (TCM).

Prague powder #1 is used to cure all meats that require cooking, smoking, or canning. This includes poultry, fish, ham, bacon, luncheon meats, corned beef, pates, and other products too numerous to mention. It is commonly used in wet cures (brines), and is the most commonly used curing salt. Prague powder #2 is also called Slow Cure because it is specifically formulated to be used for making dry-cured products, such as pepperoni, hard salami, Genoa salami, prosciutto hams, dried farmers sausage, capicola, and more. Every pound contains one ounce of sodium nitrite, and also 2/3 ounce sodium nitrate.

The tangy flavor of cured meats is, in part, the taste of nitrite, but the powerful flavors associated with curing are also products of the natural aging processes that happen over time. As food sits in a cure, enzymes inside the cells of the food break down protein into savory amino acids (like meaty-tasting glutamic acid), and fats into flavorful compounds that range from floral and citrusy to grassy and buttery. Wet-cured products are not quite as flavorful as dry-cured food because their flavors are diluted with water. The flavor of cured meats is highly concentrated, since 18 to 25 percent of the meat's original moisture is lost during the curing process.

QUICK JAPANESE PICKLED CUCUMBER

MAKES ABOUT 1 QUART

The Hindus paint a red dot, or bindi, on their foreheads as an ancient form of ornamentation that also indicates a focal point of meditation: the third eye, the site of the bright inner flame that burns in our mind's eye. People living in the warmer climates of Latin America wear a bindi of another sort, a cucumber slice stuck to their forehead to keep cool on a hot day. This practice has always fascinated me. The sure knowledge that as the afternoon wore on the wearer's sweat would salt that cucumber also made me hungry. The crisp, acidic rush of *tsukemono*, or Japanese pickles, brings focus and refreshment as an accompaniment to grilled fish, rice dishes, and sashimi. It can also be eaten on its own in a meditative moment.

12 medium Japanese or other Asian cucumbers
¼ cup shio or fine traditional salt
1 (3- to 4-inch) piece konbu (giant kelp)
Julienned zest of 1 lemon
Toasted sesame seeds, for garnish

Cut the tips off the cucumbers. Cut in half lengthwise and scoop out the seeds with a small spoon. Slice thinly and toss with the salt in a large bowl. Set aside for 5 minutes. Then knead the cucumbers with your hands for a minute or two to draw out the water. Drain off the liquid.

Bury the *konbu* in the center of the cucumbers and scatter the lemon zest over the top. Put a plate that fits easily inside the bowl on top of the vegetables. Put a weight on the plate and set aside for 1 hour.

Remove the konbu. To serve, toss the cucumbers to distribute the lemon zest, and lift the pickles from the bowl with chopsticks or a fork, shaking off excess liquid. Sprinkle with sesame seeds and serve.

PRESERVED LEMONS

MAKES ABOUT 1 QUART

One of the great pleasures of salting lies in not salting. Salt cure your lemons beforehand, cook and assemble your ingredients, serve, and let the lemon's super-salted flavors hop around the plate like Taskiouine dancers. The citrus and salt goad each other on in a warrior's dance, all white tunics and turbans and powder horns, and in your mind ring the bells of camels and the beat of rawhide tambourines. Simmer chicken in diced preserved lemon, olives, and fresh coriander for a superb tagine. Make a compound butter of minced preserved lemon, ancho or espanola peppers, and cilantro to serve over pan-fried fish. Chop preserved lemon with parsley, dill, shallots, and olive oil for a relish to top anything from rack of lamb to a goat cheese tart. And cut a strip of rind to garnish a negroni cocktail.

8 large lemons, scrubbed clean
About 3 cups sel gris
8 juniper berries (optional)
Fresh lemon juice, as needed

Cut the tips off the ends of the lemons. Cut each lemon into quarters lengthwise, leaving them attached at one end. Pack the lemons with as much salt as they will hold. Insert one juniper berry into each lemon.

Put the lemons in a sterilized wide-mouth quart-size jar, packing them in as tightly as possible. As you push the lemons into the jar, some juice will be squeezed from them. When the jar is full, the juice should cover the lemons; if it doesn't, add some fresh lemon juice.

Seal the jar and set aside for 3 to 4 weeks, until the lemon rinds become soft, shaking the jar every day to keep the salt well distributed. The lemons should be covered with juice at all times; add more as needed. Rinse the lemons before using.

SALT BLOCK GRAVLAX

SERVES 6

Impress your Jewish grandma with gravlax, or just impress yourself. Actually, my Nana preferred the cold-smoked cousin, lox, but gravlax is an incredibly easy, positively delicious way to cure salmon. The name comes from any number of Nordic fish dishes inspired by the openly morbid technique of burying in the ground (*grave*) your salmon (*lax*) with some salt cure. I like this dish because it yields a particularly moist, delicate, and lightly salted gravlax, since the salinity of the salt block does not migrate as readily into the fish flesh as a packed cure of loose salt. Also, because you don't need plates and weights, and because the salt blocks can be reused over and over again, the method boasts a certain elegance and economy of tools. See page 267 for more about salt blocks.

2 large (6 by 9 by 2-inch) blocks Himalayan pink salt
Bunch of fresh dill sprigs
2 teaspoons freshly ground white pepper
1/2 teaspoon coriander seeds
1/2 teaspoon dry yellow mustard
1/4 cup brown sugar
1 pound salmon fillet, skin on, pin bones removed
Melba toast or crackers, for serving

Cover one salt block with half of the dill sprigs.

In a small bowl, combine the pepper, coriander, mustard, and sugar. Coat the fleshy parts of the salmon with the sugar mixture. Place on the dill-covered salt block. Cover the salmon with the remaining dill sprigs. Place the second salt block on top. You now have a salt block and salmon sandwich. Wrap the whole thing in plastic wrap and refrigerate until the fish feels resilient, but not firm, to the touch. The top surface should be dry and the sides moist, and it will have lost its raw look, with the flesh having turned slightly opaque. Also, it will feel heavy for its size. This will take one day if you are using a thin fillet of wild salmon and up to three days if you are using a thick fillet of farmed salmon.

When the gravlax is ready, unwrap it completely, remove it from between the salt blocks, rinse off the seasoning, and pat dry. To serve, put the salmon, skin side down, on a cutting board and, starting at the wider end, slice thinly on a slant. Serve on melba toast or crackers. A dollop of crème fraîche or a squeeze of Meyer lemon is a nice addition.

SAUERKRAUT

MAKES ABOUT 1 GALLON

Instructed by my mother to feed the cats, I would push the door open, inch by inch, watching the sliver of light from the kitchen stab into the darkness, waiting for it to widen gradually into a triangle across the floor, bright enough to reassure me that nothing was going to attack my hand as it darted through the gap to flip on the light switch inside the garage. For a month every year, our garage changed from a dark and hazardous clutter of bikes, chainsaws, and gardening equipment to a truly terrifying place. Even in daylight I avoided the place, but when obliged to enter—such as when forced to feed the cats (whom I'd gladly have let starve), or if I really needed a bike or a skateboard—I kept a keen eye on the cinder block and plank shelves at the back, where malevolent orange enamel pots burped with sinister unpredictability. Days went by. Cobwebs formed (the better to ensnare the cats). Whenever I might show the slightest hint of getting on familiar terms with this horror—of letting down my guard—the pots would burp again, the lids would clatter, the cats would scatter, trailing cobwebs into the attic, and I would fly to my mother's legs and cling to them so tightly that she'd shriek in alarm. My reward for surviving? A measured respect for the mysteries of fermentation and a tangy mound of steaming sauerkraut bedded with boiled Polish and German sausages. It was worth it.

2 large heads (about 5 pounds each) green cabbage
¼ cup (1 small handful) finely ground sel gris,
traditional salt, or rock salt
¼ cup caraway seeds

Wash your hands very thoroughly before starting. Also, sterilize all equipment or run it through the dishwasher before using. Avoid using any aluminum vessels or utensils.

Remove the loose outer leaves from the cabbages and keep any that aren't broken. Wash the cabbage heads and the reserved leaves. Cut the cabbage heads in half, remove the cores, and cut the halves into wedges.

Slice the cabbage finely with a knife or mandoline or the slicing blade of a food processor. Put the cabbage in a big bowl and toss with the salt. Knead the cabbage and salt until the slices of cabbage become malleable and release a good deal of their water. Toss in the caraway seeds.

Pack the salted cabbage with its liquid in a clean 6-quart or 2-gallon crock. Pack down firmly but not too hard.

Trim any tough spines from the reserved cabbage leaves and cut them into sections that fit easily into the mouth of the crock or jars. Cover the salted cabbage with the reserved leaves; if you don't have any, cover with a clean white cloth such as cheesecloth or muslin. Cover the cabbage with a plate that fits inside the crock and weight down with a sterilized quart jar filled with water, or with a large plastic bag filled with water and one tablespoon of salt (that way if the bag leaks, it doesn't water down the brine). The briny juice exuded by the cabbage should entirely cover the cabbage and the plate to prevent molding. Some cabbage, particularly when it isn't very fresh, may not produce enough moisture to immediately cover everything. If so, every few hours press gently down on the weight until the moisture exuded by the cabbage immerses it fully. After one day, if you still need more brine, dissolve 1 tablespoon of salt in 4 cups of water and use to top up the crock.

Cover the crock with a loose-fitting lid or clean heavy cloth. Set aside at room temperature, 68° to 72°F. Check every day to make sure mold is not growing on the surface. If mold appears, skim off as much as possible. This affects only the surface; the cabbage immersed in the liquid below is not affected by the mold. In 5 to 7 days the cabbage should be bubbly; in my experience, if the fermenting cabbage *can* do something, it will. After a week, move the crock to a cooler place (about 55°F), such as a cellar or cool outbuilding. Fermentation may take up to 5 weeks, depending on temperature. Begin tasting the cabbage after 2 weeks. When it is sour enough for you, transfer the sauerkraut from the crock to clean glass jars, seal, and refrigerate. The sealed and refrigerated sauerkraut will keep for about six months.

SERVING IDEA: To make apple-bacon sauerkraut, cook chopped bacon until crisp. Add chopped onion to the pan and sauté until tender. Add a clove of chopped garlic and some apple slices and sauté briefly. Add the sauerkraut and heat through; finish with a little apple cider for sweetness.

FERMENTATION AND PICKLING

Curing vegetables in salt encourages fermentation, which in turn produces food-preserving acids. Plant foods are filled with benign bacteria, which grow under the right conditions and suppress the development of other bacteria that cause spoilage and disease. The good bacteria do this by being the first to metabolize the sugar in the vegetable, cutting off the food supply for the bacteria that cause spoilage. For example, cabbage contains Coliform bacteria that produce acid that creates favorable conditions for Leuconostoc bacteria, which in turn produce acids favorable for Lactobacillus. A bunch of antibacterial substances are produced along the way—notably lactic acid, carbon dioxide, and alcohol—that impede the growth of organisms that would otherwise rot the food. Not only do the fermenting bacteria leave most of the plant's nutritional substances intact, including fiber and Vitamin C, but the process of fermentation also increases the amount of B vitamins, adding aroma and tang. Although most any fruit or vegetable can be fermented, among the most common are olives, cucumbers, cabbage, lemons, and radishes. ■

GRILLING

Chaos is a friend of mine. —Bob Dylan

Cooking foods over an open fire is ancient in the extreme, but so is salting that food. Both grilling and salting were certainly among the first innovations separating us from the animals. Fire plus food plus salt remains one of the most successful recipes in human history.

There are two rules for salting grilled meat: 1. If you want a thick crust on the meat and a subtler experience of the salt's flavor, salt about thirty minutes before grilling. 2. If you prefer the flavor and texture of salt on the surface of meat, salt just before grilling.

Many cooks use kosher salt on grilled meats. Unfortunately, the moment koshering crystals affix themselves to flesh they begin to suck moisture from it. And it isn't just water: the refined sodium chloride very efficiently begins to denature the proteins of the meat, rupturing cell walls. Now powerless, the cells give up all their juicy amino goodness to the voracious thirst of the dry, porous kosher salt. Yet kosher salt's vampire nature doesn't give it immunity from fire. The moment the salt feels the heat of the fire, every molecule of moisture it drained from the meat evaporates away, leaving behind dry salt crystals on a desiccated crust of meat.

Sel gris achieves much better results. The salt is so thoroughly saturated with moisture itself that only a little moisture is coaxed from the meat, and because sel gris, unlike kosher salt, is granular and moist, that moisture has nowhere to go. So it sits there, like a lover pausing to caress a flushed cheek, until the searing heat of the fire browns and crusts it, fixing some of the mineral-rich sel gris crystals to the crust in the process. The result: moister meat with a better crust seasoned by a more mineral-rich salt. Fish, shellfish, vegetables, and fruit aren't grilled long enough to benefit from presalting. Salt these ingredients after they come off of the fire.

GRILLED SESAME SALMON WITH CYPRUS HARDWOOD SMOKED FLAKE SALT

SERVES 4

The plump pink flesh of a salmon needs so little to bring it to life that many people call it quits before they've tested its limits. The smoky-sweet flakes of Cyprus hardwood smoked lend an explosive crunch that brings a whole new vocabulary to the language of fish. The salt's cleanliness penetrates through the richer flavors, adding depth to breadth; its pastrylike crackle gives the palate something firm to hold onto amid the fish's sometime incessant unctuousness; and its lilt of golden smoke brings an oakiness that incandesces on your palate long after the fish has left the fire.

1 tablespoon black sesame seeds

1 tablespoon white sesame seeds

1 teaspoon Szechwan peppercorns, green or pink or mixed

1/4 teaspoon powdered ginger

1 3/4 pounds wild salmon fillet (about 1 1/4 inches thick), pin bones and skin removed

1 tablespoon toasted sesame oil, preferably black sesame oil

4 two-finger pinches Cyprus hardwood smoked flake salt

2 sesame leaves, coarsely chopped, or 1 scallion, trimmed and finely sliced

Preheat a covered grill to medium heat (about 375°F).

Combine the black and white sesame seeds in a small bowl. Crush the peppercorns with the flat side of a broad knife, like a cleaver or a chef's knife. Add the pepper and the ginger to the sesame seeds and stir to combine. Set aside.

Coat both sides of the salmon with 2 teaspoons of the sesame oil. Scatter the sesame seed mixture all over both sides of the salmon and press lightly into the flesh.

Brush the grill grate thoroughly with a wire brush to clean it, and coat it lightly with oil. Grill the fish for 10 minutes with the lid down, turning halfway through, until the surface is crisp and browned and the flesh feels slightly spongy when pressed at its thickest spot. Gently pull apart the flesh at the thickest part; the center should still be a translucent, darker pink. Transfer to a platter using a wide spatula.

Drizzle the remaining teaspoon of sesame oil over the fish and sprinkle with the salt. Scatter the chopped sesame leaves over the top and serve.

COST OF SERVING ARTISAN SALT

	2-FINGER PINCH (g)	$/g	COST/ SERVING
Fleur de sel	0.80	$0.09	$0.072
Sel gris	0.96	$0.01	$0.010
Flake salt	0.5	$0.06	$0.030
Shio	1.2	$0.25	$0.300
Coarse rock salt	0.7	$0.01	$0.007
Fine traditional salt	0.6	$0.02	$0.012

BUTTERMILK LEG OF LAMB WITH THE MEADOW SEL GRIS

SERVES 10 TO 12

The sheep is one of the first animals domesticated by mankind. For about ten thousand years, we've been living together and feeding each other. The true testament to the strength of our relationship is that it hasn't changed much. The passion is still alive. One secret to this long-lived tryst is that sheep are uniquely unwilling to give up their sheepy flavor, so that every time we eat them it's like a first date, or the first time, or an earlier time, or a mythic time. We've domesticated the gaminess out of most everything we eat, but every time we toss a leg of lamb on the fire we grow bushy and wild, our countenance waxing fierce amid the ghostly tendrils of burning fat and smoky mountain herbs. And after we toil over the flaming coals, the table is laid, the tapers lit, the dark wine poured. Aromatic and crackling—golden on the outside; savagely, voluptuously rosy on the inside—a leg of lamb is a meal of the ages.

Salting a leg of lamb should be approached with anticipation and reverence; this is one of the truly sacred uses of a coarse and lusciously moist salt—in other words, sel gris—in both the cooking and the finishing of the food. Any good, moist sel gris will work here, but I cannot resist calling for my own true love, the rather obscure but sublimely supple salt we have adopted as our house sel gris at The Meadow. The zesty flavors of Parameswaran's pepper—a whirl of eucalyptus, celery seed, lemon peel, and cedar—is likewise a point of precision that can lend yet more depth to the flavors of the dish.

MARINADE

1 1/2 cups buttermilk

Juice of 1 lemon

1/4 cup extra-virgin olive oil

8 cloves garlic, minced

2 tablespoons chopped fresh thyme leaves

2 tablespoons crushed black cardamom seeds

1 teaspoon ground black pepper

4 three-finger pinches The Meadow Sel Gris

1/4 teaspoon crushed red pepper flakes

LAMB

1 boneless leg of lamb (about 4 pounds), butt end, butterflied

2 tablespoons extra-virgin olive oil

4 to 6 three-finger pinches The Meadow Sel Gris or other sel gris, plus more for serving

2 teaspoons cracked good-quality peppercorns, preferably Parameswaran's

Mix the ingredients for the marinade in a large (gallon-size or larger) zipper-lock or other food-grade plastic bag. If the butterflied meat was trussed or wrapped in a butcher's net, pull off the string, rinse it, and set it aside. Put the lamb in the bag and unfold the butterflied meat so that it all comes in contact with marinade; massage the marinade into the meat briefly. Close the zipper almost all the way, squeeze out as much of the air as you can without letting any marinade seep from the opening, and zip the bag the rest of the way. Refrigerate for at least 2 hours, massaging the bag once or twice in the meantime to circulate the marinade, or you can let it chill for the rest of the day. Because marinades do not permeate meat fibers deeply, marinating for more time does little to add more flavor. Settle on a timing that fits your schedule.

Light the grill for medium-high indirect heat (about 425°F), building your fire or turning on the burners only on one side of the grill.

/ CONTINUED

Remove the lamb from the marinade. Using kitchen string (or the string you set aside earlier), truss the meat together to resemble the leg before it was butterflied: compact and thick. Pat off any excess marinade from the surface, as moisture on the surface of the meat will inhibit its ability to brown on the grill. Coat the meat with the olive oil and season it with the salt and pepper.

Brush the grill grate thoroughly with a wire brush to clean it, and coat it lightly with oil.

Put the lamb on the grill right over the heat and brown on both sides, about 5 minutes per side. If the fire should flare up, cover the grill to make the flames subside. Move the browned lamb away from direct heat, cover the grill, and cook until an instant-read thermometer inserted into the thickest part of the meat registers about 135°F for medium-rare, about 30 minutes.

Remove the lamb to a large serving platter; set aside to rest for 10 minutes.

Cut off the string and slice the lamb about ¼ inch thick. Arrange the slices on a serving platter and sprinkle them with just enough sel gris to show off the dish. Serve with more salt mounded on a small dish for the table. Leaving the meat mostly unsalted gives your guests the pleasure of sprinkling it with moist chunks of sel gris with every juicy bite.

ROASTING OPTION: If winter weather has you cooking indoors, this lamb recipe also makes a great roast. Preheat the oven to 450°F before removing the lamb from the marinade. Truss the meat as for the grill, and place on an oven rack in a baking pan. Roast for 15 minutes, then reduce the heat to 325°F and cook until the meat's internal temperature reaches 135°F for medium-rare, about 45 minutes. Remove the roast from the oven and transfer it to a platter or cutting board to rest for 10 minutes. While the meat is resting, place the roasting pan over medium-high heat and pour in ½ cup of dry white wine or dry vermouth, scraping the pan with a wooden spoon to deglaze. Slice the meat and arrange it on a serving platter, drizzle the pan sauce over the top, sprinkle with a little salt, and serve with more salt at the table.

CHIX & BRIX: SALT BRICK-GRILLED SPLIT CHICKEN

SERVES 4

We embrace the urge to grill as a rogue moment of atavism in modern life. Our primitive faculties at play, we become dissatisfied with our indoor culinary selves. Flattening a split chicken under a brick of 500-million-year-old salt and cooking it quickly over an open fire makes good on all that grilling has to offer: simplicity and dramatic impact. The salt block compresses the poultry, making it cook more quickly and seasoning it at the same time. The result is a novel flash-fired flavor, crackling crisp skin, and firmer textured meat that reinvigorates the experience of eating chicken as an authentic form of self-expression. See page 267 for more on using salt blocks.

2 (4 by 8 by 2-inch) bricks Himalayan pink salt
1 whole chicken (about 4 pounds)
2 tablespoons extra-virgin olive oil
2 cloves garlic, halved lengthwise

Preheat a covered grill to medium heat (about 375°F). When the grill is hot, brush the grill grate thoroughly with a wire brush until it is clean, and put the salt bricks on the grate. Cover the grill and heat the bricks while you split the chicken.

Remove and discard any giblets from the cavity of the chicken. Place the chicken, breast side down, on a cutting board. With a large knife, cut through the skin down the length of the spine. This may sound gruesome, but unless you have a heavy cleaver and pinpoint aim to cleave longitudinally through the spine in a single masterful stroke, use the pointy tip of a sturdy chef's knife to pierce the spine several times down its length, sewing machine style, in order to weaken it. Now you can split the spine in two by lining up the edge of the chef's knife blade with the perforations you just made, and pressing down until the chicken splits into two symmetrical halves.

Wash the halves in cold water and pat dry with paper towels. Coat them with the olive oil and rub them all over with the cut sides of the garlic cloves. If you want, you can tuck the pieces of garlic under the edges of the skin.

Put the chicken halves, skin side down, on the grill grate and, using grill gloves or thick oven mitts (or sturdy tongs, if you have them), put a hot salt block on top of each half. Close the grill and cook until the chicken skin is crisp and deeply grill marked, about 20 minutes. Remove the blocks using the grill gloves, flip the chicken halves with tongs, put the bricks back on top of the chicken, close the grill, and cook until an instant-read thermometer inserted into the inside of the thickest part of the thighs registers 160°F, 10 to 15 minutes.

Remove the salt bricks, transfer the chicken to a clean cutting board, and allow it to rest for 5 minutes (the internal temperature should reach 165°F) before cutting it into parts and serving.

PORTERHOUSE AU SEL ET POIVRE

SERVES 4

If the restaurants that produce them are any indication, the superlative steaks of the world cannot be reduced to a simple formula. Consider Le Relais de Venise L'Entrecôte in Paris, where the brisk waiter actually serves you half a steak, then gives the other half to another person, and then, just as you are finishing the last bite of your first half, he brings you another half-steak right off the grill—a miraculous second coming. Consider Raoul's in New York, where the experience of eating is suffused by an equally savory experience of sitting, drinking, observing, and conversing. The only way to rival these folks is to take matters into your own hands: an excellent steak, the best pepper, the perfect salt, and thou.

Tomes have been written on how to cook a steak. Precious little has been said on how to salt one. To cook: start with a lot of heat, finish with a little. Do the opposite with the salt: cook with no salt at all, or very little, if you really must have some. When the steak is served, choose the most beautiful sel gris you can find and let fly.

2 tablespoons good-quality black peppercorns, preferably Parameswaran's or Tellicherry

1 large dry aged porterhouse steak (2 1/2 to 3 pounds; at least 2 inches thick)

Extra-virgin olive oil

Sel gris, preferably grigio di Cervia, plus more for serving

Gently crush the peppercorns using a heavy mortar and pestle, or place them in a zipper-lock bag, press out the air, seal, and coarsely crush with the bottom of a heavy skillet or a flat meat pounder.

Pat the steak dry with paper towels and rub all over with the olive oil. Press the crushed pepper into both sides of the meat. Set aside to rest.

Preheat the grill for high to medium-low bilevel grilling. If you are using a charcoal grill this means banking your coal bed so that one side is about three times as thick as the other side. The thicker side should be blazing hot. If you can hold your hand a foot above the fire for more than 4 seconds, the fire needs stoking. If you have a gas grill, turn half the burners to high and the other half to medium-low (if you have a thermostat in the hood of your grill it will register 375° to 425°F).

Brush the grill grate thoroughly with a wire brush to clean it and coat lightly with oil. Sprinkle each side of the steak with a three-finger pinch of salt. Put the steak on the grill over high heat and cook until darkly crusted, 4 to 6 minutes per side. Move over the low fire and grill for another 10 to 15 minutes for medium-rare to medium doneness (135° to 140°F). Transfer to a platter and let rest for 5 to 8 minutes.

Cut the steak on the diagonal into 3/4-inch-thick slices and serve the slices with additional salt, making sure that each person gets some of the larger muscle (the strip loin) and the smaller muscle (the tenderloin).

HAMBURGERS WITH SEL GRIS

SERVES 6

There is only one ingredient that is used in every burger recipe. It is not the all-beef patty (burgers can be made from pork, ostrich, bison, portobello, soy, lamb, turkey); it's not the sesame seed bun (there is baguette, millet loaf, no bun at all); it's not the special sauce, lettuce, cheese, pickles, onions, etcetera, etcetera. All are optional. It's salt. You cannot make a great burger without it. I've never seen a recipe that didn't call for anywhere from a pinch to a teaspoon. Yet rarely it ever does a recipe name specifically which salt might be the best one for the job.

Salt should improve a burger in three ways. It should expand the fullness and complexity of the meat's own flavor by lending complementary mineral depth. It should produce a layering of flavors, presenting more or less of itself unpredictably with every bite. It should lend a crunch of texture that calls attention to itself by contrasting with the succulence of the meat and signaling the flavor dynamics of the sandwich to your mind and your palate. In other words, it should do its work, do it in a disciplined manner, and communicate the work it has done effectively. Sel gris is chunky, moist, and packed with fresh minerals—perfect for the job.

2 pounds ground beef chuck
¼ cup ice water
1 tablespoon extra-virgin olive oil
1 teaspoon minced garlic
3 scallions, trimmed and thinly sliced
½ teaspoon coarsely ground black pepper
6 two-finger pinches sel gris
6 hamburger buns

Light the grill for medium direct heat (about 400°F).

Using your hands, mix together the ground beef, ice water, oil, garlic, scallions and pepper in a bowl until well blended; avoid overmixing.

To form the patties, fold in 3 two-finger pinches of salt, and divide the beef mixture into six parts. Using a light touch, form six patties each no more than 1 inch thick. The patties should barely hold together.

Brush the grill grate thoroughly with a wire brush to clean it, and coat it lightly with oil. Grill the burgers directly over the heat for 6 to 7 minutes for medium, turning once.

To toast the buns, grill them, cut sides down, directly over the heat for 1 to 2 minutes.

If serving immediately, transfer the patties right from the grill to the buns. If the burgers will sit, even for a few minutes, keep the burgers and buns separate until just before serving.

Just before serving, sprinkle each burger with the remaining salt, or, alternately, serve with a dish of sel gris at the table for diners to pinch from.

BRINING

The cook cares not a bit for toil, toil, if the fowl be plump and fat. —Horace

Brining has been around for millennia, and is such an integral part of our cuisine that no one remembers where or when it first came into use. Soaking meats in a simple mixture of cold water, sugar, and salt before roasting will dramatically increase their juiciness and tenderness, but brines are especially helpful with poultry, pork, and seafood, because these meats dry out and get tough relatively quickly.

Brines work in two ways. First, salt loosens the muscle fibers that cause muscles to contract, making brined meats noticeably softer and, if not over-cooked, more tender. Second, salt unfolds the spiral structure of protein molecules, exposing more bonding sites for water. That means that brined meat can absorb as much as 10 percent moisture from a brine. Cooking dehydrates meat by about 20 percent. By bulking up the moisture through brining, you can effectively cut the net loss of juices in most cooked meat by half.

DRY BRINING WITH SEL GRIS

Try sel gris as a koshering salt. Pat it around the outside of the Thanksgiving turkey or spring chicken and let the bird rest in the refrigerator for twelve hours before roasting. Some call this technique "dry brining." The moist salt draws a small amount of moisture from the poultry, gently denaturing some of its surface proteins, and allows the bird to reabsorb the lost moisture, along with natural salts and minerals from the sel gris. When you're ready to cook the bird, pat its skin to remove the remaining salt, dry it, then rub it with olive oil and roast it as you normally would. The full mineral arsenal of the sea will come to the aid of the meat, for a surprisingly rich, hearty flavor. ■

Brines also season proteins. When water from the brine enters the meat, any flavorful components from herbs, spices, or flavored liquids dissolved in the brine are also absorbed. Meats absorb brine from the outside in, so the fibers closest to the surface get most of the benefits. But it's the surface that dehydrates most during cooking, so even a short period of brining can make meat noticeably juicier and more flavorful.

Like any cooking technique, it pays to do it right. Incomplete brining yields less juicy results, but overbrining poses far greater problems. Brines that are too salty (a medium-strength brine uses about one tablespoon of salt per cup of liquid) and/or leaving meat exposed to brine for too long makes the protein coagulate and forces moisture out of the muscle tissue; you end up with meat that is even drier than it was before it went into the brine. This potential drawback makes it especially important to monitor your brining times.

BRINING GUIDE	
FOOD	BRINING TIME
Seafood and thin fish (less than 1 inch)	about 30 minutes
Thick fish (more than 1 inch)	about 1 hour
Boneless poultry pieces, chops, and steaks	2 to 3 hours
Bone-in poultry pieces, chops, and steaks	4 to 6 hours
Roasts (less than 3 pounds) and ribs	4 to 6 hours
Large roasts or whole birds (up to 6 pounds)	6 to 8 hours
Whole large birds, such as turkeys	8 hours to overnight

FIRST PORK

A Mesopotamian tale tells of a wounded pig that ran into the ocean and drowned. After being recovered from the ocean, where it was saturated in the brine, the pork was found to taste better than unsalted meat. ■

SMOKED SALT-BRINED BARBECUED PORK RIBS

SERVES 4

Barbecued ribs are a delicacy born of the ingenuity of the poorest—the slaves and servants who were tossed bones by their masters and transformed gristly, fatty "spare ribs" into a complex delicious, finger-sucking feast—the New World equivalent of the French *potage*. The trick to cooking ribs is keeping them moist: brining is a must. Even the most delicious house-made bacon would envy the subtle woodsy notes infused from the smoked salt used in this brine. Bacony ribs glazed with a rich and spicy sauce: it's like Christmas in July.

2 cups apple cider

2 tablespoons red alder smoked salt

1 teaspoon black peppercorns, cracked

2 racks (about 4 pounds total) St. Louis–cut spare ribs or baby back ribs

ROOT OF EVIL BARBECUE SAUCE

¼ cup tomato paste

¼ cup root beer

2 tablespoons molasses

2 tablespoons spicy brown mustard

3 tablespoons apple cider vinegar

2 tablespoons Tabasco sauce

1 three-finger pinch red alder smoked salt

½ teaspoon ground black pepper

To make a brine for the ribs, mix the cider, salt, and pepper in a large (two-gallon) zipper-lock bag until the salt dissolves. Cut the racks of ribs in half and add to the brine. Seal the zipper, leaving about an inch open; push on the bag to release any trapped air through the opening, and close the zipper completely. Massage the liquid gently into the meat and refrigerate for 6 to 12 hours. If you brine the ribs overnight and won't be cooking them until evening, remove the ribs from the brine in the morning to keep them from overbrining; store them, wrapped in the refrigerator until you are ready to cook them.

Preheat a grill for indirect medium heat (about 325°F). If you are using a charcoal grill, this means banking your coal bed to one side or at opposite ends of the fire box, leaving open an area large enough to hold the racks of ribs. If you have a two-burner gas grill, turn one side on to medium and leave the other side off. If you have a three- or more-burner grill turn the outside burners on to medium and leave the center burner(s) off.

Brush the grill grate thoroughly with a wire brush to clean it and coat it lightly with oil. Remove the ribs from the brine, discard the brine, and pat the ribs dry with a clean cloth or paper towel. Put the ribs on the grill, bone side down, away from the heat. Cover the grill and cook until an instant-read thermometer inserted into the thickest part of the ribs registers about 155°F, about 1 hour.

While the ribs are cooking, bring the ingredients for the barbecue sauce to a simmer in a small saucepan, stirring as needed. Reserve one-third of the sauce for dipping at the table. Set the remaining sauce aside.

When the ribs are almost cooked, brush them with half of the remaining sauce, turn them sauce side down, cover the grill, and cook for 3 minutes. Brush the unglazed surfaces with the remaining sauce, turn the ribs sauce side down, cover, and cook for another 3 minutes.

Remove the ribs to a cutting board and cut into one- or two-rib sections. Place the ribs on a large serving platter and serve with the reserved sauce poured over the top or in a bowl for dipping.

PLUMP CHICKEN MEETS PLUMPED CHICKEN

Plumping is, theoretically, the poultry industry's attempt to brine meat, using sodium-chloride solution, chicken broth, and/or carrageenan (a derivative of seaweed). On paper, it seems like a good idea: let the bird tenderize and moisten while it's sitting in the supermarket cooler, saving you the time and effort of brining it yourself, and guaranteeing you get the best possible results by letting the experts at the chicken processing plant handle the whole process.

In practice, it doesn't work out so well.

During plumping, brine is injected into the meat instead of being allowed to soak in. The result is that moisture from the surface of the meat can be pulled toward the center where there is less water proportional to the sodium chloride of the brine; this makes the outside dry, rubbery, and easily burned while the inside is watery. The lag time between the plumping at the factory and table is also just way too long. In effect, the meat sits steeped in brine in the supermarket cooler or freezer for days longer than it should (see page 233).

The benefits to the industry, though, are clear and easily quantifiable. Brining increases the weight of the meat by adding water. Up to 15 percent of the bird's weight can legally be added salt water, so long as the package is labeled with a warning that the bird has been plumped. According to the USDA, most major plumped brands contain 7 to 8 percent salt water, adding up to about $1.50 per package at the retail level. That's $2 billion worth of salt water alone each year in the United States, much of it going to fast-food joints trying to decrease their food costs. Increased media attention may have led to a decline in the plumping of chickens, but turkeys and game hens are still almost always plumped.

Another benefit to the poultry plumpers is that, to the average consumer, their plumped poultry looks fatter, shinier, and generally more appealing. An artificially enhanced chicken breast holds the same appeal as any artificially enhanced breast: it is larger.

There is a third reason chicken producers turn to plumping: added salt means added flavor. The flavor of a chicken raised on an industrial scale is not always what one might hope for. Feeds, cages, drugs, and even the genetics of the animal itself are all engineered to convert a chick into the most profitable product possible as quickly and inexpensively as possible. The characteristics prized by industrial poultry raisers are breast size and the efficiency with which the bird converts feed into weight. Flavor is not paramount. But despite the harm done to the natural texture and concentration of flavors in chicken, plumped factory-farmed birds can pass for flavorful birds because of the tremendous amount of salt added to them.

Poultry isn't the only plumped food. Seafood, especially scallops, is frequently plumped (that is, "soaked") prior to selling to aid in visual appeal and moisture retention. Seafood brines are a solution of water and sodium tripolyphosphate (STPP). Although this concoction is not believed to be dangerous in the amounts contained in food, most governments regulate the amount of STPP that may be used to plump seafood because it substantially increases the weight, inflating the product's price. ■

ROASTING

Heat cannot be separated from fire, or beauty from The Eternal.
—Dante Alighieri

Roasted food doesn't want much—just a hot, quiet place to sit for an hour or so in privacy. Given that, a slab of beef or a chunked potato or a perfect pear will deliver delicious, concentrated flavor and the kind of gloriously deep lacquered tan that could turn a fussed-over pot roast pale with envy. Anything more is ornamentation. Except for the salt.

Roasts need salt to get their juices flowing. I know you've been told that salting meat before it goes in the oven dries it out and, if a piece of meat happened to be formed like a big water balloon, that would be the case. Salting the surface of a roast does indeed dry moisture from the surface, but no deeper, and for the ideal roast that's exactly what you want. You need a dry surface to get deep browning. Browning doesn't start until close to 300°F. Since water doesn't evaporate until the thermometer hits 212°F, browning cannot occur where water is present; this is why a dry surface is synonymous with a fabulous crust. In addition, the evaporation of water from the surface helps to concentrate all of the flavors of the flesh inside.

All you need is a light dusting. Using a lot of salt before roasting provides no greater benefit to the cooking process. On the negative side, salt crystals—especially larger ones or an excess quantity—will often absorb some of the fat from the food along with water, and then as the temperature rises the fat will react with the hot salt, turning it into blackened, bitter granules. For that reason, in most of my roasting recipes, I salt a little before the food enters the oven and then salt to taste right before or after carving.

That said, different types of meat benefit from different types of roasting and, as a consequence, different salting techniques. For example, because pork has a tendency to dehydrate and toughen at high temperatures, it is better to roast it slowly. Adding salt early on further dehydrates the meat, and does nothing to add flavor that could not be gained by salting to finish. On the other hand, beef and lamb, which are most typically served rare to medium, are better off roasted at very high temperatures to achieve a rich, dark crust and a rare center; they benefit from some salt to assist the development of that crust.

Sauce is another reason to salt lightly while cooking. A good use for roast meat juices is to serve them with the meal in the form of a pan sauce. However, because salt never evaporates, every bit of salt that dissolves in the juices as they emerge from the roast and trickle down the surface of the meat toward the pan remains in the juices. If you think about just how easily 2 or 3 tablespoons of salt can be spread over the surface of a large piece of meat such as a turkey or a leg of lamb, and consider how the food's juices are often concentrated into as little as half a cup of liquid, it is easy to imagine just how salty your sauce could end up.

I love to cook chicken and similar fowl like guinea hens at relatively high temperatures, at least to start. High heat helps the birds' skin form a wonderful crispy-golden crust. I am of two minds regarding the salting of chicken for roasting. On one hand, unsalted chicken skin develops a lovely golden crust, and then you have the pleasure of sprinkling the moist crystals of a good sel gris over the top to finish. This approach gives you the fullest experience of the luscious mineral qualities of the salt. On the other hand, salting chicken before roasting does nothing to diminish its juiciness, since the fatty skin protects the meat within. Rather, salted chicken skin constricts during cooking, creating a crisper and deeper brown crust. When you salt poultry skin before roasting, it essentially becomes a seasoned condiment to serve with the bird: chicken seasoned with crispy bits of salty chicken skin. Try it both ways and decide for yourself.

Salt cooked meat only after it has had a chance to rest. I prefer to sprinkle a little bit of salt on the cuts of a roast after carving, for a flavorful and textural jolt, and then have salt at the table so diners can season as desired.

Vegetables and fruits are roasted to concentrate their flavors and brown their surfaces. Unlike meats, roasted produce does not need to reach a specific temperature; as soon as the ingredient is tender and browned, it is done. As always, salting roasted fruits and vegetables just before eating yields maximum flavor and aroma and adds texture, all with a minimum of seasoning.

ROASTED CHICKEN WITH WINTER VEGETABLES AND SUGPO ASIN

SERVES 4

The chicken is in the oven—heat forming a golden crust that seals in the juices, salt working its silent alchemy within, denaturing some of the proteins in tough muscles making those parts more tender and flavorful. Roasting is the easiest way to cook chicken and the tastiest. All that is required to reach perfection is time and the perfect salt. Sugpo Asin, a king among salts, glowing rose-cloud white, lush and firmly crunchy, with dulcet brine notes that play lavishly (but with discipline) against the sweet tamed gaminess of poultry, honors this basic meat and vegetable meal as all basic meals should be honored—asserting the preeminence of simple home cooking as the cornerstone of eating well.

3 celery ribs, cut into 1-inch slices

1 yellow onion, cut into 1-inch wedges

2 golden potatoes, cut into 1-inch wedges

2 golden beets, 2 turnips, or 1 rutabaga, trimmed of greens, peeled, and cut into 1-inch wedges

2 carrots or 3 parsnips, trimmed of greens, peeled, and cut into 1-inch chunks

2 tablespoons extra-virgin olive oil

3 rosemary twigs, cut in half

2 three-finger pinches Sugpo Asin or Ilocano Asin (or substitute sel gris)

1 chicken (about 4 pounds), visible fat removed, washed and dried

2 tablespoons dry vermouth

Preheat the oven to 425ºF.

Toss the vegetables with 1 tablespoon of the olive oil in a large roasting pan. Stick 4 rosemary pieces into the vegetables and scatter with a three-finger pinch of sel gris and a two-finger pinch of pepper.

Sprinkle the interior cavity of the chicken with a three-finger pinch of salt and a two-finger pinch of pepper. Coat the outside of the chicken with the remaining olive oil and place the chicken, breast side down, on top of the vegetables.

Roast for 45 minutes. Reduce the oven temperature to 400ºF, and turn the chicken breast side up. It's easiest to use large tongs with one arm inserted into the chicken cavity and the other gripping the outside of the bird. Roast for 30 minutes more, or until the skin is golden brown and a thermometer inserted into the thickest part of the thigh registers 160ºF.

Remove the chicken to a carving board and let rest for 5 minutes before carving, allowing the internal temperature to come to 165ºF.

Carve the chicken and arrange in the center of a serving platter. Remove and discard the rosemary branches from the roasted vegetables and, using a slotted spoon, arrange the vegetables around the chicken.

Skim off excess fat from the juices in the roasting pan, leaving just a film of fat. Place the roasting pan on a burner over medium-high heat. Add the leaves of the remaining rosemary and the vermouth to the drippings in the pan. Bring to a boil, then spoon over the chicken and vegetables. Scatter the remaining pinches of salt and pepper over all and serve.

ROASTED MARROWBONES WITH SEL GRIS

SERVES 4

For hundreds of thousands of years, we burned bones in the fire and then broke them open to slather our food (and faces and bodies) in the butter-fine marrow. Scooped from roasted veal bones and spread on a wedge of crusty bread, marrow is so rich and flavorful that it threatens to overwhelm. And that's where the salt comes in. The strident mineral tones of a coarse sel gris penetrate through the fatty richness, letting fly its myriad dimensions—like cutting a ruby from a hunk of Burmese rock. If marrow hadn't been created by nature, it would have been necessary to invent it just to have a food that strikes so squarely at the core of the eating experience. If it weren't for sel gris, nature's felicity would all be for naught.

12 (1¹/₂- to 2-inch) center-cut pieces of veal marrowbones
Scattering of torn flat-leaf parsley leaves
Lots of thinly sliced crusty bread, barely toasted (see page 207)
4 three-finger pinches sel gris, preferably sel gris de l'Ile de Noirmoutier

Preheat the oven to 450°F.

Put the marrowbones with the cut marrow sides up in an ovenproof baking dish or skillet just big enough to hold them. Roast until the marrow retracts and sinks slightly in the center, 20 to 30 minutes. There will be a thin film of melted marrow on the bottom of the pan. Do not roast them too long, lest the marrow melt away. With that said, marrowbones of different sizes roast at radically different rates, so keep an eye on the roasting and remove the marrowbones from the pan as they are done, placing them on a large plate and covering them with aluminum foil to keep them warm.

When all the marrowbones are roasted and arranged on the plate, scatter the parsley over the plate. Serve with the toast and a small ramekin of sel gris.

To eat, dig pats of the marrow from the bone, spread on the toast, and sprinkle with the salt.

ROASTED PEACHES IN BOURBON SYRUP WITH SMOKED SALT

SERVES 4

They say we use only 10 percent of our brains. That assessment is immensely appealing. We are all potential supergeniuses with telekinetic and mind-reading powers, and could easily enjoy Heidegger or Joyce for light reading over coffee and donuts in the morning . . . if we only tried. But there is an easier way to experience the unbridled horsepower of our full consciousness: try roasted peaches in bourbon syrup with smoked salt. Your first bite will expand the boundaries of sensation separating your mouth from the rest of your body, and you'll be feeling spiciness in the warmth of your hands and smokiness in the tingling of your toes. And by the third bite your mind will have moved on to peel the black backing off the edge of the universe, filling the unending space beyond with your pounding heart.

4 large, barely ripe peaches

1/2 cup water

1/4 cup lightly packed brown sugar

1 cinnamon stick, broken into 3 pieces

1/4 cup bourbon

1 teaspoon vanilla extract

2 tablespoons unsalted butter

Greek yogurt, crème fraîche, or caramel ice cream, for serving (optional)

4 two-finger pinches Maine apple smoked salt

Preheat the oven to 425°F.

Put the peaches, stem side down, in a baking dish large enough to hold the peaches without allowing them to touch one another. Poke each peach with a fork several times to keep them from bursting.

In a small saucepan, bring the water, sugar, and cinnamon to a boil over high heat. Remove the pan from the heat and stir in the bourbon, vanilla, and butter. Return the pan to low heat and simmer until the butter melts. Remove and discard the cinnamon pieces. Spoon the sauce over the peaches.

Roast the peaches for 10 minutes, then remove the dish from the oven and brush the peaches with syrup from the bottom of the dish. Return the dish to the oven and roast until the peaches are just tender enough to pierce with a fork, about 25 minutes more. Let cool for at least 15 minutes before serving.

Serve one peach per person, with some syrup spooned over the top. Serve with a dollop of Greek yogurt or crème fraîche or a scoop of caramel ice cream, if desired. Sprinkle a two-finger pinch of the salt over each serving.

SALTING AT THE EDGE

A man cannot become an atheist merely by wishing it.
—Napoleon Bonaparte

Salt can save a meal, breathing pep into blandness, coaxing firm flesh from flab, giving form to the most elusive aromas—which is why it is one of the more abused ingredients in all cooking. Salt it a lot, the logic goes, and it will taste better. But too much salt is like listening to the car stereo with the volume turned up to the point where windows rattle in houses as you drive by: the intensity of the experience drowns out the substance of it.

Usually the result of heavy salting is food that jabs aggressively at your taste buds—or, if you're like me, makes your throat tingle and your eyeballs bulge. But sometimes the result is something else altogether: intense, maddening, raging flavor.

Standing next to a saucepot, the chef flings salt dash by dash into a sauce, descrying with each salting the shifting landscape of flavors in the concentrated liquid—lavender, perhaps, then lemon zest, then unexpected notes of chocolate and cardamom, finishing with the dark fruit notes of red wine. Thick steam and silky liquid trace the dish's entire story across the palate. Up, up, up: more and more salt falls from the chef's hand, carefully, judiciously, thoughtfully, then presto! Like a pickax striking solid gold, the sauce strikes that singular chord, an incontrovertible harmonic blend. Perfection. The dish is done.

Whether it is a pomegranate-basil sauce or fried salami and celery root salad or a wild hare and habanero etouffé, salt can be used to bring wildly diverse taste sensations together. For some cooks working in certain styles with certain recipes, it can take a heck of a lot of salt to get to this point. I call this "salting at the edge."

There are tricks to using salt with such wild abandon. First, don't use it with wild abandon. Add each crystal as you would another bit of pressure on the gas pedal. Push too far and your meal is a wreck. Second, don't do this too often. Many foods—and virtually all good fresh foods—are tasty the way they are. "Often" is obviously a highly subjective term. Which brings us to the third and most important point. Don't make salting heavily a thematic part of your cooking. It's a well-marked path to more flavor, sure, but it is also a rote and over-relied upon approach to seasoning. Adding a lot of salt often gets in the way of a better understanding of both the quality ingredients and the sound techniques that are the foundation of any good meal. Making every bite buzz alarmingly with salt can make your diners feel bewildered or overpowered, or worse, manipulated. But, boy, is salting at the edge amazing when it works. ■

FRYING

I won't eat anything green. —Kurt Cobain

Take almost any food and drop it into hot fat, and the results are delicious. All cooking techniques that use fat or oil for heat transfer are a form of frying. They go by different names—sautéing, pan-frying, deep-frying—depending on the amount of oil used, the temperature, and what is being fried, but regardless of their differences there is one thing that ties them all together: fried foods should only be salted after they're cooked.

Not only does fried food taste better with a scattering of salt crystals puncturing its richness, but adding salt too early in the frying process is downright dangerous. Salt draws water out of ingredients—especially if the pieces are small, and therefore have more surface area. Water and fat don't mix, and when the fat is hot, their lack of camaraderie can result in a good deal of spattering. For that reason alone, you should only salt fried food after it is done cooking.

There is some evidence that salt in breading or frying batter is discharged into frying oil through escaping steam and exacerbates the decomposition of the oil, which is another reason to only salt food after frying or at least to keep the salt out of the coating. Some foods may be lightly salted before being battered, as the batter will largely insulate the salted food against the hot oil.

Proper frying depends on starting out with dry ingredients. You can manually blot away excess moisture with paper towels, powder the surface with flour or starch to absorb surface moisture (in much the same way as one dusts oneself with powder after a bath), or coat the food in bread crumbs or batter to form a barrier between the frying fat and any moisture on the food.

One of the most important tricks to frying is to serve as quickly as possible after cooking. As the temperature of the food drops, oil is drawn from the surface to the interior. Blotting excess oil from the outside of fried foods before salting and serving helps mitigate this. Another reason to salt fried foods and serve them quickly is that the crunchy crispness of properly fried food is fleeting. After the food is cooked, moisture in the interior of the food continues to steam. As the steam travels to the surface, it cools, condensing back into juice just beneath the crust. It doesn't take long for that moisture to turn the crust from crisp to mush, but if the crust is salted on its surface, the salt wicks the moisture through the crust and out into the air, keeping the crust crisper for longer.

The right salt for your fried foods will vary enormously depending on the food and on the effect you are trying to achieve. Delicately fried foods like vegetable or seafood tempura can benefit from a dusting of a dry, powdery salt like Amabito no Moshio. A finely ground sea salt like Trapani can also work, though such salts are intense and will compete aggressively with the more delicate qualities of the food. French fries are substantial enough to withstand Trapani's boldness, and the hardness of the salt's crystals will provide the reassuring familiarity of a fast-food joint, albeit modestly improved. Fleur de sel is a better option. If you are making more chewy, unctuous fries of the thin Belgian or French variety, fleur de sel is essential, as the delicate crunch and mineral fullness will contribute enormously to the majesty of the food. Meats such as chicken also benefit from fleur de sel, but delicate flake salts also provide a textural complement to the crispy surface without overpowering the deep, rich flavors of the meat.

FRIED EGGS WITH FORAGED MUSHROOMS AND BLACK TRUFFLE SALT

SERVES 2

Mushrooms, noble as they may be, are not proud creatures. Poking their heads up from the loam, they stand humbly with a prepossessing calm that more or less begs us to pluck them. Fresh eggs, once you face off the fierce gaze of the hen and pull them from under her warm breast, are similarly good-natured, understated and half-smiling like the oval face of a Modigliani portrait. But dress the egg and the mushroom with a pinch of black truffle and the two rise up, swell with pride, and regale you with their tales of farm and forest.

1 tablespoon olive oil

1/4 cup finely chopped onion

8 ounces wild mushrooms (any type), cleaned and sliced

1 tablespoon chopped fresh flat-leaf parsley

2 two-finger pinches black truffle salt

Coarse freshly ground black pepper

1 tablespoon unsalted butter

4 eggs

2 slices whole-grain bread, toasted

Heat the oil in a medium-large skillet over medium-high heat. Add the onion and sauté until slightly softened, about 3 minutes. Add the mushrooms and sauté until tender, about 4 minutes. Stir in the parsley, a pinch of truffle salt, and a grinding of pepper. Transfer to a bowl and keep warm.

Wipe out the skillet and put over medium heat. Add the butter to the pan and cook until melted and foamy. Crack the eggs into the hot butter and fry until the whites are almost completely set and the yolks are still runny, 2 to 3 minutes. Turn with a spatula, if desired.

Serve by putting a piece of toast on each of two plates. Spoon the mushrooms over the toast. Top with the eggs and season the eggs with the remaining pinch of salt, and some pepper, if you want.

POTATO CHIPS WITH FLEUR DE SEL DE GUÉRANDE

SERVES 2

There are two kinds of people: those who love potato chips and those who don't exist. Making your own chips means a fresh potato, freshly fried in the freshest oil. It also means you can choose your own salt. The freshly fried potato chip is an object worthy of serious contemplation, a thing of wonder, a crispy symphony of fat and starch and salt. When the diamondlike glitter of fleur de sel throws its multifaceted might behind it, hold on to the roof.

2 large russet potatoes (about 12 ounces each), wiped clean with a damp towel

1 quart canola oil

3 two-finger pinches fleur de sel de Guérande

Slice the potatoes into paper-thin slices using a mandoline or a very sharp knife. As soon as the potatoes are sliced, put them in a bowl of ice water.

Heat the oil to 325°F in an electric deep-fryer or a heavy deep saucepan. If using a saucepan, you will need a deep-fat fry thermometer to make sure that the oil stays at a constant temperature.

Lift the potatoes from the water and arrange them in a single layer on a clean dish towel. Wrap the towel around the potatoes and wring out as much water from the potatoes as you can without crushing the slices. If the potatoes are still damp after the towel will absorb no more, transfer to another towel and wring again.

Fry the potatoes in two batches; your goal is to make sure all the potato surfaces are in contact with the hot oil, so crowding is a no-no. Stir the slices as needed to keep them separate and fry until tender enough to become floppy, but not brown, about 4 minutes. Remove from the oil with a slotted spoon and put on a wire rack set on a sheet pan to catch the drips. Let cool.

Once all the potatoes are fried and cooled, heat the oil to 375°F. Fry the once-fried potatoes in three batches until browned and crisp, 30 to 45 seconds per batch. Transfer onto a double layer of paper towels to drain. Immediately sprinkle the chips with the salt and serve warm. I like shaking the chips with salt in a paper bag to coat them better and to remove additional oil.

CHIP NOTE: Universal as the love of chips may be, not everyone agrees on what makes the perfect cut for a chip. Different chips can be turned to different purposes. Crinkle-cut chips prove best (or at least less frustrating) for dipping in clam dip. Thicker chips might do the job with steak tartare or Niçoise salad. Thinner chips may be best for light snacking with a sip of Highland single-malt whisky before or after dinner.

SAVORY POPCORN SALTED SIX WAYS

SERVES 4

The movie theater owner who first thought of charging the price of admission just for a bag of popcorn has got to be one smug cat. While Hollywood makes blockbuster motion pictures with budgets the size of some countries' gross national products, Mr. Smug whips up a batch of popcorn and drives his fork lift loaded with profits all the way to the bank. If only he hadn't stopped there he might truly have made some money.

1/4 cup corn or canola oil
3/4 cup popping corn
2 tablespoons unsalted butter, melted
2 three-finger pinches amabito no moshio salt

Heat the oil in a large, heavy pot over high heat until it just starts to smoke. Add 3 kernels of popping corn and, when they pop, add the rest of the popping corn. Cover the pot and shake gently until the corn starts to pop. Shake vigorously over the heat until the popping subsides, cracking the lid occasionally to allow the steam to escape. (Trapped steam makes the protein in the corn toughen.)

Remove from the heat and pour the popcorn into a serving bowl. Drizzle the butter over the top and toss with tongs or two butter knives to coat evenly. Divide the popcorn into six bowls and sprinkle one type of salt over each (see right). Serve immediately.

PAPOHAKU WHITE: a flavor combination of super-buttered movie theater popcorn, amusement park caramel corn, and something you might nibble on in the plush shadows of the Ritz Bar in Paris.

AMABITO NO MOSHIO: the savory one-upmanship of pasta speckled with Parmesan cheese, minus the pasta Parmesan: the Platonic form of umami.

FLEUR DE SEL DE CAMARGUE: the one-salt remedy for impromptu cocktail parties when you forgot the cheese, fruit, and prosciutto; lavished with sweet cream butter, and speckled with fleur de sel de Camargue, popcorn radiates your love and hospitality.

KALA NAMAK FINE: it's like trying to eat scrambled eggs off a subwoofer of a surround-sound movie about Mount Vesuvius erupting over the cowering residents of Pompeii. Envelop yourself in the exotic sensations of faraway lands . . . as they are being destroyed.

IBURI-JIO CHERRY SMOKED SEA SALT: flavors hover between the animate world and the eternal brightness of the elements, like stepping from an Arctic blizzard into a brothel.

BLACK TRUFFLE SALT: nature's contraband in snackable form. Lick your fingers, don't bite them.

FLAMBÉED BANANAS WITH CYPRUS HARDWOOD SMOKED SALT

SERVES 2

Whereas my second son was born without a volume control dial, my first son was born without an equalizer. The little one bellows and howls at the ceiling, pounds and slams on the floor. The big one rolls his eyes, giggles, and plays mind games, then lavishes you with smiles. Not surprisingly, their loves and fears and wants are nearly opposite, though not in the way you might expect. The big one, when he isn't politicking, just wants to create elaborate dioramas of war and space travel. The little one, when he isn't fighting, just wants to climb into your lap for a cuddle. The younger one loves to cook, the elder is a formidable epicurean. They are made from completely different machinery, as if one was crafted by a Swiss watchmaker, the other by a Tasmanian shaman. But they both love flambéed bananas with smoked salt. Cyprus hardwood smoked salt lends woody glints of bacon to the dish, while the salt's unique massive crystals lend a perfect crunch. Either way, the dish has everything. Banana sugars caramelizing in hot butter, bourbon exploding into fire, and a globe of ice cream—the whole thing set into a smoky haze, like a carnival entering a battlefield.

1 tablespoon unsalted butter

2 bananas, peeled, cut in half, the halves sliced lengthwise

¼ cup bourbon or brandy

1 tablespoon light brown sugar

¼ cup crème fraîche or 2 scoops vanilla bean ice cream

2 two-finger pinches Cyprus hardwood smoked, Halen Môn oak smoked, Maldon smoked, or Maine Apple Smoked salt

Heat a large skillet over medium heat. Add the butter and swirl around the skillet to coat the bottom. When the butter is almost completely melted, add the bananas and sauté until the bottoms are crispy brown, 3 to 4 minutes, checking by slightly lifting one edge of a piece with a spatula. Taking care not to break the slices, flip and fry the bananas until the bottoms are golden, about 3 minutes. Arrange the bananas on plates or shallow bowls.

Remove the skillet from the heat and add the bourbon. Return the pan to the heat and bring the liquid to a boil. Stir in the sugar until melted.

Scoop the crème fraiche or ice cream over the banana and drizzle the sauce over everything. Sprinkle with the salt.

OPTION: Thrill-seekers and bourbon-lovers can opt to deglaze the pan by pouring an additional 2 ounces of bourbon into the hot skillet and tilting the pan edge into the flame to ignite the boiling alcohol; then drizzle the sauce over the bananas.

PAILLARD OF CHICKEN WITH TARRAGON AND FLAKE SALT

SERVES 2

As a child walking into an Italian restaurant in San Francisco's North Beach district, I would put on a brave face and glue myself to my father's side. A cacophony of sensations would accost my nose, my ears, and my staring eyeballs. The smell of stale red wine overlaid with steaming starch. Preoccupied waitresses shoving their heavy bodies through the thick yellow air, moving from table to table with armloads of bread and heaping plates of sea creatures smoldering under garlic and basil. Greasy overhead speakers thumping from their tattered baffles; a dishwasher roaring in the back; and overlaying all, the incessant thudding of a wooden mallet slamming a defenseless piece of chicken or veal. Indifferent to my concern, my father would smile. "Howard!" the restaurant owner would bellow, wading through the crowd to deliver a tumbler of red wine. And the two would launch into boisterous talk about herbs and oils and salt, my dad gesturing appreciatively to the monster with the wood mallet and saying, "Yes, yes, chicken very thin." For much of my childhood, I thought the measure of a good restaurant was the ferocity of the butcher up front pounding flesh, and the ensuing experience of meat so wonderfully tender and mild that it melted away the world's hazards. With a flourish of flake salt to accentuate the play of texture and savor on the palate, this paillard is quick, easy, and enormously satisfying. If you like, substitute veal cutlets for the chicken, using Italian parsley in place of the tarragon.

2 split chicken breast halves

1 tablespoon olive oil

1 shallot, minced

1 tablespoon coarsely torn fresh tarragon leaves

1/2 cup white wine

2 tablespoons unsalted butter

1/4 teaspoon cracked black pepper

2 two-finger pinches coarse flake salt, such as Marlborough flakey, Maldon, or The Meadow Flake

Preheat the oven to 225°F. Coat the chicken breast halves with a thin film of olive oil. Place each chicken breast half on a sheet of foil, cover with another sheet of foil, and pound with the bottom of a heavy skillet or a flat meat pounder until very thin (about 1/8 inch thick) and the size of a small dinner plate.

Heat a large skillet (preferably cast iron) until very hot. Coat the skillet with a thin film of oil. Remove one sheet of foil from one of the pounded chicken breasts.

Using the remaining foil sheet to support the chicken, lift it on one palm and flip it over (chicken side down) into the hot pan. Remove the foil. Cook just until opaque, about 30 seconds per side.

When the chicken is done, transfer it to a plate and keep warm in the oven. Repeat with the remaining piece of chicken.

Turn down the heat to medium-low. Coat the skillet with a thin film of olive oil and sauté the shallot until transparent, about 45 seconds. Add the tarragon and the white wine. Turn up the heat to medium-high and boil until the liquid is lightly thickened, about 1 minute. Remove from the heat and swirl in the butter.

Season the chicken with the pepper and drizzle the sauce over the top. Serve immediately, finishing each plate with a flourish of flake salt.

BOILING

And he went forth unto the spring of the waters, and cast the salt in there, and said, Thus saith the Lord, I have healed these waters. —2 Kings 2:21

Salting the water for boiling or blanching vegetables can be greatly positive or vaguely negative depending on the vegetable in question. Hard, nonstarchy vegetables—everything from asparagus to green beans, carrots to peas—benefit from salt in the water at a concentration of about 3 percent (1 cupped handful, or about 2 tablespoons, of sel gris or coarse traditional salt per quart). The salt helps speed the softening of vegetables, making them cook more quickly and evenly. It also helps to minimize the loss of nutritious juices into the boiling water. The minerals, trace salts, and sugars naturally found in plants are core dimensions of their flavor and nutritional value. Cooking water without dissolved salt in it will draw these tasty elements from the plant cells, along with the vegetables' own juices.

A 3 percent concentration of salt in blanching water shifts the osmotic pressure between the liquid in the pot and the intercellular liquid in the vegetables more to the vegetables' favor. In other words, well-salted water keeps everything locked up in the vegetables where it belongs.

SALT YOUR EGG-BOILING WATER

No task confounds the home chef more surely and more thoroughly than peeling a hard-boiled egg. To make peeling easier, add three of four three-finger pinches of salt per quart of cold water, then boil the egg. Salt penetrates the shell and causes the proteins in the egg white to congeal and pull back from the inside wall of the egg shell. Cool the cooked egg quickly under cold running water, wet your hands, crack the egg, and enjoy the feeling of peeling with the experts. ∎

SALT YOUR PASTA WATER

Salting your pasta water is like rearing children: generosity doesn't spoil them, neglect does. Tradition, which is a great guide for pasta, says to salt your water to the taste of the sea, which is 3.5 percent salt in the great oceans. A gallon of water weighs 8.35 pounds (the United Kingdom's imperial gallon weighs 10 pounds), so bringing a gallon of fresh water to 3.5 percent salinity takes about 4.5 ounces of salt. But the Italians live on the Mediterranean Sea, which at about 3.8 percent is even saltier than the ocean. So figure an easy 4 to 5 ounces of salt for pasta water. This is two handfuls (about 1/2 cup) of salt per gallon of water! It's a lot, but salt your pasta heavily and the dish will behave itself wonderfully, and oftentimes there will be no need to salt the sauce at all.

Take pasta, well-seasoned from salted pasta water and cooked al dente, and add fresh vegetables and herbs or some lightly sautéed garlic, cream, and white wine. The flavors are left free in their childlike innocence to pursue butterflies across a blond pasture of fresh noodles. ■

However, salting the water for boiling starchy vegetables, especially large pieces of potato, will cause the outsides of the vegetables to become mushy before the insides are done. So for potatoes it is best to salt the vegetable after cooking.

It pays to salt water for boiling pasta with a heavy hand. Salt not only helps to flavor the noodles, but it limits the gelation of starch, reducing the amount of water-soluble nutrients lost during cooking and keeping the stickiness to a minimum. Heavily salted pasta water allows more salt to be absorbed into the pasta as it cooks. This gives the pasta more flavor, sure, but it also sets up the pasta to play the role that Italian tradition has defined for it as the foundation for fresh ingredients or a sauce. A classic Italian pasta dish is a case study in simplicity, so the quality of the ingredients is directly proportional to the quality of the dish. Use good salt in your pasta water.

Although it is true that salted water boils at a higher temperature than unsalted water—so theoretically food cooked in salted water should cook faster—at 3 percent concentration, the boiling point of water rises by only 1° or 2°F—hardly a significant change, and not enough to affect the cooking time of most ingredients.

When cooking dried legumes, you can reduce boiling times by adding salt to the soaking liquid. At a concentration of about 1 percent (8 three-finger pinches or 2 teaspoons per quart of water), salt hastens the softening of hard bean fibers by displacing magnesium from pectins in the cell walls, thereby making them easier to dissolve.

PASTA MARGHERITA WITH FIORE DI CERVIA

SERVES 4

Behind the jubilant liquid tomato smile of pasta margherita lies an intellect of herbs and garlic. The one covering for the other is a seduction of sorts, an invitation that propriety prevents you from accepting too eagerly. Sprinkle your margherita with the crystalline sweetness of Fiore di Cervia, the fine salt from the balmy Adriatic flats south of Ravenna, and marvel as the tart-sweet play of tomato and pasta asserts itself. Ennobled by the salt's fruity warmth, the sauce is freed of its ties to the herbs that first defined it. Eyes open, head borne aloft, your margherita is as beautiful in body as in spirit.

2 small handfuls sel gris

12 ounces small pasta, such as farfalle or conchiglie

2 large ripe tomatoes (about 8 ounces each)

1 clove garlic, minced

1/2 cup chopped fresh basil leaves

3 tablespoons extra-virgin olive oil

4 two-finger pinches Fiore di Cervia salt

Freshly grated Parmigiano-Reggiano cheese to taste (optional)

Bring a large pot of water to a boil over high heat. Add the sel gris and stir to dissolve. Add the pasta, stir to separate the noodles, and allow the water to return to a boil. Reduce the heat so that the water boils gently and boil until the noodles are barely tender, about 10 minutes.

While the pasta is cooking, remove the stem scar from the tomatoes with a small knife. Cut the tomatoes into thin slices, the slices into strips, and the strips into a fine dice. Combine the tomatoes and garlic in a pasta serving bowl.

When the pasta is done, drain it and shake off most of the water. Don't worry if it is still a little wet. Toss the pasta with the tomatoes, basil, and oil. Serve, then finish with the remaining salt over the top and toss. Top with freshly grated cheese, if desired.

BLANCHED SPRING PEAS WITH SAFFRON CRÈME FRAÎCHE AND CYPRUS FLAKE SALT

SERVES 4

Peas are so perfect on their own, it's a wonder it ever occurred to anyone to cook them in the first place. But fortunately someone did. A trillion peas later, after endless refinements on the art of making a pea more perfect than a pea, the French Laundry created its cold pea soup, a spring rain cloud of viridian sugars skimming a truffled forest. But before Thomas Keller could make his soup, we had to grow up watching Julia Child chiding us about making the blanching water incredibly hot, and salting it, and treating the pea with the utmost love and care. It was Julia Child who rescued cooked peas from the ignominy of creamed cafeteria concoctions, restored their preciousness, and gave them back to us like so many incandescent pearls rolled from the fair hand of nature. A drop of saffron cream shot through with a taut bolt of salt cradles and charges this blanched pea with its own electricity.

1 pinch saffron threads

2 teaspoons vermouth

¼ cup crème fraîche

1 small handful sel gris

1 pound hulled fresh spring peas or frozen green garden peas, thawed

4 two-finger pinches Cyprus flake salt

Bring a quart of water to a boil in a saucepan over medium-high heat.

Meanwhile, crumble the saffron into the vermouth in a small bowl and set aside until the vermouth turns golden, about 5 minutes. Mix in the crème fraîche.

Add the sel gris to the boiling water. When the water returns to a boil, stir in the peas and boil for about 3 minutes, until the peas are bright green and tender. Drain thoroughly.

Serve the peas dolloped with the saffron crème fraiche and seasoned with a pinch of Cyprus Silver per serving.

BAKING

Of all smells, bread; of all tastes, salt. —George Herbert

The structure of baked goods is built on gluten, the protein in wheat doughs. Gluten is strengthened by salt as positively charged sodium ions and negatively charged chloride ions attach themselves to the charged portions of wheat proteins, keeping those charged parts from repelling one another, thus encouraging the protein strands to come closer together and bond more thoroughly.

Though some traditional breads are made without salt (see page 207), most bread recipes call for salt (usually in a quantity of about 2 percent of flour weight) to improve the flavor of bread as well as its texture and rise. Unrefined salts that contain calcium and magnesium have been shown to improve the strength of gluten better than salts that are almost pure sodium chloride. In sourdough breads, unrefined salt may also help limit the gluten-damaging activity of the souring bacteria.

When making baked goods that are leavened with beaten egg whites, such as soufflés or sponge cakes, it is best to add salt to the other parts of the batter rather than directly to the beaten egg. As salt dissolves and breaks into its ionic forms, the negatively and positively charged ions compete with proteins for bonding sites, thereby reducing the number of protein-to-protein bonds and weakening the structure of the egg foam.

When salting the outside of a batter or dough before baking, avoid moist salts like sel gris, which will dehydrate rapidly in the heat of the oven, sucking fat from the dough up to the surface where it will burn to an unsightly dark color. Cookies, pastries, and piecrusts are wonderful with salt glistening on their tops, but confine your salt choices to rock salts, very dry evaporated sea salts, or thin flake salts.

SOFT PRETZELS WITH HICKORY SMOKED SALT

MAKES 6 LARGE PRETZELS

Most flat breads carry with them a long list of social and culinary baggage. Pita, matzo, injera, casava, rieska: you have to take the bread's cuisine with you to the table. The pretzel is unique because you can take it wherever you want! It's a snack food through and through, though its twisted form is steeped in folklore and symbolism. The first pretzels were made in monasteries in the seventh century, and given out on church feast days. The shape is said to represent a child's arms in prayer. I think a better resemblance is found in the image of two wrestlers drinking beer—which monks also invented. The smoky majesty of Maine hickory smoked salt is a miracle that the monks would surely have prayed for.

1 cup warm water (110º to 115ºF)
2 teaspoons dry yeast
1 teaspoon sugar
4 tablespoons extra-virgin olive oil
2 teaspoons fine traditional salt
2 3/4 cups bread flour, plus more if needed
1/4 cup cornmeal
3 tablespoons baking soda
6 three-finger pinches Maine hickory smoked salt

To prepare the pretzel dough, combine the warm water, yeast, and sugar in a large bowl, stirring until mixed. Let sit until foamy, about 5 minutes. Add 3 tablespoons of the olive oil, the fine traditional salt, and the flour and stir until a kneadable dough forms.

Turn onto a floured surface and knead until the dough is smooth and elastic, about 5 minutes, adding more flour as needed to keep the dough from sticking to your hands or the work surface. Try to add as little flour as possible.

Coat a large bowl with the remaining tablespoon of oil and add the dough, turning to coat it with the oil. Cover and let rise until doubled in bulk, about 1 hour in a warm spot or overnight in the refrigerator.

Preheat the oven to 425ºF. Sprinkle the cornmeal over the bottom of a large rimmed sheet pan; set aside.

Punch down the dough until most of the air is released, then divide the dough into 6 equal pieces. Lightly flour your hands and a work surface. Roll and stretch each piece of dough into a rope about 18 inches long.

To form a pretzel, lay a dough rope out straight on the floured work surface. Take one end of the rope in each hand. Bring one end of the rope in a loop about 1/2 inch across the center. Bring the other side of the rope across the first side so that it crosses the center of the rope at about the same point and so the overlap is about the same. To form the knot in the center of the pretzel, uncross your hands if you haven't already and grab the end of the rope closest to each hand. Cross the end of the rope over the top, forming a twist at the center of the pretzel. The rope should now be in a shape that resembles a pretzel. Push or pull as necessary to even it out and press the ends onto the knot so they stay in place.

Bring a quart of water to a boil in a large skillet. Stir in the baking soda and adjust the heat so the water barely simmers. Carefully set a pretzel in the water and simmer until it puffs, about 20 seconds per side. Lift it from the pan with a slotted spoon or spatula, allowing the excess water to drip back into the skillet, and place it on the cornmeal-coated sheet pan. Repeat with the other 5 pretzels.

Sprinkle the tops of the pretzels with the smoked salt, and bake until golden brown, 12 to 15 minutes. Remove to a cooling rack and let cool for at least 20 minutes, to allow the pretzels to firm up and get a little chewy. Eat within 24 hours.

CHERRY PIE WITH PAPOHAKU

SERVES 8

Imagine running through the tessellated shadows of the forest with a mustard jar of just-caught pollywogs and a sharpened stick for a spear, scrambling up the levee and lunging into culverts, your dog baying ahead in the distance. You slip on a wet log, stumble, catch yourself on the mossy shoulder of a boulder, oblivious to the mud and moist lichen flecking your arms. You are lean, quick, alert, leaping streams and plunging through dense brush. Lungs filled with the crisp air, perspiration on your back, eyes wild with happiness—you are free, alive, home. The old hound nuzzles up to your hand as you mount the porch steps, your mother's greeting at the screen door, the aroma of cherry pie on the windowsill, your life a storybook distilled in the sweet mirth of salt.

2 three-finger pinches Papohaku white or Kona salt

3 cups all-purpose flour

1/2 cup (1 stick) cold unsalted butter, cut into teaspoon-size pieces

6 tablespoons very cold shortening, cut into pieces

8 to 10 tablespoons ice water

2 pints sour cherries (about 3 pounds), stemmed and pitted

2 cups confectioners' sugar

1/4 cup cornstarch

1 tablespoons currant jelly mixed with 1 tablespoon water

To make the crust, crush 1 pinch of salt between your fingers and combine with the flour. Using two knives or a pastry cutter, cut the butter into the flour until the pieces are the size of large grains of rice. Cut in the shortening in the same way. Sprinkle with the ice water and continue mixing the dough with a pastry cutter or fork just until all visible dryness disappears and the dough is still slightly crumbly. Form the dough into 2 disks. Cover tightly with plastic wrap and refrigerate for at least 30 minutes.

Preheat the oven to 400°F.

When the dough is chilled, unwrap and flour one of the pastry disks and roll it on a floured board with a floured pin until between 1/4 and 1/8 inch thick. Line a 9-inch pie pan with the pastry round, gently easing the crust into the pan, trimming as needed to leave a 1/2-inch overhang all around. Poke holes over the bottom of the crust with the tines of a fork and refrigerate while you make the filling.

To make the filling, toss the cherries in a large bowl with the confectioners' sugar and cornstarch. Set aside.

Roll out the other disk of dough in the same way, and cut into 1/2-inch-wide strips. Remove the pastry-lined pan from the refrigerator. Weave the strips of pastry on top of the filling to make a lattice top. Trim the edges of the lattice top crust so that it extends about an inch past the rim of the pan all the way around. Fold this overhang under the rim of the bottom crust and crimp the edges with your fingers, sealing the top crust to the bottom.

Bake until the pastry is browned and the filling can be seen bubbling through the openings in the crust, about 50 minutes.

Just before the pie comes out of the oven, melt the jelly mixture in a small saucepan. As soon as the pie comes out of the oven, brush the lattice with melted jelly and sprinkle the remaining pinch of salt over the top, aiming for the crust lattice. Let cool for at least an hour before serving.

BALI RAMA OATMEAL CHOCOLATE CHIP COOKIES

MAKES 18 MEDIUM COOKIES

In the physical universe, there is precious little closer to perfection than an oatmeal chocolate chip cookie. Unlike standard cookies, they are never cakey or disappointingly hard, not too sweet, with the butter and oats finding common cause in each other's virtues. So how do you improve upon perfection?

Topping these cookies with a beautiful flaky salt brings out the cow in the butter, the hills in the oats, and the jungle in the chocolate. Topping them with the salt rather than just adding it to the batter sets the salt free to work its mojo with each of the ingredients as they combine in your mouth.

For these cookies, I prefer Bali Rama Pyramid sea salt, which has really cool hollow pyramidal crystals and a great, snappy impact. The advantage of using a flake salt here is that it remains delicate even after baking. The Bali Rama Pyramid salt does a spectacular job of bringing just enough drama to the cookies to make them sparkle while keeping everything mellow enough to assure they remain a comfort food. Other good choices are Cyprus flake or Halen Môn, or, in a pinch, any good fleur de sel.

1 1/2 cups all-purpose flour

1 teaspoon baking soda

1 two-finger pinch Bali Rama Pyramid salt, coarsely ground with your fingers

2 1/2 cups regular or quick oats (not instant)

1 cup (2 sticks) unsalted butter, softened

1/2 cup granulated sugar

1 cup packed brown sugar

1 1/2 teaspoons vanilla extract

2 eggs

2 cups dark chocolate morsels

2 three-finger pinches flake salt, such as Bali Rama Pyramid

Preheat the oven to 350°F and line two cookie sheets with foil.

Mix together the flour, baking soda, the two-finger pinch of Bali Rama Pyramid salt, and oats in a bowl; set aside.

Beat the butter, granulated sugar, brown sugar, and vanilla in a large mixing bowl by hand until well combined. Don't overmix. Add the eggs and beat by hand until well combined. Stir in the flour mixture and beat well by hand for about a minute. This will develop some gluten in the batter, which will help the cookies hold their shape and stay chewy. Stir in the chocolate morsels.

Scoop rounded tablespoonfuls of batter and place them about 2 inches apart on the prepared cookie sheets. Sprinkle the cookies with the flake salt and bake just until the edges are browned and the centers are still soft, about 8 minutes.

Remove from the oven and let rest for 3 minutes. Using a small spatula, transfer the cookies to a cooling rack and allow to cool for at least 20 minutes before devouring. These cookies stay fresh for nigh upon a week if stored in a cookie jar shaped like Winnie the Pooh.

SALT CRUST

There is nothing new except what has been forgotten. —Marie Antoinette

Many countries have a tradition of cooking in a salt crust, but the French are crazy about it. Fish (*daurade en croûte au gros sel*), crustaceans (*queues de langoustes en croûte de sel*), fowl (*magret de canard en croûte de sel*), beef (*côte de boeuf en croûte de sel*), lamb (*gigot d'agneau en croûte de sel*), vegetables (*artichauts en croûte de sel*) and even cheese (*reblochon en croûte de sel*)—all are given their time in hot salt. Cooking in a salt crust does an amazing job of dehydrating the surface of food enough to concentrate its flavors while sealing in enough of the moisture normally lost through cooking to make everything incredibly moist, tender, and aromatic.

The salt crust tradition is alive and well in contemporary cuisine, but with a tragic twist: sel gris has been replaced by kosher salt. Replacing the supermoist, balanced crystals of sel gris with the ragged, dried, refined crystals of koshering salt is tantamount to abandoning the wood-fired oven in favor of a microwave. Where the sel gris harbors 13 percent moisture within its crystals, kosher salt has none. The moment the koshering crystals of kosher salt touch the exterior of the food they set about sucking out all moisture possible, only to release everything into the oven as it heats. Salt crust made with koshering salt is formed from moisture extracted from the food. Salt crust made with sel gris is formed from the moisture of the salt. This is the way salt crusts were originally made, and it's how they should still be made today.

SALT CRUST-ROASTED PARTRIDGE WITH FIGS AND CHOCOLATE-BALSAMIC SYRUP

SERVES 4

Don your chain mail and broadsword. Ancient food, harbinger of tragedy and regret, roast partridges spur thoughts of delicious violence, provoking a savage appetite spurred by rich flavors and primal aromas. Daedalus, who built the labyrinth that held the Minotaur, flung his brilliant disciple Perdrix off a roof, only to have him transformed into a partridge by the goddess Athena, who has a thing for geniuses. One of the oldest partridge recipes comes from the French, who would encrust foods in salt to protect them from the scorching heat of the oven. The guards of the Aigues-Mortes salt fields, had they survived being massacred by invading Burgundians, would surely have appreciated this dish. The Burgundians were eventually massacred as well, and their bodies buried in a tower filled with salt. Athena would have approved of their ingenuity, and of salt crusting in general, though it is doubtful that she would have approved of this choice of bird for the roasting.

2 cloves garlic, minced

2 tablespoons chopped fresh rosemary

4 juniper berries, crushed

1/2 teaspoon freshly ground black pepper

4 partridges (8 to 10 ounces each), or squab, cleaned, washed, and dried

4 large fresh figs, stems removed

2 tablespoons extra-virgin olive oil

4 pounds sel gris

1/4 to 1/3 cup water (optional)

1/2 cup balsamic vinegar

1/2 ounce bittersweet chocolate

Preheat the oven to 400°F.

Mix together the garlic, rosemary, juniper, and pepper in a small bowl. Rub the partridges inside and out with the mixture and stuff a fig into the cavity of each bird.

Heat the oil in a large skillet over medium-high heat. Put as many of the birds as will fit comfortably in the pan and brown as evenly as possible all over their surfaces, about 2 minutes per side. Repeat until all of the birds are browned. Set aside to cool for 15 minutes.

Have ready a large casserole dish just large enough to accommodate the four birds. Press the sel gris between your fingers. It should be moist enough to stick together. If it isn't, stir in a few tablespoons of water until the salt is moist enough to cling together when firmly pressed.

In the casserole dish, make four 1/2-inch-thick oval pads of the sel gris, each just large enough to hold a bird. Place a bird on each oval and pack the remaining salt around each bird until it is completely encased. Bake for 30 minutes.

While the birds are roasting, boil the balsamic vinegar in a small saucepan or skillet until reduced by half. Remove from the heat and swirl in the chocolate until melted; keep warm.

Remove the birds from the oven and let stand for 5 minutes. Break the salt crusts and brush off any salt clinging to the surface of the partridges. Remove the figs from the cavity and arrange on four plates, along with the birds. Drizzle with chocolate-balsamic syrup and serve.

RIB STEAK IN SALT CRUST

SERVES 4

One of the great diversions of life in France is an intimate evening at the local bistro, where mainstays of French food are reduced to their basic elements for quick, casual dining. *Côte de boeuf en croûte de sel* is among the great bistro dishes: beef rib steak, cut tremendously thick, perfectly cooked, and served piping hot with a little herbed butter. Roasted potatoes can accompany the dish, but it is perhaps best to leave the steak to itself; the dish is so simple, so satisfying, that you will likely find yourself thinking of little more than another sip of good red wine and a nice green salad to round things off. This preparation calls for a lot of salt, but fear not, the resulting steak will be seasoned to perfection. Whatever you do, use moist sel gris, never desiccating kosher salt, for your salt crust.

1 tablespoon olive oil

1 two-rib bone-in rib steak (about 3 pounds and 2 to 3 inches thick)

1 teaspoon freshly cracked black pepper

2 pounds sel gris, such as sel gris de l'Ile de Noirmoutier

2 to 5 tablespoons water (optional)

Leaves from 2 rosemary sprigs

HERB BUTTER

4 tablespoons unsalted butter, softened

1/2 clove garlic, minced

2 tablespoons finely minced fresh herbs, such as Italian parsley, rosemary, and/or thyme

2 two-finger pinches fleur de sel de Camargue

Preheat the oven to 425°F.

Heat a heavy iron skillet over high heat for 10 minutes until very hot. Add the olive oil and swirl to coat the bottom of the pan. Pat the surface of the steak dry and season with the cracked pepper. Brown the steak on both sides, 1 to 2 minutes per side.

Have ready a baking dish just large enough to hold the steak. Press the sel gris between your fingers. It should be moist enough to stick together. If it isn't, stir in a few tablespoons of water until the salt is moist enough to cling together when firmly pressed.

Spread the sel gris 1/2 inch thick in the baking dish. Scatter half the rosemary leaves over the salt. Place

the steak on top and scatter the remaining rosemary leaves over the steak. Pack the salt around the steak until it is completely encased. Bake for 30 minutes for rare, or 40 minutes for medium-rare.

While the steak is roasting, make the herb butter. Mash together the butter, garlic, and herbs in a small bowl with a fork until well blended. Gently stir in the fleur de sel, trying to keep the salt crystals as intact as possible. Set aside.

Remove the beef from the oven and let stand for 5 minutes. Break the salt crust, brush off any excessive salt adhering to the steak, and remove to a cutting board. Cut into thick slices, arrange three or four slices on each plate, and serve with a generous ball of herbed butter.

COOKING ON SALT BLOCKS

For me, habit is just a synonym for death. —Juliet Binoche

Everyone knows about salt on food, but what about food on salt? Massive, candy-pink slabs of Himalayan salt offer a whole new medium on which to prepare and serve food. Arranging slices of green apple, pear, and mozzarella on a platter of Himalayan salt will season all three to perfection. Slice salmon sashimi on a salt slab and watch the fish grow pale and firm, gently curing at the table before you eat it. Thick blocks of Himalayan salt can be heated on the stove to temperatures in excess of 600 degrees to sear sea scallops, flank steak, or duck breast. At the other temperature extreme, you can freeze the block to zero and whip up a lightly salted frozen custard on it.

When you cook on Himalayan block salt, several things are happening at the same time: the heat of the block sears and browns proteins, melts fats, and caramelizes sugars, while the salt subtly dehydrates the surface and seasons the food. Together the heat and salt work in wonderful harmony, producing unique salty-toasty-caramelized flavors and delicately crisped surfaces as thin as a single layer of glaze on porcelain.

When food is cooked on Himalayan salt blocks, moisture from the food dissolves the salt in the block, which can then transmit too much salt to whatever you are cooking. For that reason, it is important to get the block hot enough that it immediately evaporates any moisture coming from an ingredient.

The presence or addition of fat is another consideration. Salt isn't fat soluble, so if you cook a very fatty food (such as duck breast) on salt, or put oil on the block while cooking a food that is moist but not fatty (such as summer squash), there will be less interaction between the salt and the food.

Perhaps the most challenging part of cooking on Himalayan salt blocks is heating them. As far as cooking surfaces go, salt is relatively soft. As it heats, it will naturally develop cracks and crevices. Over time, these will grow until eventually your salt block breaks. Just how long a salt block will last depends on the natural flaws in the block, how evenly you heat it, what you cook on it, and how carefully you clean it. The basic rule is: the slower you heat it, the longer it will last. Preheat the block slowly at very low heat for fifteen minutes, then allow at least 30 minutes to heat your salt block at medium to high heat to the desired cooking temperature.

An unoiled salt block gives very few visual clues as to its temperature, though it will tend to whiten a little as it nears 500°F or so. However, as with any pan, you can tell the approximate heat by holding your hand about three inches away. If the heat feels uncomfortably intense, the block is ready. If it just feels nice and warm, it's not hot enough. No matter how tempting, do not touch a salt block that's heating or cooling. Wait until you know the block is at or near room temperature.

SALT BLOCK OWNER'S GUIDE

A boulder of Himalayan rock salt emerges from the darkness of a sixteenth century mineshaft in Pakistan and explodes into light. It has been 500 million years since the sun last warmed this salt as it collected on the shores of a primordial sea. Otherworldly, its crystals catch and refract a lightshow of alizarin, vermillion, rose, and blush. Earth's abiding creativity is yours to enjoy. Here are some basic guidelines that will help you make the most of Himalayan pink salt.

Buying

Before shopping, decide what you want to use your salt block for. If you are going to use it for serving foods at room temperature or cooler, pick a block for its flaws, the fissures and colors that give the block some personality. Choose a block in whatever dimension you wish, noting that thinner blocks often catch the light beautifully, while thicker pieces offer their imposing physical presence to the table. If you aim to heat it, plainness is preferable.

When shopping for a Himalayan salt block for cooking, to choose blocks that are at least 1 inch thick, and preferably 1½ inches thick or more. My preference is to use 2-inch-thick blocks. Be sure the block is free of either large patches of impurities or clearly defined strata of impurities. The block should be consistently translucent. Very opaque or milky coloration is often an indication that the salt crystals are not densely packed. Moisture can get inside these blocks and cause them to pop, sometimes violently, when heated. On the other hand, more opaque pieces can be the most beautiful to look at, and they make excellent plates for serving room temperature or chilled foods.

Utensil Use

Use a stainless steel spatula when sautéing on a salt block, and don't be afraid to put some muscle into it. Himalayan pink salt is not a nonstick surface. Bits of cooked food will adhere to the surface of the salt. If you use a Teflon or rubber spatula when turning or removing the food, a layer of that beautifully browned and salted surface will likely be left on the block. To get the most flavor and the prettiest appearance, steady the salt block by holding a corner of it with a thick oven mitt or grill mitt, and then very firmly when flipping or removing food.

Heating

Start heating the block before you even begin assembling ingredients for your dish. Set a burner on your stove to its lowest possible setting and place the block over the heat. Giving your salt block 10 or 15 minutes to warm from room temperature to 150° or 200°F allows it to evaporate out and off any moisture locked up in the matrix of the crystals, and allows the heat to spread evenly through the block, minimizing the stresses caused by expansion.

On a gas stove, increase the heat in increments every 10 minutes, from low to medium and medium to high. It should take around 35 minutes to heat a block from room temperature to its high temperature of about 600°F. On an electric stove, use a metal ring such as tart pan with a pop-out bottom, or else use a heat diffusing ring to keep the block away from direct contact with the heating element. Add 2 to 3 minutes per step, allowing at least 45 minutes total to heat. To heat on a gas or charcoal grill, follow the instructions on page 273.

This slow preheating is especially important the first time you use the block because it is the most stressful time for the block. The different mineral components and various crystalline structures and any existing cracks will all expand at different rates as the temperature rises from room temperature to several hundred degrees. Also, there may be small amounts of moisture within the salt itself, accumulated along the road from the womb of the mountain in Pakistan to your kitchen counter. Heating the salt block very slowly the first time gives the crystals an opportunity to form the microfissures that lend a little extra elasticity to the block, and also gives any moisture time to escape. This extra care during first-time use greatly extends its lifespan.

Maintenance

To keep your salt block looking pretty, remove it from the fire before or immediately after the food is cooked. As juicy slices of flank steak come off a sizzling hot salt block, things get exciting: guests become unruly, you yourself are hungry, and we often forget to turn off the heat immediately. This is especially true when you're using a charcoal grill. Charcoal heat can't just be turned off—even gas grills can take considerable time to cool down—and the salt block is a heavy, scary-looking white-hot thing that does not invite handling. The salt block is thus left to continue toasting in the 700°F temperatures of your charcoal kettle grill.

Don't let this happen. Keep several pot holders or grill mitts on the table by the side of the grill and remove the salt block from the fire just before the food is finished. This both gives you greater control as you remove the food from the salt block and means you can race straight to the table once you do so, allowing the salt block to cool down and minimizing the amount of blackening from the cooked proteins. Clean the salt block as soon as it has cooled to room temperature, usually a few hours later. Removing any carbon or excessive food will keep your block cleaner and better-looking for longer.

Cleaning and Storing

Be sure the block is fully cooled to room temperature before washing. Wet the salt block lightly under warm water, then scrub vigorously at any areas where food has stuck or any areas that appear glazed, as happens with cooked fat. Rinse with water again to wash clean. If necessary, repeat this process until satisfied. Note that no salt block will ever return to its full preheated splendor. Pat the block dry with a clean rag or paper towel and set the block on a drying rack. Store the block in a place where humidity is at a minimum or wrap salt blocks in several layers of paper towel and seal in a plastic bag to store. I keep some of mine on the windowsill, except during periods of major, protracted rain storms . . . which happen all too frequently in Portland, Oregon.

SALT STONE-BAKED DINNER ROLLS

MAKES 1 DOZEN ROLLS

Crusty, chewy, salty dinner rolls whose textures and flavors play wonderfully off the slowly melting pat of sweet cream butter you place inside: these are the perfect accompaniment to the salad or cheese course, and will provide an irresistible distraction from the main course of prime rib or leg of lamb. If you have children, keep the rolls on reserve until after the kids say they can't eat another bit of their meat or veggies. Then sit back and behold how they magically create enough room for a marathon runner's share of salty-yeasty carbs.

1 recipe soft pretzel dough (page 259), minus smoked salt
3 (8 by 8 by 2-inch) blocks Himalayan pink salt
1 tablespoon olive oil

Prepare the pretzel dough as described up to the point that the dough is risen and punched down, but before it is punched down and divided.

Cut the dough into 12 pieces. Roll a piece into a ball, then stretch the top of the ball over itself, making a sort of seashell shape. Squeeze the edges together so the dough ball is smooth and shiny on one side and has a creased seam on the other. Place the ball, seam side down, on a sheet pan and move on to the next. After you have formed all 12 rolls, cover with plastic wrap and let stand for 1 hour in a dry warm place.

While the rolls are proofing, place the rack in the lower third of the oven and preheat the oven to 400°F.

Heat the salt blocks as described in Heating on page 269.

Remove the plastic wrap from the rolls, and push down lightly on each of them to create flatter rolls roughly the shape of bagels without holes. Brush the tops with a thin film of olive oil, making sure that the oil does not drip down the sides and collect underneath the rolls, where it will inhibit the salt from interacting with the dough. Using a small spatula, transfer the rolls onto the salt blocks and close the oven door. Bake for about 12 minutes, until puffed and pale brown.

Transfer the rolls to a cooling rack with a spatula and let cool for at least 15 minutes before serving. Turn off the oven and allow the salt blocks to cool in the oven before removing and cleaning them (see opposite page).

GRILL-FRIED BACON AND EGGS

SERVES 2

The only place to start with something so absurd yet perfect as this dish is in the middle. The bacon is ready to flip in about a minute and a half. The edges get super-crispy (who has ever noticed before that bacon has corners?), while the lean inside stays wet and meaty. And the fat actually firms and ripples, like lardo that's been working out. Suspense builds when you flip the bacon and crack the eggs on top. It's awful—like watching a landslide threaten to wipe out your village—as the egg whites run toward the edge of the hot brick, but the salt is so hot they rapidly lose steam (pun intended) and sizzle to a halt, with at most just a few rivulets dribbling over the sides of the block. The whole thing is done in less than 5 minutes. Take a bite and things get weirder still, with the sheen of salt simmering underneath the egg and bacon instead of on top, and a jumble of textures—creamy, crunchy, chewy, juicy, fatty, fleshy, and eggy.

1 (8 by 8 by 2-inch) block Himalayan pink salt
4 large eggs
8 slices baguette
2 tablespoons olive oil
4 thick slices bacon
Freshly cracked black pepper to taste

Put the salt block on a gas grill, set the burners to low, and cover the grill. After 15 minutes increase the heat to medium, and after 15 minutes more increase the heat to high. Heat 15 minutes more. (If you are using a charcoal grill, you will need to preheat the block on a stove as described on page 269. Once the block is preheated, build a medium hot charcoal fire and transfer the hot block to the grill 15 minutes before cooking, using heavy grill or oven mitts.)

Crack the eggs into individual ramekins, teacups, or other small containers; set aside.

Brush the bread slices with oil and set aside.

When the salt block is very hot (you should only be able to hold your hand above it for 2 or 3 seconds), lay the bacon slices on the block so they are parallel to one another and separated into two groups of 2 slices each. Cook until sizzling and browned on the bottom, about 3 minutes. If the coals should flare up, douse with a spray of water. Try not to get any water on the salt block.

Flip the bacon. Carefully pour 2 eggs on top of each group of 2 bacon slices. Pour slowly and guide the eggs with a small spatula so that they land right on the bacon. The eggs will start to set up as soon as they hit the salt block. Don't worry if some egg white runs over the edge of the block. Cover the grill and cook for 3 to 4 minutes, until the white is set but the yolk is still runny.

During the last minute, toast the bread slices over the moderate heat area of the grill.

Lift each portion of bacon and eggs off the grill onto a warm plate. Add the toast and season the eggs liberally with freshly cracked black pepper. Using a grill mitt, oven mitt, or pot holders, remove the salt block from the grill grate and set aside to cool before cleaning and storing (see page 270).

HIMALAYAN SALT BOWL CHOCOLATE FONDUE

SERVES 4

Is it a gimmick, or is it a serious cooking technique? Is it both? Who cares? Preparing and serving chocolate fondue in a bowl of primordial pink salt is easier, makes a snazzier presentation, and tastes better than conventionally prepared chocolate fondue. Salt bowls, which weigh in excess of six pounds, provide phenomenal thermal stability. This makes it very difficult to overheat the bowl and burn the chocolate. Once heated to the desired temperature, the salt bowl stays warm, keeping the fondue beautifully liquid during its fleeting existence before it's gobbled up. And the salt. Because salt isn't soluble in fat, the chocolate itself just luxuriates in the bowl, doing nothing. It's the touch of heavy cream that transmits a kiss of salt to the fondue's liquid body. Try cherry, orange, or traditional Angostura-style bitters to vary the flavors.

1/3 cup heavy cream

1 heavy bowl of Himalayan pink salt (pint or quart capacity)

1 dash old-fashioned bitters

2 cups dark chocolate chips (60 percent cacao or darker is preferable)

2 bananas

24 strawberries, washed and greens trimmed

Remove the cream from the refrigerator so that it loses its chill.

Place the salt bowl on a stove burner over low heat and allow to warm for 30 minutes.

When the salt bowl is warm, about 125°F, add the cream and heat until just warm to the touch, about 3 minutes. Add the bitters and stir in 1 cup of the chocolate chips. When the chocolate is mostly melted, add in the remaining chocolate and stir until completely melted.

While the chocolate is melting, peel the bananas and slice into 1/2-inch thick rounds. Arrange the strawberries and bananas on a serving plate.

With oven mitts, remove the salt bowl from the heat and place on a trivet. Serve the fruit with long skewers for dipping into the chocolate.

To clean the salt bowl, allow to cool, moisten and scrub with a nondetergent scrub pad, rinse under cold water, and pat dry with a clean cloth or paper towels.

SALT BLOCK-GRILLED FLANK STEAK

SERVES 4

Flank steak has to be pretty much the best thing this side of getting a foot rub while drinking a root beer float. But it's tough. It's ornery. There is a common strategy to making flank steak supple enough to eat without popping your jaw out of joint: marinating. I've made coffee and ginger marinades, lime and tequila marinades, smoked salt and chile pepper marinades, vinegar and sugar marinades, you name it. Every time, great steak. But think of the poor steak: a wonderful, flavor-packed piece of meat subjugated to intense acids and sugars and salts. What if you're a purist, racked with guilt? The flank steak puts you in a quandary. How do we get the elemental flavor out of a meat that resists the teeth? As usual, the solution to every quandary is to think outside the box, or in this case, outside the pan.

The two simple tricks to this dish (if you can call steak seared on a giant block of salt a dish) are cutting the meat thin, against the grain, and cooking it fast at a high temperature. Oh, and *don't* cook it on indifferent steel, but on a block of glowing, flavor-packing, tenderizing Himalayan pink salt.

1 (two-pound) flank steak
1 (8 by 8 by 2-inch or larger) block Himalayan pink salt

Cut the flank steak lengthwise along the grain of the meat, creating two long strips. Then, turning the piece perpendicular to the blade of your knife, cut the strips across the fiber of the meat into 1/4-inch-thick strips, each about 2 to 3 inches long. Set aside.

Heat the salt block on a stove, as described in Heating on page 269.

To test whether the block is hot enough, place one piece of meat on the block. It should sizzle vigorously (or however it is that a piece of meat sizzles when it is *really* sizzling). Alternatively, use an infrared thermometer, or try to hold your hand 2 or 3 inches away from the block. If you can't, it's hot enough.

Place about 12 pieces of steak on the block, or as many as the block will hold without the pieces touching. After 5 seconds (yes, just five seconds), flip and cook for another 5 seconds. Repeat with the remaining steak and serve immediately.

Make sure the salt block is off the heat, and let it cool to room temperature before cleaning and storing it (see page 270).

SALT BLOCK-FRIED DUCK BREAST WITH DUCK FAT-FRIED POTATOES

SERVES 2

Salt isn't fat soluble. On the face of it, this statement might not exactly make your spine tingle with excitement. Another unsexy observation: solid fat melts when heated. But combined, these two fatty facts provide the basis for one incomparably delicious meal. Heat a Himalayan salt block and toss on a duck breast, fat side down. The fat will immediately melt, but because salt isn't fat soluble it will not dissolve, and the duck breast will pick up only the faintest trace of salt. When you flip the breast to the lean side, the moisture on the surface of the meat will start to flow and the meat will take on a beautiful glaze of salt that carries the whole dish. Meanwhile, you can fry potatoes in the hot fat glazing the salt block! Simple as this dish may seem, it makes the best duck breast I have ever eaten. Serve with a good Rhône or Languedoc wine.

2 (8 by 8 by 2-inch) blocks Himalayan pink salt
2 duck breasts (about 1 pound each), skin on
2 yellow potatoes, such as Yukon gold
2 tablespoons Dijon mustard (optional)

Heat the salt block on a stove, as described in Heating on page 269.

While the blocks are heating, wash and thoroughly dry the duck breasts and the potatoes. Trim any excess fat from the duck breasts, leaving a good layer of fat under the skin covering the meat. Slice the potatoes into 1/4 inch-thick rounds.

Put a duck breast, fat side down, on each of the hot salt blocks and cook until the fat starts to render off the duck in a small pool, 2 to 3 minutes. If a flare-up occurs (I've never had this happen), turn off the burner, wipe off any dripping fat, and relight. Rub the rounds of potatoes in the fat and arrange them close together around the edges of the salt blocks. When the fat on the duck breast has shrunk to a golden square, 8 to 10 minutes total, turn the breasts flesh side down using a metal spatula, being careful to scrape the surface of the block to remove any adhering fat. Turn the potato rounds as well. Cook duck and potatoes together for another 4 to 5 minutes, until the bottom side of the duck is lightly browned.

Remove the duck and let it rest for 5 minutes. Continue to fry the potatoes until golden, another 4 to 5 minutes. Remove to paper towels to absorb excess fat from the surface.

Slice the duck breasts across the grain into 1/4-inch strips, arrange on plates with the potatoes, and serve with a dollop of Dijon mustard to accompany the potatoes, if desired.

Make sure the salt block is off the heat, and let it cool to room temperature before cleaning and storing it (see page 270).

SAUCING

The critic has to educate the public; the artist has to educate the critic.
—Oscar Wilde

Sauces are liquid by definition, but it wasn't always the liquid in the sauce that people were looking for. It was the salt. Sauce comes from the Latin *salsus*, which came from *sallere*, the verb "to salt," which came from the Latin *sal* or *salis*. Sauces are at the heart of culinary traditions that have given us everything from the regal *filet mignon a l'espagnole* to a simple biscuits and gravy.

We normally think of a sauce as a concentrated liquid that is salted enough that the sauce seasons the entire dish. But a sauce can also be deconstructed, expanding a dish's flavor across liquid and crystalline realms. Crusty meats and steamy vegetables under silken folds of sauce studded with salt crystals are moistened and enriched by the liquid and at the same time defined and accentuated by the salt. Sauces are an open invitation to explore the dramatic tension of salt resisting and eventually succumbing to the moisture of food.

Some sauces include a few sautéed cubes of pancetta or other salted meat, which provides the extra kick of salt that makes further salting unnecessary (though blanching these ingredients will reduce their salt content considerably). Mussels and clams cooked in their own juices create their own intense, briny sauces without help from any added salt.

At the extreme end of the saucy continuum, you can take out the liquid altogether. Combine salt and a handful of herbs and spices and pat it over the food. This is called a rub. The salt achieves two essential functions here: it captures aromatics from the herbs and spices, giving those volatile organic materials a more enduring crystalline body to live in; and it draws out juices from the food it is rubbed on. These juices then combine with the herbs and spices in the rub to make a sauce right on the surface of the food.

OEUF MAYONNAISE

SERVES 4

Eggs barely hard-cooked, dolloped with housemade mayo: without this simple, affordable bistro food, I would surely have perished under a bridge on the banks of the glittering Seine. A few bucks buys you a seat at a rickety table on a busy street for as long as you wish, leaving you free to jot remembrances and ideas as you soak up the sights, sounds, and smells of Paris. A crust of baguette dipped in the heavenly silkiness of real mayonnaise, a bite of egg, a sip of crisp lager, and you will want for little else in life, ever again, so long as you live. The waiter will scrupulously not talk to you. The beauty who spares you a cigarette flashes only a fleeting smile before vanishing. You are free, wonderfully alone. Most of my jotted remembrances and ideas revolved around my unending astonishment at just how good real mayonnaise can be. To emphasize the distinction between the ethereal wholesomeness of handmade mayo and the gelatinous goop that comes from a jar, I still refer to it by its breathy French name—just say it: *oeuf mayonnaise*. Homemade mayonnaise normally calls for a sprinkle of salt, but dissolving the salt in the sauce is a missed opportunity. Sprinkling little rubies of coarse alaea salt over a plop of mayonnaise reveals the clandestine romance of salt and sauce, animating this inscrutable dish, drawing attention to its splendors, and lending a glimpse of Paris to your day.

4 large eggs

4 three-finger pinches sel gris

2 egg yolks, large

1 teaspoon fine Dijon mustard

1 teaspoon fresh lemon juice or white wine vinegar

3 grinds finely ground black pepper

1 cup sunflower oil

1 clove garlic, peeled

4 leaves iceberg or other large-leaf lettuce

8 two-finger pinches coarse alaea volcanic salt

1 crusty French baguette, sliced diagonally into thick pieces

Start with all ingredients at room temperature. Put the eggs in a small pan, cover with cold water, and add the sel gris. Cover the pan, place over high heat, and bring to a boil. Turn the heat down to a simmer and cook the eggs for 8 minutes. Drain, cool the eggs under cold running water, and refrigerate.

Combine the egg yolks, mustard, lemon juice, and pepper in a mixing bowl. Beat with a whisk until the yolks turn foamy and pale yellow. Slowly drizzle in the oil 1 or 2 tablespoons at a time, whisking continuously to emulsify the oil with the egg. The yolk-oil mixture should thicken as more oil is added. Continue until all the oil is incorporated and the mayonnaise is as thick as pudding. Insert the garlic clove in the middle of the sauce. The mayonnaise can be refrigerated to store (tastes best within a week).

Meanwhile, peel the eggs, slice in half, and arrange them atop the lettuce on 4 serving plates. Put a large dollop of mayonnaise over each of the egg halves and sprinkle with the alaea salt. Serve with the baguette slices.

MANGO SALSA WITH HAWAIIAN BLACK LAVA SALT

SERVES 6

Sauce is basically salt in liquid form, gussied up with any manner of delicious glutamates, lipids, acids, and aromatics. There are nuances, sure, but the nuances are, well, nuances. Sauces can be more than that. Mango salsa is an example of a sauce so succulent that it challenges the raison d'être of the food for which it was created. Tacos, empanadas, tortilla chips, hamburgers, pizza—all become mere delivery vehicles for the lush, tart, spicy salsa. All the more so when the salt is introduced as a distinctive ingredient in its own right. Confettied with onyx black or garnet red crystals of Hawaiian salt, this salsa brings a firecracker pop of festivity that celebrates saucing not just for flavor, but as visual and textural celebration of food. Use it atop anything from fried fish tacos to green salad to yogurt to steak.

2 ripe mangos

1 red chile pepper such as medusa head, red serrano, or red jalapeño pepper, minced

3 tablespoons minced red onion

Juice of 2 limes

3 tablespoons minced fresh cilantro leaves

1 three-finger pinch coarse Hawaiian black lava salt or alaea Hawaiian salt, plus more for sprinkling

Using a sharp knife, cut the flesh of the mangos from the pits, leaving two halves with the skin still on. Make parallel cuts 1/4 inch apart into the cut surface of each mango half, slicing through the flesh but not through the skin. Make another set of cuts the same way, this time running perpendicular to the first cuts to make squares. Slice the mango cubes from the skin by inverting each mango half and running your knife carefully between the flesh and the skin.

Combine the mango cubes with the chile, onion, lime juice, cilantro, and salt in a bowl and refrigerate for about 1 hour before using. Mix gently, sprinkle with the salt, and serve with an additional small bowl of salt on the side.

CONFECTIONERY

With water purify their hands, and take
The sacred offering of the salted cake. —Homer

Black and white, hot and cold, loud and quiet—put them together and what do you get? Gray, tepid, and subdued. But try the same thing with flavors and watch out. Instead of uniting, they fight, and in the clash of ax on shield, sparks start to fly.

Take sweet and salt, so closely identified in our minds as opposites that they practically bark at each other from across the table. Thrown into the same arena, they battle spectacularly on behalf of more flavor. Chocolate-covered pretzels, salted caramels, honey-roasted peanuts, prosciutto and melon, crème brulée with bacon bits. As is often the case, it pays to respect salt and sweet alike, letting the ingredients speak their piece as autonomous ingredients. Each should be granted its own role. This is because rather than meshing into a new and phonetically improbable flavor ("swalt"?), the pair refuse to combine. Instead they vibrate—sweet/salt/sweet/salt/sweet/salt. As soon as our palates try to commit to one of them, the other appears, and your mouth is left with the amusing if inexplicable flavor equivalent of a dog chasing its tail.

FLEUR DE SEL AND SMOKED SALT CARAMELS

MAKES ABOUT 64 CARAMELS

Like the inventor of the airplane, the creator of fleur de sel caramels is contested. Was it George Cayley, father of aerodynamics, who invented it in 1799; or Jean-Marie Le Bris in his horse-drawn "albatros artificiel"; or John J. Montgomery in his glider; or Otto Lilienthal, Octave Chanute, or Percy Pilcher? Some say it was the Wright brothers. The arguments tend to get political and technical. The French have been making fleur de sel caramels for some time. Some say salted caramel came from the New World, where salt water was used in confectionary. But it's all but certain they never made use of great salt. However, the Americans, prone to exaggeration, have succeeded in burning the sugar to the point where the caramel treads somewhere between a dessert topping and a meal. Blend burnt caramel with good salt and little stars of flavor glimmer from within the impenetrable vastness of the caramel. Look skyward. Machines for soaring among the stars might never have been invented had the salted burnt caramel come first.

1 cup heavy cream
5 tablespoons unsalted butter, cut into pieces
1¹/2 cups sugar
¹/4 cup agave syrup or invert sugar (see sidebar)
¹/4 cup water
2 three-finger pinches fleur de sel
2 three-finger pinches smoked salt, such as Halen Môn oak smoked

Line the bottom and sides of an 8-inch-square baking pan with parchment paper or foil and spray with oil; set aside.

Bring the cream and butter to a simmer in a small saucepan; remove from the heat and set aside.

In a medium-sized heavy saucepan over medium heat, heat the sugar, agave syrup, and water, stirring until the sugar dissolves. Boil, gently swirling the pan, until the sugar turns a dark golden color (350°F on a candy thermometer).

Carefully stir in the cream mixture (the mixture will bubble vigorously) and boil, stirring often, until the liquid reaches 248°F, about 12 minutes. At that point, a drop of the mixture dribbled into a glass of cold water will form a ball that will be firm enough to lift up but flexible enough to flatten between your fingers (soft-ball stage).

Remove the sugar from the heat and quickly stir in the fleur de sel. Immediately pour into the prepared baking pan. Sprinkle with the smoked salt. Allow to cool at room temperature until firm, about 1¹/2 hours more.

Invert onto a cutting board and peel off the paper. Cut into 1-inch squares and wrap each piece in a 4-inch square of wax paper or cellophane, twisting the ends to close.

INVERT SUGAR: If you can't find agave syrup, you can use invert sugar instead. It's very easy to make, and assures your caramel will come out smooth and silky. Mix 3 cups granulated sugar, 1¹/2 cups water, and the juice of ¹/2 lemon in a saucepan over medium-high heat. Bring to a boil, then lower the heat and simmer for 30 minutes. The resulting invert sugar liquid can be stored indefinitely in a small plastic container.

HIMALAYAN SALT BRITTLE

MAKES ABOUT 1/4 POUND

Clear the decks. Salt brittle brings salt and sugar together as an edible mosaic. Eat it on its own, or serve a shard of salt brittle alongside paprika pork chops. Serve with fruit salad or endive salad with walnuts and Roquefort cheese. Crumble over unsweetened yogurt, oatmeal, or chili con carne. Himalayan salt is hard to use because—well, because it's *hard*—but its rocky texture and gemstone beauty contribute brilliantly to brittle.

1 tablespoon unsalted butter, plus more for greasing
1 cup sugar
2 tablespoons agave syrup
1 two-finger pinch of baking soda
1 tablespoon coarse rock salt, such as Himalayan pink

Grease a sheet pan and a metal spatula liberally with butter and set aside.

Put the sugar in a large nonstick skillet and cook over medium-high heat, stirring occasionally with a wooden spoon, until the sugar begins to melt and lump up, about 5 minutes.

Add the agave syrup. The mixture will start to foam. Stir constantly as the mixture thins and turns a deep amber, and the lumps start to melt. When almost all the lumps are gone and the sugar is the color of George Hamilton's tan, turn off the heat.

Immediately stir in the tablespoon of butter and the baking soda. The liquid will become very foamy for a second. Stir until the foam is no longer streaky, about 10 seconds, and immediately pour onto the prepared pan, scraping as much of the melted sugar from the pan as possible with your stirring spoon.

Sprinkle the salt over the top of the sugar and count to twenty-four. The edges of the sugar pool should now be firm. Slide your spatula under the sugar all the way around to loosen from the pan, and flip it over.

Working quickly, stretch the sheet of sugar to about 1/16-inch thickness before it becomes too brittle to move. The easiest way is to carefully push it with your hands into a larger, thinner sheet. If some parts are thinner than others, don't worry. If your hands are very sensitive to heat, you can wear latex gloves, but it's harder to work the sugar that way, so I advise you to suck it up and use your hands. It won't be that hot. When the sugar is too brittle to move, stop pushing and let it cool.

Break into shards and serve. The drier the environment, the longer the brittle can be stored. Kept in an airtight glass jar or resealable plastic bag, it will retain its snappy texture for at least one week.

CHILE CHOCOLATE ALMOND BARK WITH SALT CRYSTALS

MAKES ABOUT 3/4 POUND

Remember the peanut butter cup commercials? Man and woman, so happy in their busy day, walking around with snacks in their hands, the sky above the color of a blue slushie the houses plastered in marzipan pastels, a happy-sounding tune of endless comic surprise piped through the air, the world a perfect place. Then—whoopsie, so clumsy of me—they smack into each other, exchanging flavors, and a wonderful new treat is born. Introducing nuts to chocolate is all well and fine and, sure, millions have been made on the combination. But if only the candymakers had the temerity to take the next step, something truly delicious could have come of it: chocolate, nuts, and a faint wave of chile heat all strummed like harp strings by the dexterous fingers of a luscious salt. Use this recipe to explore new dimensions of your favorite chocolate by trying it with a variety of salts. Choose the type and quantity of chile depending on your desire for heat.

1 cup whole almonds, skins on
6 ounces dark chocolate (about 70 percent cacao), broken into pieces
1 or 2 dried Thai bird chiles or piquín chiles
3 two-finger pinches flake salt, fleur de sel, or sel gris, or a combination

Preheat the oven to 400°F.

Place the almonds on a sheet pan big enough to hold them in a single layer and toast in the preheated oven until browned and crisp, about 8 minutes, stirring once. Remove from the oven and let cool.

Melt 4 ounces of the chocolate together with the chiles either in a covered microwave-safe bowl in a microwave oven at full power for 2 minutes, or in the top of a double boiler set over barely simmering water.

Chop the remaining chocolate finely. Remove the melted chocolate from the heat and mix with a whisk until smooth. Add the finely chopped chocolate in 2 or 3 batches, whisking in each addition before adding another. The chopped chocolate will "seed" the melted chocolate with solid chocolate crystals, encouraging the bark to firm without developing "bloom," a filmy white glaze that both mars the appearance of the candy and causes it to go stale more quickly.

When the chocolate is smooth, remove the chiles (they should be the only lumps). If you are working in a double boiler, remove the top from the bottom.

Using a rubber spatula, fold the almonds into the chocolate until the almonds are completely coated and the chocolate begins to firm up. It is important that the chocolate is firm enough to mound around the nuts without being runny. If the chocolate is too runny, let stand for 1 minute and try again.

Pour and scrape the chocolate onto a medium to large sheet pan and spread it into a rough rectangle about 1/2 inch thick. Sprinkle the top with the salt and allow to set at room temperature until hard, about 2 hours. When the chocolate is solid, cut it into shards and serve. Store in a cool, dry place for up to four weeks. Do not refrigerate, as this will ruin the chocolate.

HONEY ICE CREAM WITH SUGAR MAPLE SMOKED SEA SALT

SERVES 4; MAKES ABOUT 1 QUART

Dairy and smoked salt go together like rainbows and lollipops. Only better. The rainbow's beauty is nice, but one can only speculate at its flavor, and you outgrow lollipops. Homemade ice cream is another matter. Swapping the bright intensity of sugar for the dewy softness of honey lends gusto to the meteorological event happening in your mouth. The interplay of pungent salt amid the cream's frozen opulence of sweet smoke and vanilla bolsters the soul with prismatic beauty all its own.

2 vanilla beans
3 cups half-and-half
1/2 cup aromatic honey, such as eucalyptus, avocado, or heather
4 extra-large egg yolks
2 two-finger pinches maple smoked sea salt

Cut the vanilla beans in half lengthwise. Scrape out the seeds with a small spoon. Put the seeds and pods in a medium saucepan. Add the half-and-half and honey and stir to dissolve the honey. Heat over medium heat, stirring from time to time, just until tiny bubbles form around the edges of the pan, about 8 minutes.

Remove the pan from the heat and let the mixture steep, covered, for 1 hour. Remove the vanilla pods and discard. Mix in the egg yolks and cook over medium-low heat, stirring constantly, until lightly thickened and a thermometer reads 170°F, about 10 minutes. Remove from the heat.

Cover and refrigerate the ice cream batter until thoroughly chilled. Transfer to an ice cream maker and freeze according to manufacturer's instructions. Scoop directly from the ice-cream maker for soft serve, or store in a freezer for at least 1 hour for firmer ice cream.

Serve scoops sprinkled with a little smoked salt.

DRINKS

We lived on flowers. So much for sustenance. —Samuel Beckett

Your lips are among your body's most sensitive membranes. They are gatekeepers of all you eat: the first line of defense against foods you should not eat, and at the same time, the provokers of appetite, relaying untold reams of data to the brain about the food or drink you are about to take in. There are no taste buds in the lips of an adult human, but salt trips all kinds of electrical circuits across the lips' moistness, stimulating a sensation of pungency, of mineral richness. And, of course, the lips detect unfathomable intricacies of texture.

The rim of a cocktail glass is a magnificent opportunity to show love to your lips. Expensive and masterfully crafted liquors, precious drops of freshly-squeezed fruit juices, thoughtfully chilled glasses, visually exciting garnishes—all these bow in a show of respect to that first rush of salt. But industrial refined sodium chloride in the form of kosher salt or table salt ("margarita salt"), no matter how nicely packaged or flavored, does nothing so much as present a filter of chemical artificiality between your cocktail and your mouth. A beautifully crystalline, delectably crunchy, delicately mineral, infinitely complex artisan salt with your cocktail gives your lips the primal yet sophisticated satisfaction they are due. And the lips do the talking, spreading the word to the rest of your mouth and to your throat, belly, and brain, letting everything know that all is well and good and right. You can feel it, even in the tingling of your skin.

Salt gives shape to a variety of ingredients in a cocktail. It subdues and rounds out acids in fruit juices and fermented beverages like beer and wine. It mutes bitterness to reveal depth in herbs and spices whether they be vermouths, tonics, or basil muddled with cardamom. It penetrates through sugars in liquors, syrups, and juices and brings to light the refreshing interplay of salted sweetened, sweetened salted flavors.

Cocktails and salt can come together in any number of ways. A salt rim is the most dramatic, assigning salt multiple roles as garnish, as the first blush of flavor, and as a layer of texture and flavor that shifts the quaffing of a liquid mixture into a more varied, agreeably unpredictable experience. The salted rim is one of the few examples of the salt actually constituting a sort of course in a recipe. You have the liquid and the salt, both on more or less equal terms. The autonomy given salt on such occasions suggests that the salt itself can serve as a foundation for creativity. Try crushing dried pasilla peppers and Himalayan pink salt together with a mortar and pestle for a fragrantly spiced salt-rimmed margarita. Pound a juicy-sweet Korean or Italian sel gris with lemongrass to rim a mango daiquiri.

A variation on the salted rim is the salted wrist. A bite of tart lemon from the rind, a lick of bracing sea salt from the side of the wrist, and a slug of tequila or mezcal have propelled the best of us from the calm waters of the beach to the frenzy of a Cabo San Lucas nightclub.

Salt can be sprinkled right on ice cubes. The salt perches there for a while, but also sets to work melting the ice, slowly slipping tendrils of salt into the chilled alcohol. In addition to shifting and expanding the flavor profile of the drink, it also contributes to a layering of flavors and very subtle shifts in viscosities among the swirling liquids in the glass.

Salt can be mixed directly into the cocktail itself, say, sprinkled into the tomato juice of a Bloody Mary—or the grapefruit juice of a Salty Dog, either varying or augmenting the usual salt rim. Another briny variation is the dirty martini, in which the olive's heavily salted pickling brine is dashed into the cocktail.

Probably the most venerable cocktail salting is that delivered indirectly via a pickled garnish: the olive in a martini, the pearl onion in a gimlet, the pickled string bean or okra in a Cajun martini or Bloody Mary.

Salt also performs another role in a cocktail. It allows us as drinkers to engage in the mixocological process, exploring our subtlest appetites. Sip from a broad crescent of the salted rim and feel it in the flush of your cheeks. Skirt the salted side in favor of the residue of the last sip's salt to reboot your system with the raw flavors of the cocktail. Then lick a fleck from the edge between sips for the heck of it. Drink a martini, then nibble the olive; or nibble an olive, then drink the martini. Premeditated or instinctual, examined or habitual, these variations on the salting of each sip are your own creations, private expressions of your own cocktail artistry, the poetic interlocution of tongue, lips, and flavor.

DRINKING CHOCOLATE WITH TAHA'A VANILLA SALT

SERVES 4

When chocolate was introduced to European aristocrats from the New World, it was consumed largely in the privacy of the bedroom. Finishing a chocolate drink with the fragrant crunchy spark of Taha'a vanilla salt would not have been a good idea in this setting—it would surely have escalated things to the point where the presence of the bed weighed too heavily on everyone's minds, turning a purely social invitation into something rather more.

1 cup heavy cream

2 cups milk

12 ounces dark chocolate (about 70 percent cacao), finely chopped

4 two-finger pinches Halen Môn Sea Salt with Taha'a Vanilla

Heat the cream and milk in a small saucepan over medium heat until steaming but not boiling. Stir in the chocolate and keep stirring until completely melted. Remove from the heat and let cool for 30 minutes. This step helps to thicken the chocolate.

Reheat over very low heat, stirring often, until steam rises from the surface. Stir in the salt and serve in warm cups.

SWEET MURRAY RIVER SIDECAR

Imagine strolling home along the long dusty road after a hard day in the fields. At the crossroads you encounter a gaggle of tow-haired youngsters sitting at a card table. "Sidecar, mister?" they shout. The sidecar is a lemonade drink for grown-ups. A touch of salt opens up the entire experience, makes it restorative. Citrus playing tag with sugar, chilled juice teeter-tottering with warming alcohol, the entire drink alloyed with salt's wisdom and captured beautifully in a glass of coppery liquid.

1 three-finger pinch Murray River flake salt

1 tablespoon sugar

3/4 ounce fresh lemon juice, plus more for wetting rim

1 1/2 ounces Cognac or good brandy

3/4 ounce triple sec

1 strip lemon zest

Combine the salt and sugar on a flat plate. Wet the rim of a highball glass with the lemon juice. Place the glass upside down on the plate to rim it with the salt and sugar. Put the glass in the freezer.

Combine the Cognac, triple sec, and the 3/4 ounce lemon juice over ice in a shaker and shake well for 5 seconds. Remove the glass from the freezer and strain the drink into the glass. Garnish with a twist of lemon zest. This drink can also be served on the rocks: pour ice and liquor into an old-fashioned glass rimmed with the sugar-salt mixture.

BOURBON ON THE ROCKS WITH IBURI-JIO CHERRY SMOKED SALT

SERVES 1

Some bourbons, though they may come from deep in the Kentucky heartland of America, bear within them all the smoky mystery of a single malt Scotch brewed on the edge of a peaty moor in Scotland. To revel in the delicious tension of these two great whiskey regions, smoky up your bourbon with a pinch of smoked salt on the rocks. Take the sensation to its near-ridiculous extreme by making that smoked salt Iburi-jio Cherry, a soft and supple deep-sea salt cold-smoked with cherry wood from that much newer but dead-serious whiskey-making region, Japan. The salt brings just a hint of smoked bacon aroma that whets your appetite even as the drink slakes your thirst.

2 ounces bourbon whiskey, such as Woodford Reserve or Baker's
Scant two-finger pinch Iburi-Jio Cherry salt

Fill a rocks glass half full with large ice cubes. Pour the whiskey over the rocks; it should come not more than two-thirds of the way to the top of the ice. Sprinkle with the salt. Inhale. Imbibe.

ALAEA HAWAIIAN BLOODY MARY

SERVES 1

Life is so important. There is something you really need to say. But the high voltage coil of iron-rich Alaea Hawaiian salt rimming the Bloody Mary glass at your finger draws you like an electromagnet. The first sip trips the circuit and sends the electrical charge through your body, electrifying your nervous system, vibrating your body, rebooting the brain stem. The surge of spicy tomato juice, tangy citrus, and vaporizing horseradish courses through you. A nibble at the turgid stalk of celery returns things to rights, but by now you are far away, refreshed, restored, forgetting what it was you wanted to say.

Fine alaea Hawaiian salt
Juice of 1/4 lemon
2 ounces vodka
2 dashes celery bitters
6 drops clam juice
6 drops Worcestershire sauce
1 teaspoon horseradish
3 to 6 drops Tabasco sauce
3 grinds coarsely ground black pepper
3 ounces unsalted tomato juice
1 long, fine celery stalk, leaves still attached, for garnish

Put a three-finger pinch of alaea salt on a flat plate. Wet the edge of a tall highball glass with the squeezed-out lemon rind. Place the glass upside down on the plate to rim it with salt.

Combine the lemon juice, vodka, bitters, clam juice, Worcestershire, horseradish, Tabasco, pepper, tomato juice, and 1 two-finger pinch alaea salt in a shaker over ice. Stir thoroughly for 5 seconds, pour the liquid and ice into the glass, and garnish with the celery.

KONA SALT AND COCOA-RIMMED PLANTATION RUM

SERVES 1

Rum is distilled from various sweet products of sugarcane. Playing off rum's sweet origins, a touch of citrusy-sweet chocolate adds intrigue to the strident heat of the alcohol, and a touch of salt unifies everything in a rush of flavor that would make Willy Wonka jealous. Cocoa powder can be substituted for the cacao beans or nibs, though it lacks their nutty fullness. No liquor cabinet should be without a small bottle of honey-smooth, smoky, tangerine-flavored Rangpur lime syrup. Made from the lime's peel and juice, it is great not only to wet the rim of a cocktail glass, but also as a mixer in mojitos and margaritas. Kona deep sea salt is big, with a firm backbone of mineral and a glint of fresh fruit sweetness that bring harmony through leadership rather than brute force.

1 three-finger pinch Kona sea salt or Papohaku white salt

1/2 teaspoon cacao beans or nibs, pounded into powder with a mortar and pestle

1/4 teaspoon Rangpur lime syrup or agave syrup

1 1/2 ounces good dark rum, such as Westerhall Plantation Rum

Combine the salt and powdered cacao on a flat plate. Wet the rim of a highball glass with the lime syrup. Place the glass upside down on the plate to rim it with salt and chocolate. In this case, less is more, so go easy on the salt-chocolate mixture. Drop a handful of ice cubes into the glass and pour the rum over. Inhale, touch the rim with your tongue, sip, and enjoy.

JAL JEERA

SERVES 4

The true taste of a place is found in its little oddities, and northern India is no exception. Nowhere are the distinctive attitudes and sensibilities of a people better captured than in the lemonade of northern India. *Jal jeera* is Hindi for "cumin water," but it's the wild and unruly yet ultimately constructive influence of India's famous, sulfuric kala namak salt that lends this drink its edge. It's traditionally drunk before a meal, but any hot day provides a great excuse to duck into the shade, mix up a tall iced glass of jal jeera, and tilt your face up to the sun to offer a prayer to the sun god Surya.

2 tablespoons whole cumin seeds

4 teaspoons fresh cilantro leaves

2 teaspoons sugar

3/4 cup fresh mint leaves

2 tablespoons fresh lemon juice

1/2 teaspoon kala namak salt

4 cups cold water

1/2 lemon, cut into 4 wedges, for garnish

4 mint sprigs, for garnish

Preheat the oven to 450°F. Line a rimmed baking sheet with foil.

Pound the cumin in a mortar and pestle until cracked, then spread on the prepared baking sheet. Roast for 3 to 5 minutes, until fragrant and lightly toasted, being careful not to burn.

Add the cilantro, sugar, and mint to the mortar and crush with the pestle into a paste. Combine the paste with the toasted cumin, lemon juice, and kala namak in a large jar (at least 1 1/2 quarts) and mix thoroughly. Add the water and some ice; seal the jar and shake vigorously. Pour ice and all into 4 tall glasses, garnish with lemon wedges and mint sprigs, and serve.

SALTY DOG WITH A PEACHY BOLIVIAN ROSE RIM

SERVES 1

The venerable Greyhound is made with vodka or gin and grapefruit juice, and if you salt that hound, you get a Salty Dog. So goes the logic. But logic is dull—or lonely. Vodka craves company. Its pure grain simplicity is receptive to a host of improvements that would wither under gin's herbaceous glare. And who doesn't love a peach, with all that it conjures—from climbing fruit trees to sipping Bellinis? And with the right salt—like a springwater fresh Bolivian Rose salt—the vodka and peach open up with a smiling opulence that quells the furor of even the surliest god.

1 three-finger pinch Bolivian Rose salt
Dash peach bitters
2 ounces vodka
5 ounces fresh grapefruit juice

Put the salt on a flat plate. Wet the rim of an old-fashioned glass with the peach bitters. Place the glass upside down on the plate to rim it with salt.

Combine the vodka and grapefruit juice with a scoop of ice cubes in a shaker, shake vigorously for 5 seconds, and pour into the glass.

VARIATION: For a Salted Chocolate Chihuahua, substitute tequila for vodka and rim the glass with chocolate bitters and salt.

THE MEADOW MARTINI

SERVES 2

Salting is a way. It's the path you take. It lets you discover a passage through the brambles, defines the terrain ahead, sets you on a lost trail, and, toward the summit, reveals key ledges and handholds. The better your use of salt, the higher you can climb and the more enjoyable the ascent. And the view from up top is worth it. The Meadow Martini is a diamond-perfect expression of salt's power to offer the clearest imaginable view of the most magical possible vista. Crushed Tasmanian pepperberries send blossoms of hydrangea crimson into the translucent liquid of the gin, unleashing extravagant botanical flavors. Tasmanian pepperberry (*Tasmannia lanceolata*) is sometimes used as a substitute for Szechuan pepper, though it harbors none of the heat and frankly bears no resemblance. If you can't locate any, substitute a few petals of dried hibiscus or just enjoy your martini in its classic perfection, an arc of Shinkai Deep Sea salt as its only embellishment. Shinkai imparts to the lips the felicitous texture of confetti, and the unalloyed flavor of happiness itself.

6 Tasmanian berries

4 ounces excellent gin, such as Citadelle, Miller's, or Bombay Sapphire

1 three-finger pinch Shinkai deep sea salt

1 lemon wedge

Gently crush the peppercorns with the flat edge of a kitchen knife. Combine the peppercorns and gin in a glass beaker or jar. Allow the peppercorns to infuse into the gin for 5 to 10 minutes.

Meanwhile, put the salt on a flat plate. Rub the rims of two martini glasses with the lemon wedge. Place each glass upside down on the plate to rim it with salt, then place in the freezer for at least 5 minutes.

To make the cocktail, put one scoop of ice cubes in a shaker and strain the gin over the ice. Allow to stand for 15 seconds, then very gently stir for 5 seconds. Allow to stand for another 15 seconds. Remove the martini glasses from the freezer, gently stir the gin again, and strain it into the glasses. Serve.

MARLBOROUGH FLAKEY MARGARITA

SERVES 1

Salt makes tart things taste sweeter (and, oddly, cuts the sweetness of sweet things to bring out their subtler flavors) and mellows the sharpness of alcohol. The salted rim of the margarita is iconic because it capitalizes on all the opportunities lurking within the sweet-tart-alcohol bite of the cocktail; because it is beautiful; and because it revives us with every sip. The salted rim allows margaritas to be served on the tart side, so this recipe calls for more fresh lime juice and less triple sec than is commonly recommended. As tempting as it may be to bring out the heavy guns and rim the cocktail with more massive flake salts, I often prefer the fine crystalline froth of Marlborough flakey. It gives a truly satisfying crunch, like the feeling of stepping on powdered snow—a welcome sensation when drinking a margarita in the waning heat of a late summer afternoon.

1 three-finger pinch Marlborough flakey salt
1/2 juicy lime
1 1/2 ounces silver tequila (100 percent agave)
1/2 ounce triple sec

Put the salt on a flat plate. Squeeze the lime juice into a shaker and rub the rim of a margarita glass with the wet, squeezed-out rind. Place the glass upside down on the plate to rim it with salt.

Add the tequila, triple sec, and a scoop of ice to the shaker and shake vigorously for 10 seconds to thoroughly foam the mixture. Pour the drink, ice and all, into the glass.

VARIATIONS: This drink can be served up or blended, as well as on the rocks. For an up cocktail, combine the ingredients, shake vigorously for 10 seconds, and strain into a chilled martini glass. For a blended drink, combine the lime juice, tequila, and triple sec in a blender with a scoop of ice, blend for 15 seconds, and pour into a margarita glass.

Resources

HOW TO SHOP FOR SALT

PACKAGING: If a salt contains moisture, be sure it is sold in a resealable container. Any moist salt sold in cellophane or a box should be avoided if possible. Dry salts such as flake, rock, and dry traditional salts may be shipped in porous containers.

BULK BINS: Bulk salts are every bit as good as salts sold in individually sealed packages, provided the bins are well sealed to keep in moisture—preferably lined with glass or food-grade plastic. Salts bought in bulk bins should be stored in airtight containers.

TINS: Salt is hygroscopic, meaning it collects moisture from the open air. Combined with moisture and oxygen, salt will quickly rust metal. Avoid buying any salt product that comes in tins, unless the tins are small enough or your consumption is rapid enough that you can beat the inevitable rust. Most tins are coated to ward off rust, but the moment you remove and replace the lid, grinding a few fine particles of salt between the lid and the container in the process, rust will start to form. At The Meadow, we sell one-ounce tins of popular salts for rapid consumption, but tins larger than that tend to rust in the spice cabinet.

EXPIRATION DATES: Most salts do not spoil, ever. Some can grow stale. Wet salts will lose their moisture, and dry salts may take some on. Again, sealed containers are helpful for keeping salt in its best possible condition. Some salts, such as kala namak, do have minerals or compounds like sulfur that react with moisture and oxygen in the air, making the salt lose some of its potency. Kala namak should be bought coarse if possible and ground as needed to benefit from its full aromas. Other salts, such as smoked or infused salts, will indeed go stale if left unsealed.

Guidelines for shelf life:

- Fleur de sel, sel gris, moist traditional salt, and shio in a sealed glass container will last indefinitely.

- Flake, dry traditional, and rock salts will last indefinitely under dry to moderately humid conditions, indefinitely in cardboard or other containers.

- Smoked, blended, and infused salts will last one year in a sealed glass container.

WHERE TO SHOP

There are a good many retailers offering a selection of salts, though their organization and level of description vary enormously. A good many tend to just re-sell or repackage salt from a small circle of salt importers. Below are a few of the more established websites for salt shopping. All have excellent customer service, in my experience, and source a good portion of their selection directly from salt makers. Importing salt from every corner of the globe takes experience and concentrated effort, so the businesses that specialize in salt tend to have more expertise and better selection than generalists.

SPECIALTY SALT RETAILERS					
	STOREFRONT	INTERNET	WHOLESALE	VARIETY	WEBSITE
The Meadow Portland, OR New York, NY	yes	yes	yes	high	www.atthemeadow.com
Saltworks	no	yes	yes	moderate	www.saltworks.us
Salt Traders	no	yes	no	limited	www.salttraders.com
Kalustyans New York, NY	yes	yes	some	limited	www.kalustyans.com

Index